THE PROFESSIONAL PRACTICE SERIES

The Professional Practice Series is sponsored by the Society for Industrial and Organizational Psychology (SIOP). The series was launched in 1988 to provide industrial/organizational psychologists, organizational scientists and practitioners, human resource professionals, managers, executives, and those interested in organizational behavior and performance with volumes that are insightful, current, informative, and relevant to organizational practice. The volumes in the Professional Practice Series are guided by five tenets designed to enhance future organizational practice:

1. Focus on practice, but grounded in science
2. Translate organizational science into practice by generating guidelines, principles, and lessons learned that can shape and guide practice
3. Showcase the application of industrial/organizational psychology to solve problems
4. Document and demonstrate best industrial and organizational-based practices
5. Stimulate research needed to guide future organizational practice

The volumes seek to inform those interested in practice with guidance, insights, and advice on how to apply the concepts, findings, methods, and tools derived from industrial/organizational psychology to solve human-related organizational problems.

Previous Professional Practice Series volumes include:

Published by Jossey-Bass

Managing Selection in Changing Organizations
Jerard F. Kehoe, Editor

Evolving Practices in Human Resource Management
Allen I. Kraut, Abraham K. Korman, Editors

Individual Psychological Assessment
Richard Jeanneret, Rob Silzer, Editors

Performance Appraisal
James W. Smither, Editor

Organizational Surveys
Allen I. Kraut, Editor

Employees, Careers, and Job Creation
Manuel London, Editor

Published by Guilford Press

Diagnosis for Organizational Change
Ann Howard and Associates

Human Dilemmas in Work Organizations
Abraham K. Korman and Associates

Diversity in the Workplace
Susan E. Jackson and Associates

Working with Organizations and Their People
Douglas W. Bray and Associates

The 21st Century Executive

The 21st Century Executive

Innovative Practices for Building Leadership at the Top

Rob Silzer

Editor

Foreword by Eduardo Salas

JOSSEY-BASS
A Wiley Company
www.josseybass.com

Published by

 **JOSSEY-BASS**
A Wiley Company
989 Market Street
San Francisco, CA 94103-1741

www.josseybass.com

Jossey-Bass books and products are available through most bookstores. To contact Jossey-Bass directly, call (888) 378-2537, fax to (800) 605-2665, or visit our website at www.josseybass.com.

Substantial discounts on bulk quantities of Jossey-Bass books are available to corporations, professional associations, and other organizations. For details and discount information, contact the special sales department at Jossey-Bass.

We at Jossey-Bass strive to use the most environmentally sensitive paper stocks available to us. Our publications are printed on acid-free recycled stock whenever possible, and our paper always meets or exceeds minimum GPO and EPA requirements.

Library of Congress Cataloging-in-Publication Data

The 21st century executive: innovative practices for building leadership at the top / Rob Silzer, Editor.—1st ed.
    p. cm.—(The professional practice series)
    Includes bibliographical references and index.
    ISBN 0–7879–5287–7
    1. Executives. 2. Leadership. 3. Management. I. Silzer, Robert Frank.
II. Series.
HD38.2 .A167 2001
658.4'092—dc21

2001004592
FIRST EDITION
HB Printing 10 9 8 7 6 5 4 3 2 1

To my mentors:
Mrs. Stark, Mrs. Matt, Ralph Zech,
Glenn Schuermann, William Anthony,
Robert Hauhart, Russell Clark,
Lloyd Lofquist, Marvin Dunnette,
Wally Borman, and Dick Jeanneret

Contents

Part Three: Understanding Executive Perspectives

Foreword

Good leaders do great things for organizations. Good leaders inspire, motivate, provide a vision, set goals and strategies. Good leaders make thorough but fair decisions. Good leaders successfully manage conflicts, demands, and requirements both within and outside the organization. Good leaders move organizations to levels they have never been or thought they could be. There is no question—good leaders contribute significantly to the success and viability of their organizations. But good leaders are hard to find and develop. Moreover, despite decades of leadership research, we still struggle and debate whether leaders are born or made, what personality characteristics leaders should have, what behaviors leaders should exhibit, and what behaviors leaders should not show. A cursory review of the literature raises more questions about leadership than provides answers. The leadership literature, especially that which focuses on top or executive leadership, is fragmented and piecemeal, and what is really known about that kind of leadership is hard to find. But I know there are efforts under way to better integrate and summarize the literature and to clearly uncover and highlight what we know about leadership. This book is one such effort. It provides some much-needed answers, and it tells us what it takes to be a leader at the top.

Rob Silzer and associates have taken on in this volume an elusive and difficult problem—the nature of leadership at the top. And they have provided those interested in developing and promoting leadership with a set of well-articulated insights about what it takes to be successful at the top of organizations. The authors of this volume offer very valuable information for defining, developing, coaching, training, rewarding, and selecting leaders. There is information on understanding global executives and how to succeed as a top executive. There is even information on why top executives fail. The chapters in this volume are full of practical tips and

guidelines that, we hope, will help executives and HR practitioners with processes and mechanisms to ensure the success of their
leaders. We all owe Rob for putting this volume together.

SIOP's Professional Practice Series Editorial Board continues
to promote and encourage volumes that highlight that the science
of industrial/organizational psychology can provide practical guidance to those who manage people in organizations. We hope this
volume is an illustration of what we can offer.

September 2001   Eduardo Salas
                            University of Central Florida
                            Series Editor

Preface

Corporate executives over the last twenty years have become highly visible and influential on both the American and the global stage. Once they were relatively hidden to the general public and known only to their industry peers. Now, however, they are media stars and their views carry a great deal of weight in economic, political, and even cultural debates. They leverage the financial clout of their organizations as well as their own personalities to gain influence in areas far beyond their primary executive responsibilities in the organization.

Many if not most business managers yearn to be executives so they can make strategic decisions and run their own business or business unit. They are also attracted to the public attention and financial security that can accompany an executive position. This seems to be the new career goal of many business graduates now entering organizations. Clearly the rush of managers into technology firms, both start-ups and blue chip technology, has been partly due to their executive career ambitions, although the flood of available stock options was also an incentive.

Recently, however, a little business reality is settling into the economy. Executives are being turned over almost faster than they are being hired (Bianco & Lavelle, 2000; Charan & Colvin, 1999). There is less tolerance now for inexperienced or ineffective executives in either the technology sector or the rest of the business world. Many individuals are realizing belatedly that they are poorly suited or not ready for an executive position. Just recently a chief executive officer boot camp was started to help newly appointed chief executive officers get up to speed and to reduce the 20 percent annual turnover in chief executive officers (Symonds, 2001).

Currently there is widespread interest in executives, in what leads to executive success and failure, and in how organizations can build an effective executive team. The executive group in an organization can determine the success or failure of that organization. With the widespread holding of corporate stock equities in the American population there is great public interest in the success of each organization. Corporate decisions that were virtually ignored several decades ago now attract outside scrutiny because they can significantly and rapidly affect investment in the company and the stock price. Now stocks seem to fluctuate more rapidly with each quarterly earnings report. The decisions made by executives can have great impact on those financial reports. As a result the importance and visibility of executive decisions seem to have increased in the last decade or so.

Defining an Executive

The term *executive* has been misused, which has led to some confusion. In particular, one well-known leadership training company inappropriately labels everyone who goes through a particular training program as an executive with little attention to the actual positions the participants hold. This lack of careful distinction of executives from lower-level directors, managers, and independent contributors confounds some of the writings and publications about executives.

Similar to the grade inflation reported in educational institutions, there has been widespread title inflation in organizations. The term *manager* no longer guarantees that a position has any direct reports or even that the incumbent must manage project work involving others. In one organization all exempt personnel have a manager or leader title. Similarly the term *executive* is being diluted by companies that disseminate the officer or vice president title deep into the organization. One New York financial services organization has over 1,500 positions that carry at least a VP title. It would be a real stretch to consider all of them executive level positions.

For the purpose of this book executives are defined as general managers, corporate officers, and heads of major organizational functions and business units. This includes people in positions reporting to the chief executive officer and, in large organizations, the chief executive and divisional officers for major business units. The contributors to this book have been encouraged to focus on executives and not on chief executive officers or management roles.

Clearly the executive role is a complex one. Not only are there challenging goals and objectives, but there are a wide array of internal and external constituencies to face and a rapidly changing business environment. It's something like a five-dimensional chess game with a range of known and unknown opponents who keep changing the rules in each of the dimensions. An executive needs to be effective in a number of areas and at a number of different levels at once. Failure in any one area can lead to ineffectiveness and in some cases a short tenure.

Goals of the Book

The primary focus of this book is to discuss issues related to executive effectiveness and success. The increased attention now given to executives has placed a premium on the knowledge and experience of building an effective executive team. Unfortunately there has been limited professional communication about executive success, with a few exceptions (Levinson, 1981; Kotter, 1982; Hambrick, 1988; Nadler & Spencer, 1998). Most of the focus has been on chief executive officers rather than on the broader group of executives.

There are a number of people, internal and external to organizations, who have a vast knowledge of executive effectiveness and extensive experience in working with executives. This book is an attempt to capture and share their knowledge and experience with others. The specific goals for this book are

- To focus on executive effectiveness and success.
- To recruit seasoned professionals as chapter authors and have them share what they have learned about executives.
- To include a broad range of perspectives on how to build effective executive leadership.

It will be up to you as you read to determine how well this book meets these goals. The chapter authors are a highly seasoned group. Each chapter has one or more authors with at least 20 years of professional experience working with organizations, and most have worked extensively with executives. Their 300 years of combined experience speaks for itself.

The book should be a stimulating source of ideas for a wide range of readers including corporate executives, human resource executives, business consultants, and university professors. It also supports SIOP's goal of sharing our knowledge and learnings more broadly in the business world.

The chapters are arranged into three sections. Part One provides an overview of executive success and failure and executive personalities. In Chapter 1 Jeff Sonnenfeld discusses executive failure and how learning the lessons of failure can lead to later success for an executive. Tony Rucci, in Chapter 2, reviews the traits that appear to contribute to executive success and emphasizes the importance of establishing and sustaining specific business practices. Leslie Pratch and Harry Levinson, in Chapter 3, examine executive personality characteristics and argue for a structural approach to identifying individuals who will emerge as effective leaders.

Part Two focuses on ways to build and manage effective executives. The assumption here is that successful executives are both born and bred—and thus the result of careful selection, focused development, and financial encouragement. In Chapter 4, I explore the complexity of executive fit to an organization and identify a number of selection factors that can lead to executive success. Janet Spencer, Carlos Rivero, and David Nadler, in Chapter 5, review the contribution of executive teams to an organization and introduce the strategic enterprise as a new paradigm of organizational design that leverages executive teams. George Hollenbeck, in Chapter 6, provides a refreshing review of executive coaching along with useful criteria for evaluating the effectiveness of coaching efforts. In Chapter 7, Val Markos draws on his extensive executive development experience to discuss a range of approaches that can be used to develop and train executives while also contributing to organizational success. And in Chapter 8, Marianna Makri and Luis Gomez-Mejia survey a range of executive compensation and benefit tools and show how they can motivate and direct an executive's focus on short-term and long-term performance.

In Part Three, the authors survey the issues and perspectives of specific groups of executives. Karen Lyness, in Chapter 9, provides a comprehensive review of the issues associated with women and people of color who seek or attain executive-level positions. In Chapter 10, Doug McKenna and Rob McKenna present an insider's view of the priorities and characteristics of executive leaders in the new technology economy and how they might be different from other executives. John Fulkerson, in Chapter 11, provides the success factors and characteristics of distinguished global executives and ways to grow and develop them. And to put everything in perspective, Larry Bossidy and Marcia Avedon, in Chapter 12, offer the views and insights of a highly regarded and particularly effective chief executive officer on the key factors that contribute to executive success.

Acknowledgments

Numerous individuals have contributed to this book—not least the thousands of executives and organizations that have taught the authors what they know about executives. In addition, intellectual mentors and peers in organizations, in consulting firms, and in colleges and universities were invaluable in providing insights and guiding the way. I have listed my mentors in the dedication.

I would also like to thank the chapter authors for their commitment to this project and their responsiveness to requests and deadlines. Their hard work is evident in the chapters. Many of them also reviewed other chapters and gave me valuable suggestions for improving the chapters and the book.

From the beginning the editorial board of the Professional Practice Series and Eduardo Salas, the series editor, saw the value of having a volume on executives and gave me the support to carry it through to completion.

And finally I am indebted to my editor at Jossey-Bass, Julianna Gustafson, who has provided unwavering support and enthusiasm for this book even when some important deadlines had to be shifted to accommodate some authors. It has been a joy to work with her and the Jossey-Bass team.

In the end, however, it is the readers who will have the last say on the usefulness of this book. My hope is that current executives and human resource professionals and the next generation of professionals working with executives will use it as a stepping stone to learn what is currently known and then expand upon that knowledge. This can only lead to more effective executives and ultimately to more successful organizations.

New York, New York   Rob Silzer
September 2001

References

Bianco, A., & Lavelle, L. (2000, December 11). The CEO trap. *Business Week*, pp. 86–92.

Charan, R., & Colvin, G. (1999, June 21). Why CEOs fail. *Fortune*, pp. 69–82.

Hambrick, D. C. (Ed.). (1988). *The executive effect: Concepts and method for studying top managers*. Greenwich, CT: JAI Press.

Kotter, J. P. (1982). *The general managers*. New York: Free Press.

Levinson, H. (1981). *Executive*. Cambridge, MA: Harvard University Press.

Nadler, D. A., & Spencer, J. L. (1998). *Executive teams*. San Francisco: Jossey-Bass.

Symonds, W. C. (2001, June 11). Basic training for CEOs. *Business Week*, pp. 103–104.

The Authors

Rob Silzer is managing director of HR Assessment and Development, Inc. For the past 25 years he has consulted with managers and executives at over 100 organizations to leverage psychological knowledge and expertise to accomplish business objectives. He has specialized in executive and management leadership, team selection and development, and strategically driven HR systems. He recently coedited *Individual Psychological Assessment: Predicting Behavior in Organizational Settings* with Richard Jeanneret and coauthored *Human Resource Development: A Study of Corporate Practices* with Rosemary Slider and Michael Knight. He regularly writes articles and delivers workshops and symposiums on leadership, executive selection and development, HR practices, psychological assessment, and succession planning for psychology professionals and organizational clients. He has served as president of NY Metropolitan Applied Psychology Association, president of PDI-New York, senior human resources director at a major U.S. business corporation, adjunct professor at the University of Minnesota and New York University, and on the Editorial Board for *Personnel Psychology*. He holds a Ph.D. from the University of Minnesota in both industrial/organizational psychology and counseling psychology, an M.S. in social psychology from Florida State University, and a B.S. in experimental psychology and chemistry from Southern Illinois University. He is a frequent mountain trekker and scuba diver around the world.

Marcia J. Avedon is vice president, human resources, Honeywell International. She earned her B.A. in psychology with honors at the University of North Carolina at Wilmington (1983) and both her M.S. (1986) and Ph.D. (1989) in industrial/organizational psychology from George Washington University. She joined AlliedSignal in 1995 and held positions in the corporate office and business units in human resources and organization development. She led the integration of the compensation programs during the merger of AlliedSignal and Honeywell in 1999. Her earlier experience includes senior consultant, organization development and staffing, and manager, succession planning, for Anheuser-Busch Companies and director, organization and management development for their Campbell-Taggart baking subsidiary. She began her career consulting with Booz·Allen & Hamilton.

Avedon has published articles and spoken publicly on selection systems, executive development, succession planning, and organization development. She serves on the Advisory Board for the University of South Carolina's Masters in Human Resources program, and also on the Board of the Jersey Battered Women's Services.

Lawrence A. Bossidy is chairman and chief executive officer of Honeywell International, and also served in this capacity at AlliedSignal from 1991 to April 2000. AlliedSignal acquired Honeywell Inc. in December 1999 and assumed the Honeywell name. Prior to joining AlliedSignal, he was vice chairman of General Electric and chief operating officer of GE Capital. He worked for GE for 34 years, beginning as a financial management trainee. He worked in various management roles in corporate audit and as a general manager in numerous industries. He serves on the board of directors for Merck & Co., Champion International Corporation, and J.P. Morgan & Co. He is a member of the Business Council and the Business Roundtable and holds a B.A. in economics from Colgate University. He currently writes and speaks to top executives on business and leadership topics.

John R. Fulkerson is currently vice president for organization effectiveness at Cisco Systems, Inc. His Ph.D. is from Baylor University. The majority of his career has been focused on executive development and organization effectiveness issues with international and global enterprises. He first worked on the selection and development of intelligence officers for the U.S. government, then was a principal in a consulting firm, and also served as an HR vice president in the financial services industry. He spent almost 15 years with PepsiCo working with leadership and organization development issues across all divisions (snack foods, beverages, restaurants) both globally and from a corporate perspective. He also has experience in the retail industry, with a not-for-profit organization dedicated to the development of presidents and chief executive officers, as well as in the marketing communications and advertising industry. He has written on global HR practices, diversity, cross-cultural effectiveness, executive development, and leadership. He is often a featured speaker addressing issues related to the international and global development of individual executives and organizations.

George P. Hollenbeck is an organizational psychologist specializing in executive leadership development; he consults, teaches, and writes about leadership, and has taught at Boston University, Texas A&M University, and the Center for Creative Leadership. His career includes positions as the human resources executive at Merrill Lynch in New York with worldwide responsibility for human resources, as vice president—organization planning at Fidelity Investments, and as senior director—executive education at the Harvard Business School.

After receiving his Ph.D. from the University of Wisconsin, he worked at IBM and the Psychological Corporation, and Harvard Business School's Advanced Management Program. He is a Diplomate of the American Board of Professional Psychology, and a licensed psychologist in New York and Massachusetts.

His writings include the 1999 article "Behind Closed Doors: What Really Happens in Executive Coaching," and the 2001 book *Frequent Flyers: Developing Global Executives,* coauthored with Morgan McCall. He is an avid fisherman.

Harry Levinson is clinical professor of psychology emeritus, Department of Psychiatry, Harvard Medical School; chairman of the Levinson Institute; and former head of the Organizational Mental Health Section at the Massachusetts Mental Health Center. He created and for 14 years directed the Division of Industrial Mental Health at the Menninger Foundation. He has been a visiting professor at the Sloan School of Management, Massachusetts Institute of Technology; University of Kansas; Harvard Business School; and Florida Atlantic University, as well as at other universities both in the United States and abroad. Levinson has received numerous awards for his work with business, government, and academic organizations, and in 1992 was co-recipient of the American Psychological Association Award for Distinguished Professional Knowledge. In August 2000, he was given the American Psychological Foundation Gold Medal Award for Life Achievement in the Application of Psychology. He served as president of the Kansas Psychological Association and the American Board of Professional Psychology. He has authored 13 books, including *Men, Management and Mental Health; The Great Jackass Fallacy; Organizational Diagnosis; Ready, Fire, Aim; Psychological Man; The Exceptional Executive;* and *CEO.*

Karen S. Lyness is an associate professor of management in the Zicklin School of Business at Baruch College, City University of New York. She earned her M.S. and Ph.D. in industrial and organizational psychology from the Ohio State University. Prior to joining the Baruch faculty in 1994, she held a number of positions in human resource management, organizational development, and management research at AT&T, Avon Products, and Citicorp. Currently she conducts research and consults on women in management, "glass ceiling" issues related to women's advancement into executive positions, turnover, compensation, managerial careers and development, work-family interface, and other issues related to workforce diversity. Her research has been published in *Academy of Management Journal, Journal of Applied Psychology, Journal of Vocational Behavior,* and *Sex Roles,* and she is a member of the *Academy of Management Journal* Editorial Board.

Marianna Makri is a Ph.D. candidate and research associate in the College of Business at Arizona State University. She received her B.A. and M.A. in mathematics from the University of South Florida. Prior to starting her doctoral degree, she worked for Critikon Corporation in Tampa, Florida, and as adjunct faculty for the University of South Florida. She is currently teaching management courses at Arizona State University. She has published in the *Academy of Management Executive* and has served as a reviewer for the Academy of Management Conference as well as Organization Science. She has been an active member of the Academy of Management and has presented her research at several Academy of

Management conferences. Makri's research focuses on compensation, innovation and knowledge management, and mergers and acquisitions.

Val H. Markos is executive director of leadership development at BellSouth, addressing the assessment, selection, development, and staffing of the top 2 percent of positions in the company, the company's future leadership, and the selection systems development and validation for all BellSouth jobs. He joined BellSouth as corporate manager of human resources research.

Prior to joining BellSouth, he worked as an internal consultant in the area of personnel selection and organization development in both the private and public sectors. He has an M.S. and Ph.D. in industrial/organizational psychology from the University of Georgia and a B.A. in psychology from Weber State University in Ogden, Utah.

He has made numerous presentations at national conferences and seminars sponsored by organizations such as the American Psychological Association, the Society of Industrial/Organizational Psychology, the Human Resources Planing Society, and the American Society for Training and Development. He currently serves as chair of the Management Education Alliance, an alliance of corporations, major business schools, and historically minority business schools aimed at improving the business education of minority students. He has competed in 12 marathons and 9 triathlons since 1990.

Luis Gomez-Mejia is a professor of management in the College of Business at Arizona State University. He received his M.A. and Ph.D. in industrial relations and a B.A. in economics from the University of Minnesota. Prior to entering academia, he worked for eight years in human resources for the City of Minneapolis and Control Data Corporation. He has served as a consultant to numerous organizations since then. Prior to joining ASU, he taught at the University of Colorado and the University of Florida. He has served on the editorial board of the *Academy of Management Journal* and is editor and cofounder of the *Journal of High Technology Management Research*. He has published more than 60 articles appearing in management journals such as *Academy of Management Journal*,

Administrative Science Quarterly, SMJ, Industrial Relations, and *Personnel Psychology.* He has also written or edited a dozen management books. He has been ranked among the top nine researchers in productivity, and has received numerous awards including "best article" in the *Academy of Management Journal* (1992) and Council of 100 Distinguished Scholars at Arizona State University (1994). His research focuses on macro HR issues, international HR practices, and compensation.

D. Douglas McKenna is a senior consultant in leadership development at Microsoft, where he is responsible for supporting the development of the company's current and future leaders. He joined Microsoft in 1993, after 15 years as a professor in industrial/organizational psychology at Wheaton College, University of Minnesota, and Seattle Pacific University. He was hardly a newcomer to Microsoft in 1993, having worked almost continuously for the company as consultant beginning in 1985. He holds a B.A. in psychology from Seattle Pacific University and a Ph.D. in differential psychology from the University of Minnesota.

Robert B. McKenna is an associate professor of organizational behavior and director of the Organizational Behavior Program at Seattle Pacific University. He is president of McKenna & Associates, an organizational development consulting firm specializing in leadership development and program evaluation and serving a variety of clients including Microsoft and Boeing. He holds a B.A. in business and an MBA from Seattle Pacific University, and a Ph.D. in organizational psychology from Claremont Graduate University.

David A. Nadler is chairman and chief executive officer of Mercer Delta Consulting, LLC, and serves on the board of directors of Mercer Consulting Group, Inc. He has consulted at the chief executive officer level of major corporations for the past 25 years, specializing in the areas of large-scale organization change, executive leadership, organization design, and senior team development. He has authored or edited numerous articles and 14 books on organization change, leadership, executive teams, and organization design, including *Organizational Architecture, Competing By Design, Executive Teams,* and *Champions of Change.* He has served as chairman of the Delta Consulting Group from its founding in 1980 through its acquisition by Mercer. He holds a B.A. in international affairs from George Washington University, an MBA from the Harvard Business School, and an M.A. and Ph.D. in psychology from the University of Michigan. He is a member of the Academy of Management and a Fellow of the American Psychological Association.

Leslie Pratch advises senior business leaders on the human dimensions of executing corporate strategy. Her clients include family-controlled and closely held corporations, large professional partnerships, financial service firms, and Fortune 500 industrial corporations. Her primary focus is to help corporations identify and groom the most promising future senior executives. Her consulting career began at the University of Chicago, when she advised Arthur Andersen how to groom the partners identified as having the greatest potential to bring in new business. She later attended Northwestern's medical school for clinical training, where she studied successful older executives to determine what in their psychological makeup accounted for their success. Curious if these qualities were also characteristic of younger executives, she convinced the business school at the University of Chicago to fund a study on the personality predictors of effective business leadership. She replicated the findings, which were published in peer-reviewed academic journals. She holds an MBA from the University of Chicago, a Ph.D. in clinical psychology from Northwestern University Medical School, an M.A. in human development from the University of Chicago, and a B.A. in religion from Williams College.

J. Carlos Rivero works in the area of action research, with an emphasis on organizational assessment and change measurement at Mercer Delta Consulting, LLC. He is responsible for Mercer Delta's Organization Research Group, and is co-chairman of the firm's Intellectual Capital Board. He formerly served as a faculty member at George Washington University and Columbia University, and has held internal consulting positions at AT&T and Goldman, Sachs & Co. He holds a B.A. from Columbia University and an M.A. and Ph.D. in industrial/organizational psychology from New York University.

Anthony J. Rucci is executive vice president and chief administrative officer for Cardinal Health, Inc., a $38 billion Fortune 100 global health care products and services company headquartered in Dublin, Ohio. Prior to Cardinal, he gained over 25 years of business experience as a senior officer with two other Fortune 100 companies, Baxter International and Sears, Roebuck & Co. He ended his 15-year career at Baxter in 1993 as senior vice president for corporate strategy, business development, and investor relations. Between 1993 and 1998 he was executive vice president and senior administrative officer for Sears, and chairman of the board of directors for Sears de Mexico from 1995 to 1997. He has also been dean of the College of Business Administration at the University of Illinois at Chicago. He holds Bachelor's, Master's, and Ph.D. degrees in industrial and organizational psychology from Bowling Green State University.

Jeffrey A. Sonnenfeld is the associate dean for executive education at Yale University's School of Management as well as the founder, president, and chief executive officer of the Chief Executive Leadership Institute in Atlanta. Previously, he was a professor at the Goizueta Business School of Emory University. There he founded the Center for Leadership and Career Studies, which he ran for 8 years. Prior to this, he spent 10 years as a professor at the Harvard Business School. His research, publications, and consulting address issues of top leadership development, executive succession, and board governance. He received his A.B., MBA, and D.B.A. degrees from Harvard University.

Janet L. Spencer works in the areas of executive team development, organization architecture, strategy formulation, and large-scale organizational change at Mercer Delta Consulting, LLC. In addition to consulting, she acts as co-chairman of the firm's Intellectual Capital process, and head of marketing. Most recently she served as a principal for W. Warner Burke Associates, Inc., working with senior executives in the management of large-scale culture change. She holds a B.A. in psychology from Clark University and an M.A. and Ph.D. in organizational psychology from Columbia University.

The 21st Century Executive

PART ONE

Defining Executive Effectiveness

CHAPTER 1

Deciphering Executive Failures

Jeffrey A. Sonnenfeld

We are surrounded with recipes for leadership success. Publications ranging from popular periodicals to scholarly journals and all forms of electronic media map out accessible-seeming paths to the top. Despite these inspirational tales of triumph, rare is the life saga without its hardships. When we consider the proud autobiographies of chief executive officers such as *Mean Business* by Al Dunlap of Sunbeam and *Odyssey* by John Sculley of Apple, we are reminded of the fleeting nature of fame. No sooner had these books been shipped to the bookstores than the debris that caused the ultimate career derailment of each of these leaders began to surface.

Great leaders are not protected by their renown once they reach the top. Despite their great vaults of resources they become vulnerable because they are seen as having painted a bull's-eye target on themselves while becoming more careless, and even reckless. This theme of caution at times of triumph appeared prominently in the great Kinks ballad "Celluloid Heroes":

> Everybody's a dreamer, everybody's a star,
> Everybody's in showbiz, it doesn't matter who you are.
> For those who are successful, be always on your guard,
> For success walks hand in hand with failure along Hollywood Boulevard.

Perhaps it is possible to reverse this admonition. Not only is success coupled with failure, but also perhaps career failure can actually enhance career success.

Can Failure Breed Success?

Going back in history, one of the great icons of the success myth, Horatio Alger, was, in fact, a victim of great career disappointment himself. Alger's name has long been synonymous with the epitome of business success, but his life and work are largely a social invention.

The rags-to-riches formula that ran through his stories was heavily drawn from such original authors as Charles Dickens, Herman Mellville, Mark Twain, and Benjamin Franklin. The stories profiled poor children who attained moderate success, but not great wealth. Alger himself was a fugitive former preacher who died in poverty, regarding himself as a failed writer. The success aura posthumously attached to his name was actually the creation of a crafty magazine editor who fed a nation at war, an image of a triumphant author who profiled success in others (Sharhost & Bales, 1985).

A core value—one that differentiates the false folklore of unbroken success from the genuine qualities of folk heroes across nations and over the ages—has been the theme of resilience from failure. The anthropologist Joseph Campbell (1949) has provided us with the building blocks of robust oral and written stories of folk heroism. Whether it is Moses, Jesus, Mohammed, Buddha, Odysseus, Aeneas, Chuchulain, or Tezxatlipoca, the great folk heroes were often of humble origin. They possessed inspiring visions that symbolized the dreams and aspirations of their people, and then, after a chain of successes, they overcame devastating setbacks.

More recently, Howard Gardener's (1990) study of great historic figures, *Extraordinary Minds,* similarly identified a set of common qualities that described these "influencers." Gardener did not believe that core intelligence, lucky breaks, or even an untiring spirit were the characteristics that made a difference. Instead, he posited that the great figures he chronicled possessed a candid appraisal of their own strengths and weaknesses, were effective at keen analysis of unique situations, and mastered the capacity to reframe past setbacks into future successes. The crushing nature of defeat did not deflate them but rather energized them to reengage with even greater gusto. In addition, it was not the magnitude of the setback that set these people apart. It was how brilliantly they managed to construe their losses.

Thus the "comeback kid" imagery is hardly restricted to sports and politics. Overcoming adversity is a fundamental aspect of transformational leadership. The recovery from life's challenges helps to build the near-superhuman, larger-than-life aura that is so critical to the heroic identity (Sonnenfeld, 1988). Many contemporary business leaders, such as Robert Pittman, president of AOL/Time Warner, Bernard Marcus, founder of huge home-improvement retailer Home Depot, Steve Jobs, founder of Apple Computer, and business media mogul Michael Bloomberg, are great enterprise builders who were only momentarily traumatized when forced from major leadership positions before rebounding.

Pittman was pushed out of Time Warner in 1994, having previously cofounded the MTV music channel and led Warner Ventures into taking over Six Flags Amusement Parks. He went on to top jobs at Century 21 and AOL only to return in 2001 as president of the combined AOL/Time Warner media colossus.

Marcus was fired as chief executive officer of Handy Dan's Home Improvement in a fashion he felt was intended to maximize public humiliation. Bloomberg was fired from Salomon Brothers, the only employer he ever had, before promptly launching what became a sprawling media empire (Bloomberg, 1997; Lowry, 2001). At age 32, Steve Jobs was forced out of the firm he had created when he was 21. He founded a new enterprise that was bought by Apple, ultimately returning him to his old throne (Pollack, 1997).

Years earlier, we might have turned to such far-ranging business leaders as Ross Perot, Edward Land, Henry Ford, and Thomas Edison to similarly remind us of the catalyzing force of failure. Ross Perot took a great loss in 1974 when the two Wall Street investment houses he owned collapsed.

Both of Henry Ford's first two automobile manufacturers, the Detroit Automobile Company in 1899 and the Henry Ford Motor Company in 1901, were market and financial failures. Polaroid founder Edward Land once told me how bitterly he had to fight when he was twice outmaneuvered and almost crushed by infringements from Kodak. Even the brilliant wizard Thomas Edison had been profoundly outmaneuvered by tycoon Jay Gould. Edison lost the rights for substantial telegraphic inventions. Subsequent business history, however, shows that such failures were empowering rather than paralyzing events in the lives of these storied leaders.

Why Leveraging Failure Remains a Mystery

Thus it would seem strange that the intricacies of failure are not studied with the same intensity as is the siren of success. The closest brush with failure that appears in popular and scholarly literatures is through insights on avoidance. For example, the classic psychological study of longitudinal career success by Douglas Bray, Richard Campbell, and Donald Grant (1974)—*Formative Years in Business*—revealed the importance of a good early start. With initial supportive supervision and appropriate early assignments, a self-fulfilling success syndrome could build up momentum where good positions are followed by more good positions.

Failure can curtail such momentum. A dozen years ago, the Center for Creative Leadership pioneered this important field by looking at fast-track managers who stayed on track versus those who lost their trajectory with greatness.

Despite the wisdom of learning from lessons of honest history that historians and philosophers from Santayana onward intone, even historians often approach the collective wisdom as guidelines to avoid political or diplomatic failure rather than the means of recovering from a bad call or a devastating fall. We often look at the factors that led to a national leader's defeat and, at most, shake our heads in amazement at the phoenixlike revivals of leaders such as Richard Nixon, Michael Dukakis, or Bill Clinton. The reasons we do not see a more enthusiastic embrace of failure are tenfold:

1. *Our society so worships success that we are afraid of associating with a possible contagion of failure.* Unless we look successful, people may have to distance themselves from us.

2. *The self-esteem cost of failure is so painful our whole identity can be imperiled by even acknowledging defeat* (Matheny & Cupp, 1983). A lifetime of personal dreams and the aspirations of others in your

life may seem to have ended. People feel lost with no career road map; a sense of anomie or a directionless and powerless type of depression can set in.

3. *The victims of defeat are angry with themselves and ashamed.* They may feel liable for the losses to those in their family and those coworkers they feel they have let down. They believe, often correctly, that without their business card, they are worthless to others around them. They view their failure as a character flaw and not an injustice in their prior work environment.

4. *The victims of failure often believe that they can disguise their defeat by superficial wordsmithing.* This is the proverbial and always unconvincing, "Resigned to pursue other interests." They may believe that they can control speculation or that no one else really knows what happened (Freudenberger, 1974). No one is fooled by these pathetic efforts to sweep things under the carpet, to bury the truth, but victims cling to the hope that if they hide under the covers, perhaps the monster will go away. Friends may encourage this by counseling, "Why bring attention to this? Fewer people know than you think." The reality is, those you fear knowing about the setback will either know or become immediately aware the moment you are a candidate to enter their work environment.

5. *Others around the victim are similarly embarrassed.* Practicing face-saving management techniques (Goffman, 1959), they advise the victim in avoidance practices. Thus with Polonius-like wisdom they recommend, "Move on! Don't wallow in your misery!" when one attempts to analyze what has happened. Or, "Take a vacation. You need a break from the stress," when the victim rationally seeks to understand and possibly confront the source of the stress.

6. *People may think they lack sufficient resources to take on the restoration campaign.* Taking on a campaign to prove your valor is not easy. It may require winning over skeptical investors, amassing legal armament, convincing influential political forces, affiliating with credible and cleaner third parties, or having the courage to start over—proving yourself again with little fanfare or infrastructure.

Ironically, those born to wealth or prominence feel this weakness especially keenly. Perhaps not having scraped for crumbs of support before climbing the ladder rung by rung, they do not know where to begin. After Tom Oliver left the presidency of Federal Express quite suddenly, he left Memphis for Atlanta to run a tiny, floundering technology firm. He soon escaped when Bass PLC called, asking him to take the reins of the Holiday Inn lodging empire. For this reason venture capitalists often seek to invest in those who, in fact, have previously faced failure.

7. *The lack of knowledge about recovering from failure creates a circle of ignorance.* People do not know how to confront failure so they just try to hide from it. "With no guides to follow why experiment with my life? What if challenging defeat doesn't work? Perhaps I'll just exacerbate the damage."

8. *The double-edged sword of celebrity may create liability out of a former asset.* The more career successes someone has and the more prominent someone becomes in their profession or industry, the better known their setback will be. Thus fame can morph into infamy. This abrupt transition often hits accomplished people quite hard. Literary scholar Leo Braudy wrote in *The Frenzy of Renown* (1986) that many people either seek or endure public recognition in the belief that fame will liberate them from the shackles of conventionality and the dangers of powerlessness. This is akin to what has been labeled by psychologists as *idiosyncrasy credits* (Hollander, 1964). There may be a cushion of material comfort in being a celebrity, but the fall from great heights is only more painful and the recovery more complicated than the smaller-scale disasters of lesser-known lives.

9. *Elevation and celebrity, however, is never guaranteed to be permanent.* The vulnerable nature of leadership reputations creates barriers. When catastrophic career setbacks attack superachievers, known most for their enormous success, we now see them as failing in a public spotlight. They have lived very public lives and now confront their personal losses in that spotlight of attention. President Jimmy Carter, widely regarded as the greatest U.S. ex-president, once confided to me, "It is especially hard starting over when you've been fired. Especially if you've been fired by the public."

10. *High-profile successful people are often used to believing themselves self-reliant in sharing their advice and resources with others.* They don't like the uncomfortable position of being on the receiving end. Rather than feeling it is now payback time, they often believe that seeking or accepting advice, credibility, and finances from other parties makes them look and feel even weaker. Relying more on the generosity of others, they need to shift from familiar power bases

like formal authority, coercion, and resource control to those based more upon referent power or identification with the suffering and obligation or friendship.

The Tasks for Recovery

The path for recovery is rarely a rapid one but is often far more achievable than is believed. The first step must be some sort of working analysis of the situation. The second step involves decisive actions whereby the victim regains a sense of mastery over life and career. Both these steps have several components. The initial goal should be to gain an accurate assessment of current strengths and weaknesses as well as an accurate assessment of the opportunities. The ultimate goal should be to recast the leader's image as back in charge.

Am I to Blame?

Too often when this is attempted, the victim becomes confused between situational attribution (it's all their fault) and dispositional attribution (it's all my fault) (Jones & Nisbett, 1971). Too much of either risks vilifying innocent parties, shielding the career victim from an accurate awareness of personal complicity, or blaming the victim. The reality may well be a mix of the two perspectives. At the same time, there actually are such entities as innocent victims and genuine villains and a balanced perspective—putting blame on both houses—is not necessarily accurate. Both dispositional and situational filters must be used to thoroughly understand the failure event even though a balanced sharing of culpability is inappropriate.

These dispositional questions—which must be considered—have to do with how the victim possibly contributed to this failure:

Did you accurately assess your talents or were you over your head in competence, experience, or necessary relationships? Early career leaders often seek the celebrity and power or "bright lights and trumpets" before they are ready. Often in fast-growing enterprises people find that their skill sets were not growing with their job demands. After mergers, ambiguity in roles and job requirements is common. Did you possess the cross-functional competence needed for a new managerial position? After becoming chief executive officer of

Coca-Cola following the death of legendary Roberto Goizueta, the financially brilliant Douglas Ivester was unable to appreciate complex global realities requiring new sensitivities to local issues and appreciation of diversity challenges and domestic bottler problems, and was removed from office.

Was your leadership style an issue? Sometimes people can exhibit what to others may look like impatience, lack of responsiveness, impulsive responses, defensive posturing, destructive hoarding and turf protection, arrogant exercises of power, ego-driven decisions, and personal pampering and grandiosity. Was constructive confrontation not well handled in situations of high conflict? Could well-placed humor or more careful listening have made a difference? Recent chief executive officers of Kellogg and Procter & Gamble have been removed from office, in part due to the accusations of high-handed, abrasive tactics.

Was your character ever an issue? Has your integrity or reliability ever been questioned by others and insufficiently resolved? Are you considered trustworthy and reliable? Are you seen as impartial and open-minded by all? Is your basic business judgment and street savvy respected? Al Dunlap has recently been indicted along with his outside auditors on misrepresentations in revenue recognition. Similarly, accusations presently surround the past leaders of CUC/Cendant and McKesson/HBOC in the aftermath of troubled mergers. No career recovery is possible until society believes accountability and justice have been served. By contrast, convicted of securities crimes, financier Michael Milken is back in action. He may still dispute the fairness of the charges against him, but after a $1 billion fine, two years in prison, and a lifetime ban from returning to the securities business, he is a thriving, respected, and popular entrepreneur in new technologies and education as well as a generous philanthropist.

Have you stayed on top of your firm's strategic mission? Do you understand the changing nature of your business and your industry? Is the mission correct and current? Twenty-five years ago, the visionary founder of Polaroid, Edwin Land, was informed that his prize project, an instant motion-picture system he called Polavision, was doomed by the emergence of home video. He berated the financial analysts and his own staff, insisting on his own correctness and crying out, "The bottom line is in heaven." Soon thereafter his board removed him from office.

Have you become entangled in the technological ball and chain? Lately, leaders have become enamored with information technology advances that may create electronic sinkholes. Bosses can become too insular, detached from social contact, micromanaging, and overwhelmed by data overload. Recently, even technology titan and Intel co-founder Gordon Moore exclaimed that his biggest technology barrier was getting through the avalanche of personal e-mail he receives every day.

Are you unable to leave the shop floor behind? Sadly, the present generation of workplace leaders is failing as community leaders. Political scientist Robert Putnam points out in *Bowling Alone* (2000) that involvement in civic groups has shrunk 50 percent in one generation. In my own surveys of chief executive officers, I have found that 84 percent spend two hours a week or more in recreation but only 32 percent spend that much time in civic organizations and only 4 percent spend that much time in political activities. Valuable perspectives on changing interests and competing needs in our diverse society are being lost on some of our leaders. As a result, many have lost the access to critical friendships for moral grounding, objective advice, and external influence networks.

Have your defensive filters kicked in? Have you started to believe only your flattering press clips? No one ever told Alexander of Macedonia that he was Alexander the Great until he so labeled himself. He then started to believe this fiction and invented a royal lineage tracing his ancestry to Achilles to further burnish his image. Grandiosity has destroyed many promising leaders. They can become intoxicated with the trappings of office and the vanity of a heroic identity.

Does your family understand what happened? Is your family a strong support system for you? How has your setback affected them? Are they concerned about your sense of loss? Have you communicated well with them and listened? What have they lost in terms of prestige and security? Are they interested in joining you in battle (and able to do so)? Do they pay too a high price for your personal campaign?

How has the trauma of the failure affected you? Do you seem more anxious? Does your intensity frighten people? What do you do to release the strain? How does the threat of external scrutiny and judgment feel? Are you able to withstand the career and financial uncertainty? How do you explain yourself to friends and family?

Do you have friends or professionals to turn to for needed advice and counsel? How sturdy is your physical health? What do you lose sleep over? How is your temperament?

What do you want to do with the remainder of your career? Do you want to reclaim what you lost or build something entirely different? Will you be able to recapture lost career momentum on the same track? Is there anything liberating for you from this setback given the timing, your life circumstances, and your present interests? Is this the right time for a career switch? These sorts of dispositional appraisals are critical because failure often hits successful people when their very success blinds them from needed remedial work. No one can learn without feedback from the surroundings.

Successful leaders often feel too busy for reflection and, as action-oriented people, are rarely the reflective type. Furthermore, a leader's success record often intimidates people from raising necessary challenges feeling that they themselves are of "mere dust and ashes" by comparison. Finally, the leader's imposing style may lead some intended messengers to conclude that those who carry bad tidings will be shot.

Are THEY to Blame?

When we turn to situational analysis, it is important to consider the many aspects of the external and internal work setting.

First, the culture-strategy-style fit must be reviewed. It is possible that a utility was not as well suited to your skills as an ad agency or a biotech firm would have been. The failure may have been one of selecting the wrong workplace for your interests. For example, elsewhere I refer to "Baseball Teams" (cultures that value novelty and invention and heavily recruit outside star talent); "Academies" (cultures that prefer to develop new ideas from within, offering consistency rather than first-mover advantages and internal functional career pipelines); "Clubs" (cultures offering reliability and slower, generalist careers); and "Fortresses" (cultures in distress requiring a survival ethic and trouble shooting skills such as cold, cross-functional analytic decision making) (Sonnenfeld, 1988).

It is unlikely that the same individual would flourish equally well in such diverse cultures. Often a superstar performer in one culture may seem too glitzy, too pushy, too sluggish, too cold, too analytical, too touchy-feely in another. Different cultures have different assumptions, values, time frames, theories of justice, norms of communication, styles of conflict resolution, and appearances. I've also indicated that different qualities of charismatic leadership such as personal dynamism, recognition, setting a credible example, and establishing high expectations matter more in some cultures than others (Sonnenfeld, 1989; Sonnenfeld & Peiperl, 1988).

Another appraisal must be done on the governance system—who was in charge and who had voice over what matters? Could you trust your boss? Were you set up to take the blame for someone else's bad decisions? Where could you go for grievances if you felt that you were not being treated fairly and seek an appeal?

Are any of these mechanisms available to you now? Are you exposed to your board of directors? How comfortable are they with management's performance? How knowledgeable are they? How independent are they from management? Is the information they get heavily filtered? Who are the key decision makers on the board? Do they invest the proper time to know what is really going on? Is there a clear succession plan? Does the board care about your situation? How can you get their attention? Do you have the resources to get your voice heard through internal channels, litigation, or the media if necessary?

A third type of situational assessment looks at the stakeholder profile. Were other interests on the outside likely to have pressured the firm about you? Were internal or external political interests threatened by you? Were individual rivalries in play? Who is involved in the success of the enterprise? Who has what views on the larger strategic context? How do their interests vary? Who is plugged in and in a position to help you explain what has taken place or lobby on your behalf? What power bases did you have (such as relationships, knowledge, seniority, formal authority) versus any antagonists? Who has what resources? Will the media or key industry sources understand and believe your version of events?

A fourth type of situational assessment has to do with the work system. How do subunits in the enterprise fit together? Were some groups just designed to be in conflict? Was dysfunctional stress apparent? Were you with a losing division from the start? Did they plan to spin your unit off, harvest it, or shut it down?

A fifth type of situational assessment has to do with the reward process. Were you fairly and accurately measured? Were the proper issues tracked over the right time frame? Who handles your performance appraisal? Are they objective and knowledgeable? What sorts of behaviors and time frame were encouraged by the incentive system? Were you put in an uncomfortable position relative to competitors or colleagues given the objectives set for your business?

A sixth type of situational assessment has to do with the career system. Closely related to the culture issues, was your time frame for advancement consistent with the norms in your culture? Were you given the training and tools to do your job well? Was there a destructive or unfair contest created in the tournament for promotions? Are outside hires evaluated skeptically or given too much credit as potential saviors?

From Analysis to Action

Having taken stock of yourself personally and of your situation in general, it is important to develop a recovery plan and act on it. Some victims of failure can get so involved in assigning blame or second-guessing past decisions that they do not climb out of their career quicksand. What do you want to accomplish? What resources do you have at your disposal? What is your likely time frame? What are the consequences now if you do not succeed? The ultimate objective must involve the following steps:

1. Acknowledging and redirecting the stress
2. Showing concern for collateral victims of your setback
3. Restoring your image by rebuilding your stature
4. Regaining your trust and credibility
5. Clearing your past by charting a new future

Redirecting Stress

Looking first at redirecting the stress, we have long known that job loss is one of the most stressful events in life (Holmes & Rahe, 1967). Similarly, the losses of title and role clarity are highly destructive workplace stressors (Cooper, 1983; Cooper & Payne, 1988). Instead of taking the often-prescribed vacation from the stress to clear your head, it is generally preferable to remove the source of the stress. Thus instead of acquiescing powerlessly to the adversity by going into retreat mode, figure out a strong approach and go into attack mode (Schuler, 1981). Research on psychological hardiness indicates that to triumph over stress, people must regain a sense of control and be willing to take radical approaches (Kobassa, 1979).

Hence we see the powerful example of Henry Silverman, chief executive officer of Cendant. Following a dazzling career as a Wall Street high-flier, the merger of his original firm, HFC, into CUC resulted in the dramatic unraveling of his service empire and a tragic loss of wealth and reputation. He acknowledged the heavy toll of the stress, sought counseling, reduced his exposure to critical stakeholders, protected his family, became a health enthusiast, and—most important—began a major litigation effort with government investigators against his merger partners and auditors to prove that he and his shareholders were deceived (Barett, 2000; Colarusson, 2001).

Reducing Collateral Damage

The next action, showing concern for the collateral victims, reminds us that resilient leaders draw heavily on their support system—friends, family, and coworkers—and these people's own resources must be respected and appreciated. One career victim who got caught in an accounting firm's power struggle realized that people were avoiding him over time because each time he saw an old friend who inquired how he was, he answered in far more detail than anyone cared to hear.

In addition, innocent friends and coworkers sometimes take stray bullets intended for the target victim. When Barnard Marcus was fired from Handy Dan's Home Improvement Stores by the infamously tough turnaround manager Sandy Sigoloff, Marcus believed that his two lieutenants were also fired through guilt of association. He took them both along as co-founders of Home Depot, where they became billionaires with their 1,000-store chain of 160,000 employees and $60 billion in sales. At the time of the initial firings, their financial backer Ken Langone exclaimed, "This is the greatest news I have heard. You have just been kicked in the ass with a golden horseshoe" (Marcus & Blank, 1999, p. 37). He could not have been more prophetic.

Rebuilding Reputation

The third task is to rebuild your stature by communicating the true nature of the adversity (Scott & Lyman, 1968; Fombrun & Shanley,

1990; Elsbach & Sutton, 1992). Reputations are a crucial corporate and personal asset, painstakingly built through experience, performance, and affiliations. When a reputation is attacked, it is essential to establish a credible denial of culpability if it can be done truthfully—or a prompt apology if otherwise—along with clear redirection of responsibility for the mishap (Benoit, 1997; Staw, McKenchnie, & Puffer, 1983). That is, you want to tell just what the real story is if you are clean. You also want to reduce the apparent severity of the nature of the act (as Michael Milken sought to put his questioned transactions in the light of prevailing industry practices rather than the consequences to ultimate victims), convey the appearance of reasonable behavior (could we see ourselves in your spot), and present understandable but unpalatable motives for your adversaries' behavior (greed, rivalry, bigotry, and the like).

When Leonard Roberts was fired as chief executive officer of Shoney's restaurants, many viewed the termination as a political revolt of the old guard against Roberts's style (Romeo, 1993). However, when the *Wall Street Journal* carried a searing piece indicating that Roberts was too vigilantly policing a new affirmative action program just weeks after Shoney's settled a huge racial discrimination suit, people saw things differently. The paper quoted founder and former chief executive officer Raymond Danner as complaining, "too many niggers here. If you don't fire them, I'll fire you" (Pulley, 1992).

While some recruiters thought Roberts's experience at Shoney's made him too controversial, the chief executive officer of Tandy RadioShack saw great potential in Roberts as his successor (Palmeri, 1998). At RadioShack, Roberts led a triumphant repositioning of the firm and a stunning 18 percent annual growth rate (Grant, 2001).

Reestablishing Credibility

The fourth critical task is to regain trust and credibility. Often this means proving your heroic mettle all over again. Do people still believe that you have the right stuff? Even some of your trusted supporters may wonder if you have been worn down by the career injustice or setback. The flamboyant real estate tycoon Donald Trump had no shortage of detractors in good times. By his 20s, he was already considered New York's premier developer (Morrison,

2001). His name had been splashed garishly across many of his enormous creations. Nonetheless, caught in a real estate cash crush in 1990, he saw the bankers once eager to lend him money now eager to get it all back (Rutenberg, 1996). He personally took control of the difficult retrenchment, as described in his book *The Art of the Comeback.* By 1997 his net worth returned to $3.5 billion with booming properties (Tomkins, 1994; Blair, 2001).

Start Again

Finally, the fifth task needed for recovery is to clear the past and chart a new future. As the 1960s Frank Sinatra anthem "That's Life" proclaimed:

> That's life. And as crazy as it seems,
> Some people get their kicks riding on dreams.
> You're riding high in April, shot down in May.
> Each time I find myself falling I fall flat on my face,
> I just pick myself up and get back in the race.

This often means launching a new heroic mission or discovering a fresh new calling. Steve Jobs was fired as chief executive officer of Apple in 1985, eight years after he founded the company and five years after it went public (Carlton, 1997). Angered and hurt, he regathered his ample resources and launched Next Computer with five devotees from Apple. Their product, NeXTStep Cube, flopped—but their operating system sold. Ironically, Apple bought it for $425 million 11 years later. A year after that, he was back at Apple as chief executive officer, promoting exciting lines of new products.

Failure as the Missing Ingredient in Success

Leadership books flaunt titles featuring everyone from the *Star Wars* characters to Attila the Hun and the many bromides from successful sports figures (Sonnenfeld, 1998). When the TV shows fade, scholarly revisions show unknown weaknesses in historic figures, or the sports figures slip up, the titles disappear from bookshelves. Transformational leadership is enhanced though adversity, but our writings and teachings underplay this.

A best-selling Harvard case study of the visionary transformational airline entrepreneur Don Burr all but disappeared when his pioneering airline was forced to sell out in distress. It had made one or two bad calls affecting finances, postmerger operating challenges, and technologies, and had had to deal with changing consumer preferences and some tough moves from competitors that made for an unwieldy mix. The lessons of this great social experiment are all the more valuable not because we do not know what led to unchallenged success but because the limits of the system were tested. I found it nearly impossible to teach the great Ibsen play "Enemy of the People" to success-oriented MBA students because the heroic protagonist of the tale failed in that his neighbors forced him out of town. The lessons of recovery are hard to locate because of our discomfort in looking into failure.

The experience of failure reminds us of our human vulnerabilities and our vital interdependencies. The humbling nature of career adversity genuinely builds character. The more pervasive the public humiliation, the more battle-tested a leader becomes. Overcoming adversity teaches us to cherish our reputations, value our friends, hone our communication skills, and learn empathy for the many sufferers of injustice that surround us. As Nietzche said, "What does not kill me, makes me stronger." While few resilient leaders care to relive their setbacks or continue to grieve over old losses, they are quick to spot a fellow sufferer and offer a hand to another who has slipped into career quicksand. It's good to know the lessons of failure are not lost to all.

References

Barrett, A. (2000, March 13). The comeback of Henry Silverman. *Business Week*, pp. 128–150.

Benoit, W. L. (1997). *Accounts, excuses, and apologies: A theory of image restoration strategies.* Albany: State University of New York Press.

Blair, G. (2001). *The Trumps: Three generations that built an empire.* New York: Simon & Schuster.

Bloomberg, M. (1997). *Bloomberg on Bloomberg.* New York: Wiley.

Bloomberg News. (2001, February 28). Former Cendant executives Forbes, Shelton indicted. Available online.

Braudy, L. (1986). *The frenzy of renown: A history of fame.* New York: Oxford University Press.

Bray, D. W., Campbell, R. J., & Grant, D. L. (1974). *Formative years in business.* New York: Wiley.

Campbell, J. (1949). *The hero with a thousand faces.* Princeton, NJ: Princeton University Press.

Carlton, J. (1997). *Apple: The inside story of intrigue, egomania, and business blunders.* New York: Times Books.

Colarusson, D. (2001, April 22). Wall St. is pondering Cendant's fresh start. *New York Times,* p. B-9.

Cooper, C. L. (1983). *Stress research: Issues for the eighties.* New York: Wiley.

Cooper, C. L., & Payne, R. (1988). *Causes, coping, and consequences of stress at work.* Chichester, UK: Wiley.

Elsbach, K. D., & Sutton, R. (1992). Acquiring organizational legitimacy, through illegitimate actions. *Academy of Management Journal, 35,* 699–738.

Freudenberger, H. J. (1974). Staff burn-out. *Journal of Social Issues, 30,* 159–165.

Fombrun, C., & Shanley, M. (1990). What's in a name? Reputation building and corporate strategy. *Academy of Management Journal, 33,* 233–258.

Gardener, H. (1998). *Extraordinary minds.* New York: Basic Books.

Goffman, E. (1959). *The Presentation of the Self in Everyday Life.* Garden City, NY: Doubleday.

Grant, L. (2001, March 26). Radio Shack uses strategic alliances to spark recovery. *USA Today,* p. B-1.

Hollander, E. P. (1964). *Leaders, groups, and influence.* New York: Oxford University Press.

Holmes, T. H., & Rahe, R. N. (1967). The Social Adjustment Rating Scale. *Journal of Psychosomatic Research, 11,* 213–218.

Jones, E. E., & Nesbitt, R. E. (1971). The actor and the observer: Divergent perceptions of cause and behavior. In E. E. Jones et al. (Eds.), *Attribution: Perceiving the causes.* Morristown, NJ: General Learning Press.

Kobassa, S. (1979). Stressful life events, personality, and health: An inquiry into hardiness. *Journal of Personality and Social Psychology, 37,* 1–11.

Lowry, T. (2001, April 23). The Bloomberg machine. *Business Week,* pp. 76–84.

Marcus, B., & Blank, A. (1999). *Built from scratch.* New York: Times Books.

Matheny, K. B., & Cupp, P. (1983). Control, desirability, and anticipation as moderating variables between life change and illness. *Journal of Human Stress, 9,* 14–23.

Morrison, L. (2001, April 1). Profile: Donald Trump. *Scotland on Sunday*, p. 9.

Palmeri, C. (1998, March 23). Radio Shack redux. *Forbes*, p. 54.

Pollack, A. (1997, November 8). Can Steve Jobs do it again? *New York Times*.

Pulley, B. (1992, December 21). Strained family: Culture of racial bias at Shoneys underlies Shoney's chairman's departure. *Wall Street Journal*, p. A-1.

Putnam, R. (2000). *Bowling Alone: The Collapse and Renewal of American Community*. New York: Simon & Schuster.

Romeo, P. (1993, May 1). What really happened at Shoney's? *Restaurant Business*, pp. 116–120.

Rutenberg, J. (1996, April 7). Towering comeback for Trump. *New York Daily News*, p. 10.

Scharhost, G., & Bales, J. (1985). *The lost life of Horatio Alger Jr.* Bloomington: Indiana University Press.

Schuler, R. (1981). Organizational and occupational stress and coping: A model and overview. In M. D. Lee & R. Kanungo, *The management of work and personal life* (pp. 169–172). New York: Praeger.

Scott, M. B., & Lyman, S. (1968). Accounts. *American Sociological Review, 33*, 46–60.

Sonnenfeld, J. (1988). *The hero's farewell: What happens when CEOs retire*. New York: Oxford University Press.

Sonnenfeld, J. (1989). Career systems and strategic staffing. In M. Arthur, D. T. Hall, & B. S. Lawrence (Eds.), *Handbook of career theory* (pp. 202–227). Cambridge, UK: Cambridge University Press.

Sonnenfeld, J. (1998). Does it matter who is the boss? In D. Hambrick, D. Nadler, & M. Tushman (Eds.), *Navigating change* (pp. 98–112). Boston: Harvard Business School Press.

Sonnenfeld, J., & Peiperl, M. (1988, October). Staffing policy as a strategic response: A typology of career systems. *Academy of Management Review*, pp. 588–600.

Staw, B. M., McKenchnie, P., & Puffer, S. (1983). The justification of organizational performance. *Administrative Sciences Quarterly, 28*, 582–600.

Tomkins, R. (1994, June 31). Casinos deal Trump a fistful of aces. *Financial Times*, p. 14.

CHAPTER 2

What the Best Business Leaders Do Best

Anthony J. Rucci

Who's the most effective business leader you can think of in the 20th century? Is it Alfred Sloan of General Motors, John D. Rockefeller of Standard Oil, Henry Ford of Ford Motor Co., Thomas Watson of IBM, Jack Welch of General Electric, or maybe Bill Gates of Microsoft?

Over the past 50 years, the topic of leadership has been a focus among I/O psychologists (Yukl & Van Fleet, 1992). It is easily among the most studied and written-about areas in organizational research. And it's not just psychologists who have focused on the leadership issue. Popular culture, more than ever, seems to be obsessed with the personality and charisma of leaders, whether in business, government, religion, philanthropy, or even sports. The fascination with leaders has been evident in the annals of written history—the heroic, visionary individual who inspires others to achieve more than they conceived themselves capable of achieving, as in Homer's *Iliad* and *Odyssey*, *The Song of Beowulf*, the Bible!

The discussion to follow is about what it takes to be an effective executive in a for-profit enterprise. Do we also expect business executives to be leaders? I suppose we do. It's certainly safe to say that the most effective business executives will typically display many of the traits that would be necessary to be a leader in other contexts. But that may be too simplistic a notion. Consider the diagram in Figure 2.1. With a few moments of thought, it's actually

**Figure 2.1. The Hybrid Model of
the Effective Business Leader.**

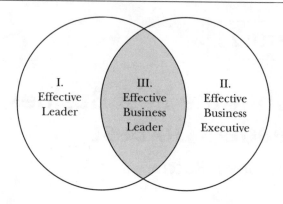

quite easy to think of examples of individuals who might fit the definition of an effective business executive, but not necessarily an effective leader. And there are certainly just as many examples of effective leaders who would be poor business executives. Lastly, there are those individuals who meet both definitions.

Take Group I, the Effective Leader Group. Few would debate that 20th-century leaders like Mother Teresa, Martin Luther King Jr., Lec Walesa, Caesar Chavez, Michael Jordan, or Jack Welch have demonstrated profound personal leadership influence. Would each of these leaders also have been effective business executives? We know Welch is, and we probably don't question Jordan's ability to do practically anything. But as for the others, you could probably generate a serious debate.

How about Group II, the Effective Business Executive who may not be an effective leader? Any list of effective business executives in the 20th century would have to include the names of successful entrepreneurs, venture capitalists, investment bankers, and inventors. That is, of the people who have created enormous economic value for themselves and others, but who would be leadership disasters in large, for-profit enterprises.

So who are the best business executives? For purposes of this discussion, they're the Group III individuals in Figure 2.1, the Business Leaders. These individuals cannot only achieve success as business executives but also meet the criteria for effective leadership. They cannot only create and sustain *economically* viable enterprises and generate acceptable economic returns for the owners of the enterprise, they can also create and sustain *socially* viable enterprises and cause others to voluntarily choose to follow their vision. In that sense, effective business leadership is a special category or subset of effective leadership. That's the group to be treated through the remainder of this discussion.

Who Decides What a Good Business Leader Looks Like?

Given that the leadership and executive effectiveness literature is so rich and robust, it might seem simple to define the criteria for being a good business leader. Just review the research literature, maybe perform some meta-analytic exercises, and you've got the answer. That approach is expressly avoided through the remainder of this discussion. No longitudinal studies will be cited and no prominent authors or researchers on the topic will be quoted. Instead, this largely (and admittedly) anecdotal discussion relies on a blend of research literature, personal experience, and simple observation of business executives.

A fundamental assumption being made is that setting the criteria for defining an effective business leader is largely an exercise in *emergent* leadership. When the board of directors appoints someone to a leadership role, that doesn't necessarily mean that the individual is a business leader, or at least an effective executive. When a business magazine puts someone on the cover, it doesn't mean that the person is a business leader. In fact, the best operational definition of a good business leader invariably comes from people in individual contributor roles in an organization. If you want to know who the best business leaders in your organization are, go ask your employees. They know. And they also know who your weakest business leaders are, even when your board of directors may not know. Too often, we fail to ask the people who know best what and who an effective leader is.

A business leader—whether chief executive officer, chief operating officer, chief financial officer, or executive vice president— is defined here as an individual whose peers and subordinates would *choose* to follow and support even if they weren't required to do so. It's the business executive who inspires commitment from others. The one who causes others in the organization to want to be part of the event, and makes them want to contribute their discretionary energy and ideas to the business leader and the enterprise. It's the business leader who evokes support for the vision based on three things:

- *Who* they are
- The *traits* they possess
- The *practices* they establish

Our focus here is the best-of-the-best. Many business executives perform adequately. The intent here is to isolate those things that seem to distinguish the outstanding business leader from the average business executive. What do the best business leaders do best?

Who They Are

Exceptional business leaders seem to have three things in common . . . the Three P's: passion, performance, and principle. Figure 2.2 reflects a brief description of these Three P's. These factors seem to characterize the best business leaders today—the ones who inspire commitment from those around them.

Passion

Exceptional business leaders have a passion for what they do every day. When the alarm goes off at 5:30 A.M., their waking thought is to want to be there as soon as they can, to make something happen. It's the passion you routinely sense in a true entrepreneur—someone who does for a living what they'd do for free if they had to. And the passion is palpable and contagious to others. Ask exceptional business leaders what they do for a living and you can visibly see their affect level change. Their energy level rises as they talk; you can feel their enthusiasm.

The passion is there whether they're the chief executive officer, the corporate treasurer, or the senior human resource executive in the organization. The chief executive officer's passion may be channeled into building the most competitive enterprise in the

**Figure 2.2. Exceptional Business
Leaders: Who They Are.**

The Three P's	Exceptional Business Leaders . . .
Passion	• Have a personal passion for what they do. They'd continue to do it if they were independently wealthy. They'd also continue to do it if they were compensated very little.
Performance	• They hate to lose. They keep score, and they set high standards. As much as they enjoy winning, they hate losing even more.
Principle	• Cheating to win doesn't count. When faced with a decision that puts profit ahead of principle, principle will always win.

industry. The human resource executive's passion may be channeled into creating the highest level of commitment possible from the workforce. The treasurer's passion may be to execute a creative, elegant debt issuance of corporate bonds. The point here is that each has a personal interest and belief in the value of what they do every day. Too often, in large enterprises, we have "professional managers"—executives who go through the motions every day, adequately executing their assigned roles but lacking a fundamental belief or excitement in the intrinsic nature of their jobs. You rarely see an entrepreneur just going through the motions. The minute that begins to happen to entrepreneurs, they're on to the next big idea or venture.

It might appear that it takes a noble cause or ideology to evoke passion. That's really not the case. Believe it or not, there are business executives who are genuinely passionate about earning more profit, higher EBITDA, or 20-basis-point reductions in expenses. No matter how anyone else may view that individual, it's their passion. No value judgment need apply. It's whatever the individual relates to at a personal level, whatever gets the person's achievement motivation and self-esteem engaged. It can be profits, core ideology, or professional excellence. All the best business leaders have passion, and others can recognize it.

Performance

Exceptional business leaders hate to lose. Coming in even second is distasteful to them. They keep score in obvious and not-so-obvious ways. They enjoy winning, but they hate losing even more. After all, losing not only reflects poorly on them, it makes them feel they've let their people down, too.

Being performance driven at a personal level manifests itself in a number of important ways. First, good business leaders set goals for themselves and others, and the goals are not easy. In fact, good business leaders typically will set goals for themselves that are far more challenging than either their manager or the organization would impose. And they write the goals down and measure progress against them. Second, good business leaders display a sense of urgency about results. Once a course of action is determined, they become immediately impatient to execute the decision and see the outcome. And third, good business leaders do not allow ineffective or even mediocre employees to remain with the organization. Other than personal breaches of ethics or trust, the quickest way for a business executive to lose credibility is to not confront poor performers. Poor performers are conspicuous to everyone else in the organization. Exceptional business executives are as demanding of others' performance as they are of their own. They are tough-minded in assessing poor performance, but compassionate in managing the individual.

Principle

Generally speaking, popular culture and the media portray senior business executives as mercenary and overly concerned about shareholders. National surveys also show a substantial level of public distrust toward business executives, as well. Unfortunately, there are some highly publicized cases that reinforce that stereotype. Executive compensation packages, which have reached incomprehensible levels, haven't helped much either. The fact is, senior business executives as a group are no different from any other slice of the population one could identify. Some business executives are not highly principled people. Some will look the other way when confronted with a convenient ethical shortcut.

But the best business leaders *never* put profits ahead of principle. The best business leaders will always defer to their principles when faced with a business issue. *Business ethics* is not an oxymoron to good business leaders. This arena of principled behavior, or principled leadership, is probably the most critical way a business executive has of gaining or losing the commitment of people in the organization. When business executives take ethical shortcuts, even once, it calls into question their trustworthiness. People in an organization see it and immediately wonder what would happen if it ever became convenient for that executive to make an expedient decision at others' expense. It's an insidious thing that can destroy the level of trust throughout an organization.

The best business leaders hold themselves and others to high standards of professional and personal behavior. They help articulate and enforce the core values of the enterprise. And they have zero tolerance for out-of-bounds behavior when it comes to matters of integrity and ethics. The very best business leaders not only establish ethical boundaries for themselves, they also possess a keen sense of the moral obligation they have toward the people they employ. They have a felt need to create a sustainable economic enterprise that allows employees and their families to experience satisfying lives and rewarding careers.

Why Do Some Executives Fail?

Before moving on to describe the traits that effective business leaders possess, it's important to ask a simple question: Why do some executives fail? It may seem out of sequence to be posing that question before completing a discussion of the traits and behaviors exhibited by good business leaders. The answer might seem obvious: executives fail when they don't possess the personal traits or practice the behaviors of effective business leaders (the ones to be described later). Unfortunately, it's usually not that simple.

Senior business executives who fail are rarely terminated for performance or skill set deficiencies. Think about it. Business executives who become chief executive officer, president, chief financial officer, or chief information officer of a major economic enterprise have usually demonstrated a consistent, sustained track record of achievement throughout their careers. Typically they've done quite well academically throughout their school years, including college and postgraduate work. (Yes, there are stunning exceptions to this assumption—Bill Gates of Microsoft or Larry Ellison of Oracle.) They've gone on to be effective at producing successful outcomes over a sustained period of time. They've established a reputation for being successful, dependable, and achievement-oriented. They've been promoted. Not just once, but six, eight, a dozen times in their careers before reaching the senior executive level in a major business enterprise. Could it possibly be that those promotions were all a mistake? That this person was really incompetent all along, and nobody recognized it? Highly unlikely.

Executives fail for one of three reasons, as shown in Figure 2.3. The overpromoted executive, typically promoted from within the firm, was a good or even excellent performer in prior assignments but simply does not possess the skills or traits necessary to perform at the senior executive level. As well-intentioned as the promotion decision was, the organization either failed to identify the criteria necessary for executive success or ignored them. Why would anyone ignore their own criteria? Typically out of a sense of obligation for prior contributions or as a reward for loyalty to the firm. This is a regrettable failure, since both the firm and the individual lose. The firm loses an otherwise competent contributor; the individual loses the fulfilling, rewarding career he or she enjoyed earlier.

The second type of failure results from an executive's inability to change. This individual has performed well in an executive-level assignment for some period of time, but fails to adapt to changing demands and conditions. Oftentimes this failure occurs after a merger or takeover by another firm. The executive fails to adapt to the new ownership's expectations, often seeming to regress to tried-and-true methods of success and overrelying on those behaviors even when it becomes obvious they aren't effective. Worse still, for the organization's sake, this failure also occurs when a successful executive begins to play it safe and defend his or her business position in the marketplace. The organization pays a significant price for this type of defensive behavior. It loses its competitiveness in the marketplace and begins a spiral of decline before the cause is identified. This is probably the single most nondiagnosed failure among business executives today.

Figure 2.3. Why Some Business Executives Fail.

Cause	Description
A. Overpromoted	These individuals fail because the organization promoted them inappropriately. Their performance in prior jobs was good or excellent, but they simply didn't possess the new skill sets necessary to move to the executive level. This failure typically occurs when executives are promoted from within their current company out of a sense of obligation for past contributions or as a reward for loyalty.
B. Inability to Change	These are individuals who have performed well for some period of time in an executive level assignment, but who fail to adapt to change. They rely on their traditional skill set and behaviors when new ideas and behaviors are required.
C. Cultural Misfit	These are individuals who have all the required skills and management practices to be successful at the executive level, but there is simply a lack of fit between the individual and the culture or values of the organization. They are often executives recruited in from outside the organization.

The third and perhaps most common reason business executives fail is a cultural misfit between the individual and the organization. It's the otherwise competent, successful executive who simply doesn't hold the same values as the rest of the executive management team. The individual who always seems just a little oblique to the tempo, rhythm, and conversation going on. Very often, this is an executive who is recruited from outside the organization with an otherwise exceptional résumé and track record. But all the interview and reference checks in the world will rarely allow for a reliable assessment of cultural fit with the organization's core values.

What is noteworthy about all three of the executive failure types described is that they rarely occur because of lapses in performance or competence. These heretofore successful individuals typically fail for intangible, subtle reasons. That's why traditional skills testing and psychological testing are not completely adequate to account for these qualitative factors.

The Traits of Good Business Leaders

You could find hundreds of studies of traits necessary for executive success. In addition, every company has its own set of criteria, written down or not, and the research literature in I/O psychology is replete with studies on the subject (Bray, Campbell, & Grant, 1974; Bennis & Nanus, 1985; Bass, 1990). How important is intellectual ability to success as a business executive? Consideration and initiating structure were the big two factors to come out of the early I/O research on leadership effectiveness (Fleishman, 1953). And popular business publications are guaranteed to have at least one article in every issue describing "the critical characteristics" of an effective leader or executive.

Figure 2.4 lists the seven key traits the best business leaders seem to possess. This list is an attempt to capture the relevant research literature on the topic, as well as summarize the popular business literature. Most specifically, this list comes from observation of good business leaders over the years.

Business Acumen

Business, like any profession, has components of science and art associated with it. The science of business is what one learns in college, and certainly in an MBA curriculum. The science is also learned by practicing the operational responsibilities of being a business manager.

In most professions, although understanding the science is a fundamental ingredient for success, it is those individuals who practice the art of the trade who typically excel. This is no less true in business. The term *business acumen* here refers to the art of being

**Figure 2.4. Seven Traits of
Effective Business Leaders.**

1. *Business Acumen*
   Assesses the financial implications of decisions and actions.
   Understands how strategies and tactics work in the marketplace.
   Balances data analysis with good judgment and common sense.

2. *Customer Orientation*
   Understands who the customers are, how they are motivated, and
   the current and future business challenges they face. Demonstrates
   a strong bias toward service, quality, and customer satisfaction.

3. *Results Orientation*
   Stays the course from start to finish. Does not confuse effort with
   results. Separates what is important from what is not. Demonstrates
   a persistent bias for action. Is tough-minded in assessing
   performance.

4. *Strategic Thinking*
   Anticipates future trends and directional shifts in the relevant
   marketplace, industry, and environment. Able to construct
   meaningful competitive strategies for addressing the knowns and
   unknowns of future business scenarios.

5. *Innovation and Risk Taking*
   Willing to explore new possibilities and approach issues differently.
   Focuses on a desire to achieve a goal rather than a fear of failure.
   Views honest mistakes as an investment in better outcomes.

6. *Integrity*
   Has an uncomplicated and uncompromising understanding of
   right from wrong, both publicly and privately. Values a fair playing
   field for everyone, and demonstrates courage of conviction for
   personal belief.

7. *Interpersonal Maturity*
   Is other-oriented rather than focused on self. Listens effectively and
   communicates ideas and opinions clearly. Is assertive while showing
   respect and positive regard for others. Considers the consequences
   of personal actions and decisions. Takes a collaborative approach
   that brings out the best thinking, attitude, and performance in
   others.

a business executive. Business acumen does not mean the ability to read a profit-and-loss statement or to calculate return ratios from a balance sheet, although those skills are necessary. The best executives have business acumen as a result of having an in-depth understanding of three critical questions about the enterprise:

- Who is the enterprise's core customer?
- Who is the competition?
- What is a realistic assessment of the enterprise's competitive strengths and weaknesses?

Understanding one's core customer is a fundamental but often misunderstood ingredient of success. Many firms assume they know the answer. Good business leaders never assume they know for very long. They're constantly asking about the demographic profile and purchasing trends of their core customer, and they talk to customers frequently. Next, good business leaders are obsessed with their competition. They know how customers assess their competitors, and they attempt to anticipate each competitor's next move. Very often, good business leaders get to know the personality of their competitors at a personal level. They include an assessment of a competitor's personality when making key decisions. Finally, good business leaders are brutally objective about their own firm's strengths and weaknesses. They view their enterprise as it really is, not as they'd like it to be.

It should be noted that business acumen is a common trait of all good business leaders, not just chief executive officers. The best chief financial officers know the answers to the three questions, as do the best senior human resource executives and the best heads of quality affairs. No matter what functional role one holds as an executive, business acumen—understanding the art of business— is a key trait to be among the best business leaders.

Customer Orientation

Customer orientation is another critical trait for good business leaders. Once they understand who the core customer is, they talk to those customers. They listen to what they say—both about their own company and also about the competition. They measure the customer's satisfaction with both product and service quality, and they take action.

At a personal level, good business leaders have a high sense of urgency about being responsive to customers. And they have a personal bias toward service. They'll pick up a phone if it's ringing. They'll get someone pointed in the right direction, and they'll interrupt what they're doing in favor of a customer's need.

Results Orientation

People who finish what they start are results-oriented. They stay focused on the desired outcome, and they do not get diverted from the goal. Good business leaders possess this trait. They are personally action-oriented, and display a high sense of urgency about results. Most important, they do not confuse effort or activity with results. Results-oriented people get to the point when they are communicating, and they emphasize the outcomes of a situation: "We won the championship"—"I graduated with a 3.8 GPA"—"We increased earnings that year by 20 percent."

Good business leaders measure things and track their organization's progress. They hold themselves accountable for results, and they intervene when progress is delayed. They also hold others accountable for their performance, and they are tough-minded in assessing the performance of others.

Strategic Thinking

As important as results are, good business leaders recognize the need to think about where the organization needs to be next month, next year, and next decade. Strategic thinking is much more than intellectual ability, although good intellectual ability in an executive never hurts. Strategic thinking has to do with abstract cognitive processes like pattern recognition, cognitive complexity, and tolerance for uncertainty. It is the ability to anticipate where markets are headed, and what the competition will do next.

Is strategic thinking the same as strategic planning? No. In fact, strategic planning processes in many organizations can actually constrain strategic thinking by forcing regimented approaches and disciplines to problem solving. Strategic thinking is an abstract reasoning process that is usually *not* linear or sequential. The most effective strategic thinkers are those who are intuitive as well as logical and fact-based.

Innovation and Risk Taking

Good business leaders take risks. They perform excellent due diligence, they are detail-oriented on facts and figures, and they demand precision. But after all those prudent activities, they do not hesitate to make the leap of faith that no set of facts can ever solidify. They recognize the power of being first to market with an idea or product.

Good business leaders not only tolerate change well, they initiate change. They're actually afraid of the status quo, and are constantly pushing themselves and their organizations for the next new idea or product. Most important, good business leaders do not view mistakes born of prudent analysis as failures. Quite the contrary, mistakes are viewed as an investment in a better ultimate outcome. And, of course, risk taking requires a high tolerance for ambiguity.

Integrity

Good business leaders meet all the traditional standards of integrity. They are honest and truthful. They are ethical, and they do not compromise themselves or their organizations. They don't cheat on travel expense vouchers. They don't use company resources for personal activities, and they don't ask secretaries to balance their checkbooks, pick up their laundry, or make family vacation travel arrangements.

In addition to these obvious indices of personal integrity, good business leaders ensure a fair playing field for others in the organization. They view their role as doing what's necessary to make others successful, not to catch others making mistakes. And last, good business leaders demonstrate courage of conviction for their ideas and behaviors. They state their opinions when they disagree, and they do not remain silent about issues in the organization. When something they've done or some idea they've had is not successful, they assume responsibility and do not look to place blame elsewhere.

Interpersonal Maturity

Good business leaders have a healthy self-esteem and are assertive but not egocentric. They are other-oriented, and they listen to people. They show a genuine respect and regard for others, and they do not abuse the power their position authority could provide. They are as respectful and considerate of an hourly employee as they are of a board member or the chief executive officer.

Good business leaders take a collaborative approach with others. They do not feel the need to do all the talking and they resist imposing a solution on others. What does it take to be a good business leader of people? It boils down to the fundamentals. You say "good morning" when you come in each day. You say "thank you" when someone has done something on your behalf. You look at people when they are talking to you to ensure they know you're listening. This is hardly rocket science, but good business leaders recognize the power in caring about employees as people.

The Practices of Good Business Leaders

Thus far, we've discussed who good business leaders are and what traits they possess. And while those elements must be present, they are not sufficient to create a good business leader. No matter how strong the personal traits, an executive who cannot introduce and sustain good practices will not be a good business leader.

So what practices exemplify good business leaders? Figure 2.5 shows the VOICE model. These five practices were identified by examining nearly 50 high-performance business enterprises (Rucci, Ulrich, & Gavino, 2000). The definition of "high performance" included criteria like superior five-year total shareholder return, high customer satisfaction ratings, and recognition as a superior place for people to work. The sample included organizations such as Cisco Systems, 3M, Southwest Airlines, Dell Computers, Harley Davidson, and the Mayo Clinic.

Business leaders in these high-performance organizations have introduced practices and organizational systems related to the VOICE components model. It's because of good business leaders that these processes and systems are sustained and improved. These practices have been shown to affect employee attitudes that are directly predictive of improved customer satisfaction, better profits, and superior total shareholder return (Rucci, Kirn, & Quinn, 1998; Schlesinger, 1994).

**Figure 2.5. Key Practices of Good
Business Leaders: VOICE.**

V	Vision	Have a purpose and create a clear line of sight.
O	Opportunity	Evaluate and develop people obsessively.
I	Incentives	Reward results and let employees share the financial success.
C	Communication	Share information widely and listen.
E	Entrepreneurship	Promote innovation and risk taking.

Vision

Good business leaders identify and communicate the purpose for their enterprise. Purpose is not strategy. It is a much more fundamental reason why an enterprise is allowed to exist by its customers (Collins & Porras, 1996). Disney's purpose is not to operate theme parks, it is to make people happy. Merck's purpose is not to make pharmaceuticals, it is to preserve and improve human life. Good business leaders articulate their company's core purpose, and it becomes a clear, elevating goal for people to be proud of (LaFasto & Larson, 1989).

In addition, good business leaders clearly articulate the core values of an enterprise. Core values are the guiding principles of an organization. These are beliefs that would not change over time, even if the company's strategy changed. The beliefs are held for their *intrinsic* value, not because they help produce profits. Truly "core" values would be maintained even if they became a competitive disadvantage for a firm. And core values need not be the Boy Scout oath. Making a profit can be a core value, if it meets the test of intrinsic value.

Good business leaders proactively communicate the enterprise's purpose and core values. They talk about these things. Most important, they attempt to create a clear line of sight from each employee's job to the enterprise's purpose. Whether you're a fork lift operator or the chief executive officer, you should be able to come to work each day at 8 A.M. seeing the connection between what you do for eight hours and the purpose, goals, and values of your organization.

This vision practice was clearly the most common characteristic among the high-performance companies. One other key practice related to vision is critical. Good business leaders hold people accountable for both their results and their compliance with the core values. The best business leaders eliminate from the organization those employees who don't share the core values, even if they are competent performers.

Opportunity

Good business leaders put systems in place to hire and develop the best people. And once they've hired good people, they give them meaningful work and decision-making authority, and they help them achieve balance between their work and personal lives.

Most important, good business leaders know the hiring template for success in their organizations. They develop criteria for executive success, and they use those criteria in disciplined selection and human resource planning systems. They are constantly assessing both performance and long-range potential, and they provide developmental opportunities for their employees. The very best business leaders spend as much of their time reviewing people as they do reviewing the financials of the company.

Good business leaders give people meaningful decision-making authority and they allow employees to act on their ideas. They give people managerial and profit-and-loss responsibility very early in their careers. And they allow people to balance work requirements with their personal lives and families.

Incentives

Good business leaders understand that even though people don't work exclusively for compensation, effective incentive systems are still a key part of an organization's success. Incentive systems need to be simple and they must pass the clear-line-of-sight test proposed earlier. They must also be consistent with the culture and values of the enterprise.

Generally speaking, good business leaders establish incentive systems with the following features:

- Rewards are performance-based.
- Rewards are tied to goals that support the strategy.
- Both financial and nonfinancial results are rewarded.
- Financial rewards are shared broadly throughout the organization.
- Individual and team-based rewards are balanced.
- Nonfinancial rewards are used liberally.

To be performance-based, incentives must be contingent upon the organization achieving certain performance goals. Those performance thresholds should be tied directly to creating value for the owners of the enterprise. Meanwhile, key contributors in an enterprise should be owners, receiving a portion of their compensation in some form of equity in the firm.

Increasingly, good business leaders establish incentive systems that reward nonfinancial outcomes as well as financial results. For example, customer satisfaction, product quality, and employee attitudes are increasingly viewed as *leading indicators* or predictors of future financial performance of an enterprise. Incentive systems should reward people for improving these leading indicators, just as they reward profit performance.

Broadly sharing the success of an enterprise is a key consideration. Good business leaders push equity participation well down into an organization. Stock options and discount stock purchase plans are two valuable ways of doing so. Profit-sharing plans and gain-sharing techniques are also excellent ways to include a broad segment of people in the performance-based incentive.

The critical component in any incentive system is the clear-line-of-sight test. Individual and team goals should be established, and those goals should relate directly and simply to the organization's strategic objectives. An employee at any level in an organization should be able to see a clear connection between individual effort, organization goal achievement, and incentive rewards. Good business leaders create incentive systems that cause employees to see how their job and effort ultimately creates positive rewards for themselves and the owners of the enterprise.

Communication

Perhaps the most overused word in management practices, *communication* is a hallmark of effective business leaders. First, good business leaders share and disseminate information broadly. Rather than hoard important information about financial performance and customers, they give people information to allow them to improve and do their jobs better. They do this through formal channels like newsletters and financial reports, but they are equally focused on informal channels like town hall meetings, staff meetings, or even hallway conversation. More than ever, people need information to do their jobs well. It's the executives in an organization who have access to the broadest amount of information. Good business leaders share information, and do it frequently and routinely.

The most overlooked and underutilized skill among business executives today is listening. Good business leaders listen to people at all levels in the organization. In fact, the best business leaders know that it takes conscious effort not to lose touch with people in large, complex organizations. They also know that politics and human dynamics cause others to be less than candid when talking to a senior executive. So good business leaders devise both formal and informal ways of staying in touch. They use employee surveys, but they also use the lunchroom to get a sense of the mood and concerns of employees. Employees at all levels in an organization know what their company does well and not so well. They also know when a company is in trouble. If business executives simply took the time to ask their own employees for impressions and ideas, they would learn a tremendous amount.

Though good business leaders communicate frequently, they recognize the importance and benefit of a simple, repeated message. In today's large, complex organizations, simplicity of key messages is a prerequisite to creating a clear line of sight for employees.

Entrepreneurship

Good business leaders possess the personal traits of innovation and risk taking, but they also establish processes to promote those behaviors in others. Most directly, they involve people at all levels in creating strategy for the enterprise. That is, they actively engage in formal strategic planning efforts, but they also informally ask for ideas and suggestions. Good business leaders not only allow mistakes, they actually encourage mistakes.

Resource allocation in an organization is a critical process. Good business leaders do not "allocate" resources to their people, they create systems that allow the best ideas to "attract" resources (Hamel, 1999). The analogy here is the open-market economy we know as capitalism. Capital in an open market flows to those enterprises that create value better. There is no chief executive officer of the global economy who decides to invest 5 percent of global capital in General Electric stock and 8 percent in municipal bonds. Capital is a pull system, not a push system, and good business leaders try to create that same dynamic when allocating resources within their organization.

The five components of the VOICE model—Vision, Opportunity, Incentives, Communication, and Entrepreneurship—are practices of good organizations and good business leaders. Most important, these five practices evoke commitment from people in an organization. Good business leaders understand that employee commitment to the goals and values of the enterprise is the seminal ingredient to creating value for the organization and its owners.

Summary

What do the best business leaders do best? That was the question posed at the outset of this discussion. I have tried to answer that question by defining the best business leaders as those who can create and sustain both economically and socially viable enterprises.

Figure 2.6 summarizes the answers to the three dimensions of effective business leaders—who they are, what traits they possess, and what practices they establish.

The definition of good business leaders has changed over the past 10 years—dramatically. Figure 2.6 reflects that change. For much of the 20th century, good business leaders displayed a militaristic, command-and-control style. The executives in an organization possessed *the* information and they were expected to have *the* answers. We have entered an explosive information-driven economic era. In today's complex, global enterprises, the best business leaders recognize that no one mortal individual can know everything necessary to run a successful organization. Giving peo-

Figure 2.6. What the Best Business Leaders Do Best.

Who they are	The Three P's: • Passion • Performance • Principle
What *traits* they possess	The Seven Key Traits: • Business Acumen • Customer Orientation • Results Orientation • Strategic Thinking • Innovation and Risk Taking • Integrity • Interpersonal Maturity
What *practices* they establish	The Five VOICE Practices: • Vision • Opportunity • Incentives • Communication • Entrepreneurship

ple a voice in an enterprise and gaining their commitment distinguishes the very best business leaders today from those business executives who are still going through the motions. Is it more demanding on the individual business executive to do the things reflected in Figure 2.6? Yes. It is much easier to be a command-and-control business leader who tells others what to do. But good business leaders recognize the value in the protocol outlined here. They also recognize that demanding though it may be, it's not rocket science.

References

Bass, B. M. (1990). *Bass & Stogdill's handbook of leadership: Theory, research and managerial applications* (3rd ed.). New York: Free Press.

Bennis, W. G., & Nanus, B. (1985). *Leaders: The strategies for taking charge.* New York: HarperCollins.

Bray, D. W., Campbell, R. J., & Grant, D. L. (1974). *Formative years in business: A long-term AT&T study of managerial lives.* New York: Wiley.

Collins, J. C., & Porras, J. I. (1996). Building your company's vision. *Harvard Business Review, 74*(5), 65–77.

Fleishman, E. A. (1953). The description of supervisory behavior. *Personnel Psychology, 37,* 1–6.

Hamel, G. (1999). Bringing Silicon Valley inside. *Harvard Business Review, 77*(5), 70–84.

LaFasto, F. M., & Larson, C. E. (1989). *Team work* (Vol. 10). Thousand Oaks, CA: Sage.

Rucci, A., Kirn, S., & Quinn, R. (1998). The Employee-customer-profit chain at Sears. *Harvard Business Review, 76*(1), 82–97.

Rucci, A., Ulrich, D., & Gavino, M. (2000). *The VOICE Model.* Unpublished manuscript.

Schlesinger, L. (1994). Putting the service-profit chain to work. *Harvard Business Review, 72*(2), 164–174.

Yukl, G., & Van Fleet, D. (1992). Theory and research on leadership in organizations. In M. Dunnette & L. Hough (Eds.) *Handbook of Industrial & Organizational Psychology,* pp. 147–197. Palo Alto, CA: Consulting Psychologists Press.

CHAPTER 3

Understanding the Personality of the Executive

Leslie Pratch, Harry Levinson

You must look into people as well as at them.
LORD CHESTERFIELD

The long-term success of a company depends on selecting the best senior managers and developing their fullest potential. There is no shortage of computerized surveys, standardized tests, 360-degree evaluations, and other instruments that aim to help select and cultivate the best. Yet experience attests that instruments alone fall short of doing the job. Human behavior in organizational settings is so complex that only a multidimensional approach that assesses the individual-organizational interface can come close to anticipating behavior over the long run.

In this chapter, we offer a comprehensive structural psychological approach to understanding the established continuity of the inner world of the executive and its influence on external behavior. This approach supplements traditional industrial and organizational approaches to leadership and executive personality.

Structural Versus Trait and Behavioral Approaches to Understanding Personality

Efforts to understand personality and predict executive behavior can be categorized in two ways (Pratch & Jacobowitz, 1997). One is a general, global way of characterizing a person according to his major styles of coping with problems. Another way of describing personality deals with one major quality of the person at a time and only secondarily attempts to understand the relations among these qualities. The latter approach characterizes most psychological models of leadership. A narrow focus on isolated traits or discrete behaviors enables researchers to achieve greater precision in understanding any one quality. Trait and behavioral approaches can be criticized, however, on the basis that individuals do not function as disjointed collections of parts but rather as more or less smoothly integrated wholes. Measuring each characteristic separately does not capture that integration. A global or structural model is useful to provide a framework into which many different specific aspects of personality can be integrated and understood in their relation to one another and to role performance.

We begin with a review and critique of the empirical literature. Building upon this review, we describe a structural approach to understanding personality and then demonstrate the utility of this approach for elucidating the complex, dynamic nature of executive personality. First, however, it is necessary to clarify the use of two key terms.

Definitions

The term *personality* has two different meanings, and it is important to keep them separate. On one hand, it refers to social reputation and to the manner in which others perceive an individual. This is personality from an observer's perspective. It concerns the amount of esteem, regard, or status that the person has within his reference groups. Personality in this sense is public and clearly linked to judgments of the person's behavior based on interpersonal performances. On the other hand, personality may also refer to intrapsychic structures, dynamics, processes, and tendencies—

intrapersonal behaviors—that explain *why* a person behaves in a certain way in specific circumstances.

The first meaning of personality refers to a person's social reputation: it is public and verifiable and can be assessed descriptively by paper-and-pencil tests (such as Jackson's Personality Research Form, 1989) and 360-degree feedback. The second meaning refers to the person's inner nature: it is private and inferable. Epistemologically, the status of these two meanings is quite different. The effectiveness of a leader depends on the perceptions of others; that is, the leader's reputation. This is the empirical phenomenon we want to explain or predict. However, a theory of inner processes, their functions and interrelations, is needed to explain or predict the bases of that reputation or effectiveness.

Corresponding to these two meanings of personality are two senses of the word *trait*. On one hand, trait refers to recurring trends in a person's behavior (that is, at the interpersonal level). To say that a person is masterful means that he tends to exert control over, influence, or direct other people or things in his environment. In this sense, the word *trait* is theoretically neutral and purely descriptive. It tells us what we may expect a person to do, but not why he would do it or when he would behave differently.

The term *trait* has also been used to denote psychological features that exist inside a person and that explain the recurring tendencies in that person's behavior (that is, at the intrapersonal level). This second use of the term describes what we may expect a person to do and explains why we should expect the person to behave that way. In this chapter, *trait* is used to denote stylistic consistencies in an individual's social behavior. The word will not be used in this chapter to denote structures or systems inside individuals.

Historical Overview

Because executives are individuals who occupy the most senior ranks of an organization, they are scarce as subjects of empirical research. The most relevant literature examines the relationship between personality and managerial or leadership effectiveness. Although executives are not necessarily leaders or managers, our overview of the industrial and organizational literature is limited to that research.

Empirical approaches to personality and leadership can be divided into three historical periods: the trait period, from the beginning of the 20th century to World War II; the behavioral period, from the onset of World War II to the 1960s; and the contingency period, from the late 1960s to the present.

Trait Approach

The earliest work in this area grew out of the late Victorian fascination with the so-called Great Man. Individuals who became leaders were understood to be different, somehow, from those who remained followers. The goal of research was to identify what unique features made an individual a leader. With the rise in the early part of the 20th century of the psychological assessment movement, personality measures were used to screen large populations for these traits. In more than 120 studies conducted over 40 years, leaders and their followers were compared on various measures of psychological traits believed to be associated with successful leadership. The measures ranged from dominance, ascendancy, and extraversion to physical appearance and intelligence. Reviews of the trait studies identified no consistent or reliable pattern (Bird, 1940; Jenkins, 1947; Stogdill, 1948).

Behavioral Approach

The perceived failure of the trait approach and the growing emphasis on behaviorism in psychology led researchers to direct their attention to the behavior of leaders. In the late 1930s, Kurt Lewin and his associates conducted a classic study (Lewin, Lippitt, & White, 1939). These researchers identified three styles, or behavioral patterns, of leadership: democratic, autocratic, and laissez-faire. The autocratic style was characterized by the leader's tight control of the group's activities and its decisions. The democratic style emphasized group participation and majority rule. The laissez-faire style involved very low levels of activity of any kind by the leader. Working in a controlled laboratory setting, the researchers examined the different effects of each style on small group productivity and morale. The democratic style was found to have slightly more beneficial effects than the other two styles.

Lewin's research is important not so much for its findings as for its conception of leadership as a behavioral style. The distinction between autocratic-directive styles and democratic-participative styles has influenced the focus of much subsequent research. A leader may either take responsibility for making decisions and directing group members or share, in varying degrees, decision-making and coordinating functions with them. What behaviors constitute the most effective leadership style has been a major topic of inquiry, whether the research was conducted in an organization, a laboratory, or an assessment center.

In the 1950s, behavioral approaches came to the forefront as research moved away from questions of traits and preconceived styles to what leaders actually do. Rating scales, interviews, and observations were used to identify the specific behaviors of leaders. Several researchers independently verified the existence of two clusters, or factors, of leader behavior. One factor related to interpersonal warmth, the use of participative, two-way communication, and concern for followers' feelings. The other emphasized task-related feedback, directiveness, and goal facilitation. The two dimensions were variously labeled *socio-emotional* versus *task-oriented* leadership (Bales & Slater, 1945) and *consideration* behavior versus *initiation of structure* (Stogdill & Coons, 1957), and *employee-oriented* versus *production-oriented* leadership (Kahn & Katz, 1953).

The identification of two reliable, behaviorally based dimensions of leader behavior was an important step forward. Nevertheless, attempts to consistently predict the effects of these behavioral styles on group and organizational outcomes were unsuccessful. Considerate leader behaviors, for example, did not appear to be reliably associated with satisfied subordinates, nor was the leader's structuring behavior consistently related to group productivity (Korman, 1966).

Several theorists have surmised that the failure of the trait and behavioral approaches was due to a view of leadership as the effect of a single and unchanging set of behaviors (Bennis, 1961; Gibb, 1954; Stogdill & Shartle, 1955). In fact, the trait and behavioral approaches failed because no one leadership style was universally successful across all situations. Only with the emergence of contingency theories could researchers finally predict leadership effectiveness with an impressive degree of consistent success (Bass,

1990a). Contingency notions propose that the leadership style that will be most successful depends on the nature of the task situation. Modern contingency models attempt to identify and categorize the most critical features of the situation and relate them to the most important aspects of leadership style and behavior.

Contingency Approach

The introduction of the first contingency theory by Fred Fiedler (1967) brought leadership research into a third phase, where it has more or less remained. Fiedler argued that two factors—the situation and the leader's orientation to the work group—determined leadership effectiveness. Specific situational parameters, such as the degrees of control, certainty, and predictability the situation afforded the leader, were crucial in determining leadership effectiveness. Fiedler also identified two leadership styles: relationship motivated and task motivated.

In addition to research that has incorporated contingency models, during the past 20 years a number of other approaches have been pursued. These include examinations of the time and process dimensions of leadership, including the nature of the complex interplay between the attributes of the leader and the needs, values, perceptions, and judgments of followers (cf. Bass, 1990b; Conger, Kanungo, & Associates, 1988; Graen & Scandura, 1987; House & Howell, 1992; Kouzes & Posner, 1987; Willner, 1984).

The Cognitive Revolution

The cognitive revolution in psychology has profoundly shaped contemporary leadership studies. Cognitive theories emphasize the role of cognitive mediation in influencing the contingencies that regulate relations between leaders and followers. A large body of research concerns the hypothesis that interpersonal actions and judgments are a function of the way in which events are construed in the minds of leaders and followers (cf. Binning, Zaba, & Whattam, 1986; Lord, 1985).

Cognitive psychology has also played a major role in recent taxonomies of managerial skills and tasks (cf. Cox & Cooper, 1988; Kanungo & Misra, 1992; Whitley, 1989). Terms such as *schemata, scripts*, and *knowledge structures* have been used to refer to underlying patterns of thinking that influence how managers interpret internal and external stimuli, and how this information is transformed into action. For example, Herbert Simon (1987) argued that constructive, reality-oriented habits of problem solving may be key components of a manager's effectiveness.

Elliott Jaques has developed a theory of eight levels of conceptual capacity (Jaques, 1996; Jaques & Cason, 1994). Each level is defined by how far into the future an individual can think or plan. The theory contends that organizations should be structured according to these eight levels, and that individuals should be chosen so that the conceptual requirements of the role match the individual's conceptual capacity.

The literature on the underlying cognitive competencies of leaders and managers emerged in the mid-1980s. This research is important because, for the first time since the early trait studies, scholars were again investigating the psychological characteristics that contribute to a leader's success across different situations and settings. Leadership studies entered a second trait era.

The Second Trait Era

Impetus for this trend was provided by meta-analyses of the early trait data (cf. Kenny & Zaccaro, 1983; Lord, DeVader, & Alliger, 1986; McCann, 1992). The findings of these analyses indicated that, contrary to earlier conclusions, certain individual characteristics, such as ego strength, stress tolerance, affective regulation, and self-direction, are linked to leadership effects across a wide variety of situations.

One individual characteristic that has been related empirically to effective leadership under stressful conditions is internal locus of control orientation (Rotter, 1966). Individuals with a strong internal locus of control ("internals") believe that events in their lives are determined more by their actions than by chance or fate. In contrast, individuals with a strong external locus of control ("externals") believe that mostly uncontrollable forces determine events and that there is little they can do to bring negative events to positive outcomes. A strong internal locus of control predicted managerial success in several field studies (Anderson, Hellriegel, & Slocum, 1977; Brockhaus, 1975; Goodstadt & Hjelle, 1973; Miller, Kets de Vries, & Toulouse, 1982, 1986).

Self-confidence, another personality characteristic, has also been related to managerial leadership. In one study, self-confidence predicted promotion to more senior levels of management at AT&T (Howard & Bray, 1988). In a study differentiating outstanding from average senior managers in six different types of organizations, self-confidence—manifested in the tendency to be stimulated by crises and other problems, rather than being distressed or overwhelmed by them—was the main determinant of managerial competency, influencing the likelihood that one of the other competencies would be expressed (Klemp & McClelland, 1986). Successful managers were described as confident during crises in a study comparing successful and "derailed" managers. A study of "critical incidents" in the work experience of more than 250 managers also indicated that self-confidence distinguished effective from ineffective managers (Boyatzis, 1982).

Emotional intelligence, as described by Daniel Goleman (1995), recently has been related to executive effectiveness (Goleman, 2000). Drawing on research on more than 3,000 executives, Goleman outlined six distinct leadership styles, which fall along the familiar dichotomy of task-oriented versus relationship-oriented styles. Each style, he contends, is linked to a different aspect of emotional intelligence, various competencies, such as empathy, relationship building, and interpersonal communication. In turn, each style has a distinct effect on the working atmosphere of a company or team, and, in turn, on its financial performance. The styles, by name and description, fall along the familiar continuum of leadership styles first identified by Kurt Lewin and his associates.

Other individual characteristics that have been related to leadership and managerial effectiveness include practical intelligence (Atwater, 1992; Atwater & Yammarino, 1993); social intelligence (Zaccaro, Gilbert, Thor, & Mumford, 1991); stress tolerance (Howard & Bray, 1988; McCall & Lombardo, 1983); response flexibility (Skinner & Sasser, 1977); the capacity for crafting a bold vision that anticipates future changes (Kotter, 1999); and self-monitoring (the capacity to monitor and control expressive behaviors in oneself; Ellis, 1988; Zaccaro, Foti, & Kenny, 1991).

Recently, some theorists have used the five-factor model of personality to organize and explain what other researchers had discovered about leadership (cf. Hogan, Curphy, & Hogan, 1994). The five-factor model relates to the structure of personality ratings (that is, trait words), which may be expressed in terms of five broad dimensions or factors—conscientiousness, emotional stability, agreeableness, surgency, and intellect. These factors are said to reflect what Hogan and his associates refer to as the "bright side" of personality. Proponents of the model argue that leadership requires the presence of bright-side traits as well as the absence of dark-side characteristics—that is, behavioral tendencies that undermine a person's ability to form a team and that may alienate subordinates.

It is important to note that the five-factor model refers to the structure of trait words, not to hypothesized inner psychological structures or systems. The model tells us about interpersonal behavior from the observer's perspective. Because individuals are predisposed to think about others in terms of these factors (Norman & Goldberg, 1966), the factors have been considered midlevel cognitive prototypes (Cantor & Mischel, 1977) or cognitive schemata (Fiske & Linville, 1980). Thus, although the five-factor model may tell us something about individual cognition, it is not a structural model of personality, as has been argued (cf. Digman, 1990).

The cognitive revolution shifted the focus of leadership research from the level of public perception (interpersonal)—the focus of behavioralism—to the level of private perception and the information-processing characteristics of leaders and followers (intrapersonal). This shift allowed research on behaviors that are observable by others and on those psychological characteristics of leaders that can be inferred.

Limitations of Trait, Behavioral, and Current Approaches

Significant progress has been made in identifying the traits, behaviors, and decision tendencies that influence managerial leadership. Unfortunately, however, research has neglected important issues in understanding personality. Fundamentally, it fails to address the relationship between overt, easily observed traits, behaviors, and decision styles of executives and their inner worlds—particularly their irrational and unconscious motives, values, and fantasies.

No matter how much they may reject the notion, executives bring their inner selves and private lives to work with them every day. From a structural perspective, this is a truism that scarcely merits comment. Yet those psychologists who typically advise organizations rarely address executives' inner worlds—to the detriment of the organization and the individual. Their work suffers from several fundamental conceptual and methodological shortcomings.

A focus on discrete personality traits or isolated behaviors. Trait theories attempt to explain and predict a person's way of thinking, feeling, acting, and reacting in a certain situation, with its specific characteristics and psychological significance, by combining values from a set of traits. Accounts of personality are framed in terms of one major quality of the person at a time, and only secondarily in terms of relationships among these qualities. Trait theories do not treat psychological functioning as a dynamic process, even when noting the importance of interactions among personality characteristics (cf. Goleman, 2000; Klemp & McClelland, 1986; Yukl, 1994). What needs to be understood is personality in all of its facets.

The trait approach leaves several questions unanswered:

- Are these traits indeed different tendencies, or do they reflect an underlying personality structure? How do attributes such as self-esteem, self-confidence, sociability, and intelligence relate to other individual characteristics, such as need for achievement, moral responsibility, regulation of affects and impulses, and an overall sense of identity?
- Do deficiencies in the latter characteristics undermine the degree to which the former attributes can contribute to a leader's effectiveness?

A focus on short-term functioning. An executive's style is fundamentally the outcome of a developmental process. Most research and applications to executives explain behavior in isolation from any developmental processes that may have led to the person's present state. It does not consider the origins of relevant aspects of the individual, the timing and environment of past and present events, and the ways those factors interact to produce current behavior. As a result, traits or behaviors seem to emerge de novo in the person. How a trait or behavior comes into being, whether it is likely to remain stable or change in subsequent years, and what factors are likely to affect its emergence and further development are rarely discussed.

The most effective executives exhibit a protean quality of resiliency and creativity, a continued readiness to *develop* new skills for coping with emergent, dynamic, and complex situations. Yet industrial and organizational psychologists, typically those most likely to be working with executives, come from academic backgrounds that give them neither the conceptual tools nor clinical training to assess the potential of individuals to grow and adapt over time. Consequently, they miss one of the most important indicators of functioning in executive roles.

A focus on behavior in the work role. The private activities, personal needs, and values of the person outside work are seen as off limits. While executives' private lives per se are their own, they bring their personal lives into their work in ways that are not always rational or easy to control. It is unrealistic to believe that events and experiences outside the professional sphere do not affect executives' formal decisions and programs. Without knowledge of a person's capacity to deal with all of life's demands as a family member, citizen, or friend, the ability to predict executive effectiveness is severely constrained.

A focus on rational, conscious thought. Conscious thought is often seen as a simple and obvious activity, resulting from a state of full self-awareness and full self-control. Less rational, frequently pathological and antisocial sides of behavior, such as neurosis, narcissism, sexuality, and exploitation of others, are minimized or ignored. Unconscious dynamic factors lead to intrapersonal conflict—and sometimes psychopathology. From a structural perspective, for example, lack of self-confidence may be a symptom of deeply rooted conflict centered on an individual's repressed infantile wishes. Executives who are unable to master career disappointments may subsequently fail because they founder on unresolved conflicts at the center of their experience with disappointment (Zaleznik, 1984).

Unconscious dynamic factors underlie the difficulty many executives have in dealing with their own and others' anger (Kets de

Vries, 1984). Efforts to appease feelings of guilt and denial of anger may lead to irrational decisions. These irrational interactions can have ruinous consequences for a business or work group, such as an excessive dependency of superiors and subordinates on each other (Levinson, 1984). If we fail to account for the impact of irrational and unconscious forces on overt behavior, we cannot predict how a manager is likely to function when put in an executive role.

Associated with these conceptual limitations is the problem that traditional executive assessments employ methods that are, on their own, unable to identify the factors that differentiate potentially effective from potentially less effective executives in pools of already highly functioning candidates. They rely on structured, objective assessment methods that tap consciously controlled thoughts, perceptions, and actions. The measures they use include behavioral rating scales, interpersonal checklists, structured interviews and role-plays, questionnaires, and self-report inventories.

Because the purpose of such measures is transparent, individuals who are well adjusted or psychologically sophisticated can easily "fake good." Individuals who are already successful by normative standards quite naturally take advantage of the structure inherent in such tests to produce what they usually correctly infer to be the appropriate image. In 1946, for example, when Robert McNamara arrived at Ford—a company he would later head—he was given a psychological assessment that asked him whether he would prefer being a florist or a coal miner. McNamara knew Ford had a right answer in mind that had nothing to do with his preferences (personal communication from a McNamara scholar).

Even putting aside the question of deliberate faking, the information obtained from self-report measures is limited. A person may be completely forthright in describing her own behavior but nevertheless still omit important data. Often this occurs because the individual lacks awareness of the conflicts and motives that shape her behavior. Especially in conditions of high emotion and conflict, a person may wish to avoid unpleasant or out-of-control states of mind. To prevent the anticipated displeasure or threat, ideas and emotions are unconsciously barred from a conscious representation that would otherwise occur. Thus what managers say about how they respond to stressful events does not necessarily reveal how they actually cope in such situations. Yet the way managers handle stressful events is an excellent lead indicator for predicting how they will deal with the sorts of issues we expect executives to handle in a successful, capable manner.

A Structural Approach to the Personality of the Executive

A structural approach is capable of overcoming the conceptual and methodological limitations noted in the preceding section. From the perspective of this framework, personality is conceived as a complex structure with characteristic, relatively stable functional dimensions that interact and respond to changing circumstances. This view assumes an internal organization of psychological processes that cannot be directly observed but that underlies the cohesiveness and directedness of personality at a single time and over longer periods of development. It also assumes that individuals have the capacity to develop new capabilities, such as the conceptual capacity to meet the increasing complexity of executive roles (Jaques, 1996). The term *structural* refers to the relations among different levels or functions of personality. A structural approach thus offers a developmental framework into which different facets of personality may be integrated and understood in dynamic relation to each other.

Interrelations among traits. A structural approach yields insights into the integrity of personality and the cohesiveness of an individual's value system. In addition, it provides a lens from which to judge the degree of self-criticism to which an executive is prone. Consequently, a structural approach can explain the behaviors developed to compensate for the ensuing feelings of inadequacy and depression. In some cases, for example, severe self-criticism may be the source of self-defeating behaviors or an inability to tolerate success.

Life-span development. A structural approach accounts for the possibility that individuals may grow and adapt. It thereby helps in judging whether an executive is likely to develop new capabilities by actively coping with challenge and change or is prone to capitulate passively to frustration. Knowing the individual's developmental history makes it possible to specify particular stressors to which an executive may be uniquely vulnerable.

Cross-domain issues. A structural approach permits inferences about a person's characteristic modes of maintaining psychological equilibrium and their transformations into behavioral patterns across domains, be they public or private. It allows us to differentiate between characterological behaviors—such as a consistent readiness to blame others—from those that occur only under certain circumstances and in reaction to specific situations.

Unconscious and irrational factors. A structural approach accounts for unconscious and irrational motivational factors that shape an executive's personality, decisions, and actions. Lack of self-confidence may arise from repressed infantile rage toward parental figures. Repressing the need to depend on others makes accepting the legitimate dependency of subordinates difficult for some executives. Fear of having to take charge, guilt for negatively appraising a subordinate, and depression upon loss of a stable supportive organizational structure are other examples of potentially unconscious influences on executive behavior.

Application of a Structural Approach

The usefulness of a structural approach in identifying which individuals will emerge as the most effective leaders among a population of already highly functioning individuals selected for their leadership characteristics has been empirically demonstrated (Pratch & Jacobowitz, 1996, 1998). The relationship between integrative capacity and evaluations of leadership effectiveness was examined in a nine-month intensive leadership development program at the University of Chicago Graduate School of Business. Integrative capacity was conceptualized as a central dimension of the structural psychological characteristic, active coping, and differentiated from the cognitive construct, integrative complexity. Self-report, semi-projective, and projective measures of integrative capacity obtained at the beginning of the program were correlated with peer and faculty ratings of leadership at the end of the program. Significant correlations ranged from .27 ($p < .05$) to .52 ($p < .001$). Intelligence and integrative capacity contributed separately to leadership. The findings support the value of examining variables related to personality structure and the use of projective techniques to assess candidates for positions of business leadership. A second study examined the effects of gender, coping, and motivational orientation in evaluating individual leadership. The data reveal significant gender differences on measures of motivation, with men showing higher levels of agentic-instrumental tendencies and women exhibiting higher levels of communal-social qualities ($p < .05$). Women exhibiting strong agentic characteristics were negatively perceived as leaders ($p < .05$). There was no relationship between agentic or communal qualities and evaluations of leadership received by male leaders. Finally, individuals with active coping tendencies were evaluated as more effective leaders for both genders. The fact that active coping predicted leadership in these two elite samples, selected for intelligence as well as other personality attributes associated with leadership potential, demonstrates the usefulness of a structural approach in assessing candidates for executive roles.

To illustrate the added benefits of such an approach for understanding, supervising, and developing executives, we describe two financial executives who are engaged in the same level of financial work in the same Fortune 500 company. Each is functioning cognitively at Elliot Jaques's Level V, with a 5- to 10-year conceptual horizon. Each is in charge of the company's financial operations in different parts of the world. The required behaviors and accountabilities of their roles, although exercised in different cultures, are virtually the same.

The executives display many of the qualities that have been positively correlated with managerial leadership: internal locus of control, practical intelligence, response flexibility, conscientiousness, achievement orientation, self-monitoring, stress tolerance, and self-confidence—manifested in the tendency to be stimulated by crises and other problems, rather than being distressed or overwhelmed by them. In addition, they have both been successful in previous financial roles, and they are conceptually on developmental tracks that could potentially put them in top management, chief executive officer, or board chairman roles.

Most of these qualities could be identified using the kinds of paper-and-pencil tests, behavioral event interviews, and simulations known by most readers. A structural approach to assessment, utilizing techniques that give information about an executive's personality dynamics, yields a more comprehensive understanding. It affords the depth of insight required for making astute developmental recommendations for executives and their superiors. Accordingly, the next sections describe the nature of such assessments and the types of information they provide.

Multimethod, Multilevel Methodology

Selection for executive roles requires finding a way to know how disturbed a candidate's thinking becomes under severe emotional stress. Even if it were possible to subject the individual to such stress, we would not want to do so for ethical reasons. Instead, we may pose such situations through confronting the candidate with vague or affectively laden stimuli. From these miniature stresses, we try to infer or predict an individual's responses to more severe stimuli.

Selection for executive leadership requires more than exposure to stressful stimuli. To predict how an individual will cope with the demands of an executive role over time, we should assess how unconscious phenomena relate to more conscious, experiential, and observable psychological phenomena (such as behaviors, values, thoughts, and feelings). This process calls for a variety of tests to tap both surface and underlying aspects of personality. Traditionally, such a battery consists of an array of assessment techniques along two separate but related dimensions, ranging from structured to unstructured, and from objective to projective.

To relate the objective-projective dimension to the structured-unstructured dimension, we can view objective and projective tests as stimuli that present differing degrees of situational constraint on behavior. According to Walter Mischel's (1977) distinction between strong and weak situations, strong situations (that is, objective stimuli) leave little room for the expression of individual differences, because everyone sees the situation in the same way, understands the expectations, and knows the sanctions for failing to comply with those demands. Such situations tend to suppress individual differences. Conversely, ambiguous situations, which contain few cues to action or information about behavioral sanctions (that is, projective stimuli), allow for greater expression of individual differences (Schutte, Kendrick, & Sadalla, 1985). One study (Monson, Hasley, & Chernik, 1981) showed that by manipulating the situational strength, researchers could systematically vary the validity coefficients from low (.13) to moderate (.32) to substantial (.42). Monson concluded that individual differences in personality would have their strongest impact on behavior in relatively unstructured, psychologically weak situations. This conclusion has practical relevance for selection for executive roles, where one is trying to assess individual differences in a relatively homogeneous pool.

In psychological assessment, there is a frame of reference of tests that are highly structured, semistructured, and unstructured. This dimension refers to the degree to which the tasks involved in a test have or do not have a high degree of specificity. Structured tests tend to be close to the concept of questions with right and wrong answers. The more the test permits the individual to use his own ideas and imagination in responding to the task, the less structured the situation is. Thus, for the most structured tests, the tasks are specific, with little opportunity for the respondent to make an individual interpretation of the task. For unstructured tests, the tasks are vague and unfamiliar, and they require that the respondent contribute much to the interpretation of the task itself. The tests within a battery are chosen so that the three levels of structure are represented.

Structured tests are typically represented in the usual self-report measures. Tasks are so highly defined that the respondent is fully aware of what is expected and has minimum choice. He is expected to find the standard answer, rather than the one reflecting personal choice, thereby eliminating the need to use his own personal resources to cope with the task. Because this task requires that the individual respond with a prescribed answer, his responses provide little information about the individual's uniqueness as a person. Indeed, the more unique the respondent's answers to self-report measures, the stronger is the inference that an internal psychological process has become so dominant that it has pervaded a situation from which the individual should be able to exclude it. By contrast, unstructured tests offer respondents minimal information regarding the demands of the task. Therefore, respondents must turn to themselves, formulate what the task involves and how to cope with it, and summon the energy to commit to a response.

The review of a person's responses to structured, semistructured, and unstructured tests thus permits comparative inferences on all three levels of personality, to assess whether the person has the capacity to cope effectively with all three types of demands—structured, semistructured, unstructured. If the respondent is not successful on all three, then it should be noted whether there is difficulty only in the more personal, unstructured situation, whether the difficulty is more pervasive and includes difficulty at the semistructured level, or whether the difficulties permeate all aspects of functioning.

This continuum of structured to unstructured situations may be mapped onto life situations to help us understand the degree to which an individual is dependent on external guidance and direction for effective coping. Our definition of the effective and emotionally healthy person is based on the concept of the capacity to cope with most of life's situations, ranging from those that permit little initiative to those that require a great deal of initiative. A battery of tests of the type just described provides a basis for judging the individual's ability to match that definition. From this description, one might expect that, for example, more effective coping on unstructured psychological tests would differentiate effective from ineffective executives. Using unstructured tests to assess an individual's coping capacity is clearly superior to observing whether the person stutters during a behavioral simulation or has a sweaty palm.

Closely related to the structured-unstructured continuum in psychological assessment is the objective-projective dimension. Objective assessment techniques—including simulations and behavioral interviews—represent clear, unambiguous stimuli that permit a high degree of conscious control over what is revealed about the self. Consequently, such techniques assess observable aspects of personality functioning. Individuals who are successful by normative standards find it easy to fall back on the structure of the test situation to produce what they understand to be the desired image. In particular, candidates for top executive roles are already quite good at behaving appropriately, and they are skilled at monitoring their responses. These individuals are likely to maintain firm, steady eye contact with their interviewers, exude poise, and shake their interviewers' hands with a cool, authoritative grip. Objective techniques are therefore poor predictors of executive functioning among managers in line for top executive roles.

Projective techniques, in contrast to objective assessment techniques, present relatively vague and ambiguous stimuli for eliciting underlying personality characteristics. One (the Sentence Completion Technique; Pratch, 1996) asks the respondent to complete several incomplete sentences (for example, "He was happiest when—"). Another (the Thematic Apperception Test; Murray, 1938) asks the respondent to make up stories that describe a series of pictures. The key to projective techniques is that, as with unstructured tests, the stimuli provide little structure to guide the response. They thereby reveal aspects of individual functioning related to underlying structural dimensions inaccessible with objective tests.

Integrated Case Descriptions

To assess the executives discussed in this chapter, the following battery of tests was used: Jackson's Personality Research Form (1989); Wechsler's Abbreviated Adult Intelligence Scale (1999); Raven's Advanced Progressive Matrices (1988); Pratch's Sentence Completion Technique (1996); and Murray's Thematic Apperception Test (1938). These tests, in conjunction with detailed developmental histories, provided information for building hypotheses and drawing conclusions regarding each executive's personality and likely performance in role.

The time-span measure of a role corresponds to the length of the longest task or assignment, from point of inception to targeted completion date. This measure provided information pertaining to the level-of-work complexity for the role (Jaques, 1996). The longest-range assignments for the roles of each of the executives have a time horizon between 5 and 10 years.

Current potential capability is defined as the highest level of work an individual could handle effectively if she possessed all the necessary knowledge and experience and was fully committed to the work. This is a reflection of the complexity of the individual's mental processing. It seeks to answer how complex a problem a person can handle effectively. Each of these executives is able to construct sequential patterns and weave multiple sequential patterns together at a symbolic level of information complexity. They are able to use abstract concepts to handle problems. Their current potential capability is appropriate for roles with assignments in the five- to seven-year range. Thus they possess the current problem-solving ability to handle the level of work required by their present roles.

Furthermore, their *future* potential capability over the next 10 years (Jaques, 1996) suggests that they are increasingly likely to process information at an abstract level of complexity. They are both likely to be able to make the transition from an operational level to the corporate level of cognitive complexity. Simultaneously, once they develop this ability to think more abstractly and strategically, their time horizons potentially could expand to the 7- to 10-year range, making them likely candidates for more senior executive roles.

Figure 3.1 shows that although the two executives are currently capable of handling the complexity of roles having a 5- to 7-year time horizon, what Jaques calls Stratum V, their developmental trajectories differ. Brian, at age 30, falls within Mode VIII; in 10 years, his potential time horizon will be between 15 to 20 years. In 20 years, he will be capable of handling the demands of a major multinational corporation, with the potential to consider and influence events affecting the company 20 to 40 years in the future. Peter is 46; he will be limited to a role having at most little more than a 10-year time horizon.

Brian Bennish, 30, VP Finance, Asia

Brian is a thoughtful, patient, hard-working, and caring young man. He is motivated to succeed at work while maintaining a loving home. His integrity is beyond reproach; he has a well-established value system that has been tested in various ways in the past. He can be trusted to do the right thing—for the company and for his family. He pushes himself hard to fulfill his responsibilities accurately and on time and expects others to demonstrate similar dedication. Brian approaches problems in an orderly, highly analytical fashion. His cognitive style is cautious and he is therefore not quick to make decisions, especially when people are not straightforward or honest. Extremely well organized, he prioritizes effectively and tries to make every minute count. He retrieves information readily, both from his own head and from the organization.

Figure 3.1. Time-Horizon Progression.

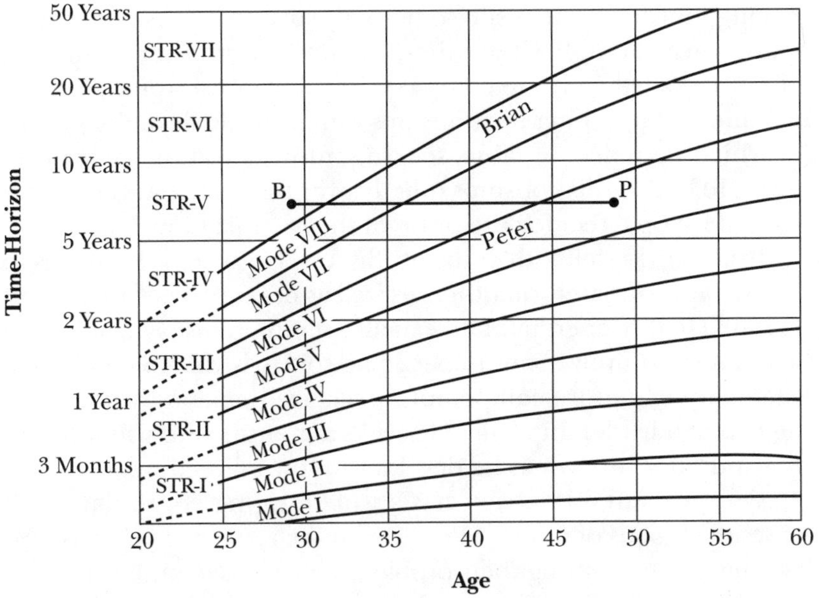

Source: Copyright © 1989, Elliott Jacques. Reprinted with permission from Jacques (1996), p. 30.

Intellectually, Brian has the capacity not only to abstract but also to be practical. He makes good use of language to draw from experience. His judgment is sound—he is thoughtful, can see the whole picture, and knows when to act but does not always do so quickly enough. He needs to trust his judgment more so that he *does* act forthrightly when appropriate.

Brian has the capacity to take charge when necessary. He takes a responsible stance toward problems and the needs of the company. He has demonstrated a willingness to go beyond arenas in which he is already secure to attack problems tactically from new positions. He is oriented toward the organization's success rather than personal aggrandizement. He has an intense wish to master new challenges and to move up in the organization as recognition of competence. He struggles internally with his ambition because of the potentially negative impact he thinks it might have on others.

Brian picks up feelings and reads body language well. In fact, he is more aware than most of subtle cues in groups. A basically trusting individual, he is still somewhat naive and does not yet recognize early enough when others are dishonest or manipulative. Highly involved with the company, he allocates serious, continuing time to developing relationships with individuals in the groups for which he is accountable, seeking information on their problems. He builds relationships quietly over time. He has the potential to develop a feel for the pulse of the organization.

Brian works well with authority figures. He accepts his needs to depend appropriately on others as well as others' needs to depend on him. He is cooperative and can also stand on his own, although he is not yet entirely comfortable doing so. He is able to yield to the leadership of a more competent, specialized person without feeling loss of a leadership role. He seeks a mentor who will listen to him and offer support as he develops his own direction.

Very presentable, Brian has a wide-ranging vocabulary, and senses the moods of others. He may earn the respect of peers for verbalizing and presenting their problems. He can see humor in most situations, including his own shortcomings. His humor is warm and affectionate. He has a natural ability to ease tension in groups. He is firm in holding his position without being intimidating. These strengths have been significant assets in cultivating his company's relationships in Asia.

Brian has a consistent high energy level, paces himself well, and can take sustained pressure. He remains calm and deliberate in stressful situations while still expressing a sense of urgency. Although he uses effective coping devices, such as consulting with others, he tends to dwell on problems and accepts more than his share of responsibility for them. Indeed, he seems to take the world's troubles onto his heart and overextends himself. In addition, when events do not unfold as expected, he becomes frightened and worried. He finds himself too tightly wound, unable to relax, and has difficulty sleeping or concentrating on matters other than work.

Brian is thoughtful about the progression of his career. Although he has not crystallized a direction for himself (and this is partly a function of age), his goals are consistent with the needs and values of his company. He enjoys teaching and working collaboratively with others. He enjoys finance and operations. He relished a previous assignment in operations because it allowed him to play in an operational role from a financial perspective. Eventually, he is interested in a lead financial role and also in general management. He appreciates the social responsibilities of such a role, and may very well develop the presence to be able to fulfill a public role.

Extremely conscientious, Brian sticks to a task and sees it through regardless of the difficulties encountered. Underlying his persistence is an optimism that stems from a confidence that a solution will be found. His self-confidence is mature and realistic, inclining him to work issues through on his own rather than rely on direction from others.

Developmental needs. Brian is well suited to move up in the executive ranks to become chief executive officer. Given the breadth of his career interests and abilities, he should continue to be exposed to increasingly broader financial and operational responsibilities. His assignment in Asia has given him valuable experience dealing with other cultures, business practices, and financial institutions in those cultures.

Brian is a talented, values-oriented person who is concerned with others, particularly with nurturing and protecting others. He has not yet figured out what he wants for himself and does not want to be told what to do. He needs a sensitive and caring mentor who is attuned to his struggles, who will sit and talk with him about life and work, and who can present a wise view, let him grow, and think about where he wants to go.

Brian's core problem is his severe conscience. On one hand it fosters his consistent integrity and pursuit of organizational success. On the other hand, it imposes on him urgent responsibility for matters beyond his control. To meet these felt obligations, he overextends himself, fearful that he may not live up to his excessive self-imposed demands and unable to temper them by himself. His harsh conscience also keeps him from fully appreciating his considerable competencies, telling him that he is not good enough. His sensitivity and wish to be helpful will make him vulnerable to exploitation—they will delay his taking appropriate action early enough to cut off the event fast enough. He may not be appropriately tough enough in situations that require critical judgment, disciplining action, and coping with manipulators.

Brian needs to be able to tolerate what he cannot do, what is beyond his immediate control. He needs to learn how to read and deal with people who are not honest and direct. He needs to learn not to blame himself for everything because his guilt can distort his understanding of what is occurring. He needs to relax and trust his judgment more. His seniors can help him to be more hard-nosed about his decisions, develop a degree of skepticism and distrust about what he is told, and to take a more forthright stand when necessary.

Structural approach—benefits. Typically, psychological assessments conducted by industrial and organizational psychologists describe the subject in his current stage of development. Few extrapolate to the future from the strengths they identify, how those strengths may become liabilities. Brian's case is illustrative. We did not simply describe his conscientiousness; we explained how his conscience demands that he care for others, assume responsibility, and behave with integrity. That severe conscience, not tempered, could give rise to stress and thereby detract from his efficiency. Brian's case demonstrates how a structural framework enables psychologists to understand the underlying cohesiveness of his personality by showing how, for example, he presently copes well with his strong internal demands on himself and maintains his effectiveness.

A structural frame of reference also affords the insight that Brian's tension, integrity, and tendency to underestimate his competency result from his strict conscience. We made these inferences from Brian's overt, public behaviors, as well as from covert, less consciously controlled communications about himself elicited in response to semi-projective and projective techniques. To Brian's potential mentors we offered advice designed to help Brian temper the demands of his conscience, gain greater self-confidence, and avoid the potential future shortfalls of being too trusting and too conscientious. This case demonstrates the added benefits of a structural approach in explaining the interrelations among overt traits, behaviors, and decision tendencies and in projecting Brian's likely future course of development.

Peter Schwartz, 46, VP Finance, North America

A recent hire from another company in the same industry, Peter primarily emphasizes giving to and getting. Warm and caring, he works to earn the respect of others. He enjoys the challenge of solving problems and gets pleasure from the work itself rather than bragging about the outcome. He is not impulsive and will not make hasty decisions. He is not aggressive or confrontational. If attacked, he will accommodate or leave. He will not fight for his position, and he needs others to accept his ideas and encourage him. He is a good team worker who generates trust, fairness, friendliness, mutual help, and regard—with creativity and good feeling.

Peter's strategy in life is to try to blend in. He is willing to sacrifice aspects of his desires or ambitions to attain harmony and good will as long as he can do the work he enjoys with colleagues he trusts and who can trust him. He has difficulty setting his own direction and is not one to create a new business, to put in a structure, to generate rules, or to guide others. He is a self-effacing, loyal employee who needs a team and a leader with rules and direction. With that, he will work hard and achieve in a way that makes others feel good. He can be the glue that keeps a group together.

Peter struggles when leaders let him down. He is not a hard-charging, directing individual—not someone to generate energy. He becomes confused when others hold conflicting views of the same situation. When he has to draw the line and control others, he may not exercise his power.

Peter's strengths, like Brian's, can become potential liabilities. He denies his aggression, funneling it constructively into teamwork efforts that make others like and respect him. His peers will expect him, because of their relative youth, to provide them with guidance, experience, and wisdom. This he can give, in his congenial style. He may disappoint them, however, if he does not behave authoritatively. In addition, he is likely to be surpassed by younger, more competitive executives who have greater potential complexity of information processing and who will exceed his pace.

Developmental needs. Peter's seniors should help him to exercise leadership and take a stance when appropriate. When others need to be called to account for their actions, he should be encouraged to give straightforward feedback on their performance. He should be supported in situations of conflict so that he is able to think clearly and take charge.

Structural approach—benefits. Peter's case illustrates the added benefit of considering an executive's phase of development, both in terms of Jaques's modes of conceptual ability and in terms of Erik Erikson's stages of adult development (Erikson, 1963). To anticipate

Peter's future course within the company, both views on development help to identify potential pitfalls and limitations. Most psychological assessments by industrial and organizational psychologists
do not explicitly address these developmental issues and their
implications.

According to Jaques's framework, Peter's current potential
complexity of information processing is adequate to handle the
role of the VP finance, North America. His *applied* capacity, however, may not be sufficient to perform the work of the role. His
maximum potential capacity is a role with little more than a 10-year
time span (see Figure 3.1).

At 46, Peter is approaching an age at which executives are expected to mentor junior colleagues. A nurturer by nature, Peter is
likely to foster the development of those who report to him
through gentle, positive feedback. Because he is uncomfortable
with the rebellious, aggressive parts of himself, however, he is unlikely to be able to help subordinates grow by telling them what
they are not doing well, what they must do to meet his requisite
standard, by when, and with what consequences for their future
prospects. His executive effectiveness will diminish as others learn
to regard him as insufficiently authoritative or capable of setting
and enforcing clear accountabilities. By accounting for the developmental tasks associated with each phase of psychological development, a structural approach allows us to help plan for executive roles and advise executives of the normative expectations associated with age-related role performance.

Discussion

These two executives possess the level of cognitive complexity to
handle the technical parts of their current roles. They also have
limitations, some of which are amenable to coaching and development, some of which are not. Each is developmentally in a different conceptual mode and a different phase of the life span.
Brian has the capacity to take a more forthright stand with appropriate encouragement. Eventually, as his ambitions crystallize and
he gains broader experience, he will simultaneously develop the
conceptual capacity that would put him in the running for the role
of chief executive officer and board member. By contrast, although
Peter can become more authoritative if his teammates and seniors

tell him to be more directing of others, he is unlikely to be suited for a position in corporate governance given the projected limits of his conceptual capacity.

Conclusions

This chapter describes a structural psychological approach to understanding the personality of the executive. Managers and consulting psychologists alike may find this approach an operationally useful supplement to traditional industrial and organizational conceptions and frameworks. Its usefulness lies in its power to explain behavior—not merely describe it—giving rise to the ability to predict with greater confidence how a person is likely to behave under various conditions. A structural approach addresses both the dynamic requirements of the role—the environment, including technical and interpersonal variables over time—and the personality of the individual being considered for that role. It considers the nuances of personality as a dynamic process. It provides a developmental framework for understanding an executive's potential to grow with the changing demands of the role. This aspect is particularly useful in executive assessment, for it is important to know how an individual will cope with the increasing demand as the level of leadership responsibility increases, to evaluate, develop, and support others. A structural approach also offers an integrative perspective capable of making sense of the interactions among various behaviors observed across the objective-projective psychological testing spectrum. It is therefore a valuable tool when assessing candidates for executive roles.

The trend in academic and industrial and organizational psychology has been to focus on isolated behaviors, traits, and decision styles. The structural approach we have described provides a means by which the continuity of various facets of personality—public and private, rational and irrational, conscious and unconscious—can be understood and integrated in dynamic relation to one another as part of an organic whole.

References

Anderson, C. R., Hellriegel, D., & Slocum, J. W. (1977). Managerial response to environmentally induced stress. *Academy of Management Journal, 20*(2), 260–272.

Atwater, L. E. (1992). Beyond cognitive ability: Improving the prediction of performance. *Journal of Business and Psychology, 7*(1), 27–44.

Atwater, L. E., & Yammarino, F. J. (1993). Personal attributes as predictors of superiors' and subordinates' perceptions of military academy leadership. *Human Relations, 46*(5), 645–668.

Bales, R. F., & Slater, P. E. (1945). Role differentiation in small decision-making groups. In T. Parsons & R. F. Bales (Eds.), *Family, socialization, and interaction processes.* New York: Free Press.

Bass, B. M. (1990a). *Bass and Stogdill's handbook of leadership: A survey of theory and research.* New York: Free Press.

Bass, B. M. (1990b). From transactional to transformational leadership: Learning to share the vision. *Organizational Dynamics, 18*(3), 19–31.

Bennis, W. G. (1961). Revisionist theory of leadership. *Harvard Business Review, 39*, 26–36, 146–150.

Binning, J., Zaba, A., & Whattam, J. (1986). Explaining the biasing effects of performance cues in terms of cognitive categorization. *Academy of Management Journal, 29*(3), 521–535.

Bird, C. (1940). *Social psychology.* Englewood Cliffs, NJ: Appleton-Century-Crofts.

Boyatzis, R. E. (1982). *The competent manager: A model for effective performance.* New York: Wiley.

Brockhaus, R. S. (1975). I-E locus of control scores as predictors of entrepreneurial intentions. *Proceedings of Academic Management,* pp. 433–435.

Cantor, N., & Mischel, W. (1977). Traits as prototypes: Effects on recognition memory. *Journal of Personality and Social Psychology, 35*, 38–48.

Conger, J. A., Kanungo, R. N., & Associates. (1988). *Charismatic leadership.* San Francisco: Jossey-Bass.

Cox, C. J., & Cooper, C. L. (1988). *High flyers: An anatomy of managerial success.* New York: Blackwell.

Digman, J. M. (1990). Personality structure: Emergence of the five-factor model. *Annual Review of Psychology, 41*, 417–440.

Ellis, R. J. (1988). Self-monitoring and leadership emergence in groups. *Personality and Social Psychology Bulletin, 14*, 681–693.

Erikson, E. (1963). *Childhood and society* (2nd ed.). New York: Norton.

Fiedler, P. E. (1967). *A theory of leadership effectiveness.* New York: McGraw-Hill.

Fiske, S. T., & Linville, P. W. (1980). What does the schema concept buy us? *Personality and Social Psychology Bulletin, 6*, 537–543.

Gibb, C. A. (1954). Leadership. In G. Lindzey & E. Aronson (Eds.), *Handbook of social psychology.* Reading, MA: Addison-Wesley.

Goleman, D. (1995). *Emotional intelligence.* New York: Bantam Books.

Goleman, D. (2000, March-April). Leadership that gets results. *Harvard Business Review*, pp. 78–93.

Goodstadt, B. E., & Hjelle, L. A. (1973). Power to the powerless: Locus of control and the use of power. *Journal of Personality and Social Psychology, 27*, 190–196.

Graen, G., & Scandura, T. A. (1987). Toward a psychology of dyadic organizing. *Research in Organizational Behavior, 9*, 175–208.

Hogan, R., Curphy, G., & Hogan, J. (1994). What we know about leadership: Effectiveness and personality. *American Psychologist, 49*(6), 493–504.

House, R. J., & Howell, J. M. (1992). Personality and charismatic leadership. *Leadership Quarterly, 3*(2), 81–108.

Howard, A., & Bray, D. W. (1988). *Managerial lives in transition: Advancing age and changing lives*. New York: Guilford Press.

Jackson, D. N. (1989). *Personality Research Form manual*. Port Huron, MI: Research Psychologists Press.

Jaques, E. (1996). *Requisite organization: The CEO's guide to creative structure and leadership*. Arlington, VA: Cason Hall.

Jaques, E., & Cason, K. (1994). *Human capability*. Arlington, VA: Cason Hall.

Jenkins, W. O. (1947). A review of leadership studies with particular relevance to military problems. *Psychological Bulletin, 44*, 54–79.

Kahn, R. L., & Katz, D. (1953). Leadership practices in relation to productivity and morale. In D. Cartwright & A. Zander (Eds.), *Group dynamics*. Orlando: Harcourt Brace.

Kanungo, R. N., & Misra, S. (1992). Managerial resourcefulness: A reconceptualization of management skills. *Human Relations, 45*(12), 1311–1332.

Kenny, D. A., & Zaccaro, S. J. (1983). An estimate of variance due to traits in leadership. *Journal of Applied Psychology, 68*, 678–685.

Kets de Vries, M. (1984). Defective adaptation to work. In M. Kets de Vries (Ed.), *The irrational executive* (pp. 67–84). New York: International Universities Press.

Klemp, G. O., & McClelland, D. C. (1986). What characterizes intelligent functioning among senior managers? In R. J. Sternberg & R. K. Wagner (Eds.), *Practical intelligence: Nature and origin of competence in the everyday world* (pp. 31–50). Cambridge, UK: Cambridge University Press.

Korman, A. (1966). Consideration, initiating structure, and organizational criteria: A review. *Personnel Psychology, 19*, 349–362.

Kotter, J. (1999). *John Kotter on what leaders really do*. Boston: Harvard Business School Press.

Kouzes, J. M., & Posner, B. Z. (1987). *The leadership challenge: How to get extraordinary things done in organizations.* San Francisco: Jossey-Bass.

Levinson, H. (1984). Management by guilt. In M. Kets de Vries (Ed.), *The irrational executive* (pp. 132–151). New York: International Universities Press.

Lewin, K., Lippitt, R., & White, R. K. (1939). Patterns of aggressive behavior in experimentally created social climates. *Journal of Social Psychology, 10,* 271–301.

Lord, R. G. (1985). An information-processing approach to social perceptions, leadership, and behavioral measurement in organizations. *Research in Organizational Behavior, 7,* 87–128.

Lord, R. G., DeVader, C. L., & Alliger, G. M. (1986). A meta-analysis of the relation between personality traits and leadership perceptions: An application of validity generalization procedures. *Journal of Applied Psychology, 61,* 402–410.

McCall, M. W., & Lombardo, M. M. (1983). *Off the track: Why and how successful executives get derailed* (Tech. Rep. No. 21). Greensboro, NC: Center for Creative Leadership.

McCann, S.J.H. (1992). Alternative formulas to predict the greatness of U.S. presidents: Personalogical, situational, and zeitgeist factors. *Journal of Personality and Social Psychology, 62*(3), 469–479.

Miller, D., Kets de Vries, M., & Toulouse, J. (1982). Top executive locus of control and its relation to strategy-making, structure, and environment. *Academy of Management Journal, 25*(2), 237–253.

Miller, D., Kets de Vries, M., & Toulouse, J. (1986). Chief executive personality and corporate strategy and structure in small firms. *Management Science, 32*(11), 1389–1409.

Mischel, W. (1977). On the future of personality measurement. *American Psychologist, 32,* 246–254.

Monson, T. C., Hasley, J. W., & Chernik, L. (1981). Specifying when personality traits can and cannot predict behavior. *Journal of Personality and Social Psychology, 43,* 385–399.

Murray, H. (1938). *Explorations in personality.* London: Oxford University Press.

Norman, W. T., & Goldberg, L. R. (1966). Raters, ratees, and randomness in personality structure. *Journal of Personality and Social Psychology, 4,* 44–49.

Pratch, L. (1996). *Manual for Pratch's Sentence Completion Technique.* Unpublished manuscript, University of Chicago.

Pratch, L., & Jacobowitz, J. (1996). Gender, motivation, and coping in the evaluation of leadership effectiveness. *Consulting Psychology Journal: Practice and Research, 48*(4), 203–220.

Pratch, L., & Jacobowitz, J. (1997). The psychology of leadership in rapidly changing situations: A structural psychological approach. *Genetic, Social, and General Psychology Monographs, 123*(2), 169–196.

Pratch, L., & Jacobowitz, J. (1998). Integrative capacity and the evaluation of leadership: A multimethod assessment approach. *Journal of Applied Behavioral Science, 34*(2), 180–201.

Raven, J. C., Court, J. C., & Raven, J. (1988). *Manual for Raven's progressive matrices and vocabulary scales: Section 4.* London: Oxford Psychologists Press.

Rotter, J. B. (1966). Generalized expectancies for internal versus external control of reinforcement. *Psychological Monographs, 80*(1), 1–28.

Schutte, N. A., Kendrick, D. T., & Sadalla, E. C. (1985). The search for predictable settings: Situational prototypes, constraints, and behavioral variation. *Journal of Personality and Social Psychology, 49,* 121–128.

Simon, H. A. (1987, February). Making management decisions: The role of intuition and emotion. *Academy of Management Executive,* pp. 57–83.

Skinner, W., & Sasser, W. E. (1977). Managers with impact: Versatile and inconsistent. *Harvard Business Review,* pp. 140–148.

Stogdill, R. M. (1948). Personal factors associated with leadership: A survey of the literature. *Journal of Psychology, 25,* 35–71.

Stogdill, R. M., & Coons, A. E. (Eds.). (1957). Editorial comments. *Leader behavior: Its description and measurement.* Columbus: Bureau of Business Research, Ohio State University.

Stogdill, R. M., & Shartle, C. L. (1955). *Methods in the study of administrative leadership.* Columbus: Bureau of Business Research, Ohio State University.

Taylor, A. (1995, February). Ford's really big leap at the future. *Fortune,* p. 134.

Wechsler, D. (1999). *Abbreviated Wechsler Adult Intelligence Scales.* San Antonio, TX: Psychological Corporation.

Whitley, R. (1989). On the nature of managerial tasks and skills: Their distinguishing characteristics and organization. *Journal of Management Studies, 26*(3), 209–224.

Willner, A. R. (1984). *The spellbinders: Charismatic political leadership.* New Haven, CT: Yale University Press.

Yukl, G. (1994). *Leadership in organizations* (3rd ed.). Upper Saddle River, NJ: Prentice Hall.

Zaccaro, S. J., Foti, R. J., & Kenny, D. A. (1991). Self-monitoring and trait-based variance in leadership: An investigation of leader flexibility across multiple group situations. *Journal of Applied Psychology, 76*(2), 308–315.

Zaccaro, S. J., Gilbert, J. A., Thor, K. K., & Mumford, M. D. (1991). Leadership and social intelligence: Linking social perspectives and behavioral flexibility to leader effectiveness. *Leadership Quarterly, 2*(4), 317–342.

Zaleznik, A. (1984). Management of disappointment. In M. Kets de Vries (Ed.), *The irrational executive* (pp. 224–248). New York: International Universities Press.

PART TWO

Managing Executive Resources

CHAPTER 4

Selecting Leaders at the Top

Exploring the Complexity of Executive Fit

Rob Silzer

Similarity breeds complacency.

An outside executive who had recently become chief executive officer of a financial services corporation once asked me for help in reviewing the current executive team that she inherited and in advising her on how to best use the existing talent. The chief executive officer wanted to turn the finances of the company around quickly but wasn't sure how to gauge and to get the best out of the current executives, who had worked together for a number of years. The company had several years of poor financial performance after four years of strong income growth and had fallen into a relaxed maintenance business approach. Most of the blame for the recent weak financial performance was aimed at the previous chief executive officer, who had left the company. The executive group had become quite supportive and collegial with each other and had a difficult time identifying what had gone wrong, except to note that the former chief executive officer had ambiguous and modest corporate goals. The executive consensus was that the company just needed some clear direction. The new chief executive officer was ready to set a clear and challenging new direction but intuitively knew that the performance problems were deeper and much more complex than just having vague and unambitious goals.

After going through a systematic and thorough process of assessing the leadership skills of the remaining executives, it became clear that the executives had a lot in common with each other—including their personal values and work styles. They were a surprisingly homogeneous group. They all had long tenure with the organization and had been selected as executives to deliver on business strategies identified eight years previously. The primary strategy was essentially to rely on standardized products and services sold to a broad range of individual clients and financial institutions. The new chief executive officer was determined to focus more on client needs and to introduce a wider range of products and services tailored to specific customer groups while at the same time updating the standard products and services.

She questioned whether the current executive team was the right match for the new strategic direction, and the assessments confirmed her concerns. The current executives were very committed to the standard products and services they had developed and were comfortable with their shared work routines and habits. There were no challengers in the group to question their group thinking. In fact, many of them had received substantial compensation for their cooperation and their team effort. You could say they were highly cooperative with each other and with the former chief executive officer. But their homogeneity and team allegiance seemed likely to lead to their downfall. No one questioned their shared assumptions or challenged the status quo thinking. They had become a cozy group with one vision but sharing the same blind sides.

The dilemma faced by the new chief executive officer is not a new problem in business. It is an old problem—whether to select executives for breadth, diverse views, and a heterogeneous team or to emphasize teamwork, alignment, and homogeneity. The easy way is to hire for homogeneity rather than for diversity. Many organizations have a clear bias toward selecting new executives similar to the existing executive group. This is particularly true when the current executives are very collaborative and team oriented, want to minimize group conflict and disagreement, and have influence in the selection decision. The search for homogeneity stems from the misperception that team member similarity and agreement correlates with team effectiveness. It has been very common in many organizations to hire all the executives against a common selection profile (except perhaps for some differences in functional skills), now more fashionably called an executive competency model.

The executive competency model is driven by several things. First, chief executive officers—who are frequently interested in maximizing immediate short-term financial performance—drive executive selection decisions to focus on a single set of narrow skills, values, attitudes that seem to be closely aligned with their short-term performance goals. They believe there is a connection between having a homogeneous executive team and achieving immediate financial results. They often do not want to deal with dissent, conflict, or even challenging questions. Needless to say they may also see this as in their own best financial interest if their personal compensation is strongly contingent on producing short-term results. Unfortunately this shortsighted approach often ignores longer-term business strategies and the need to continuously adapt to the constant change occurring in the marketplace.

Second, chief executive officers often place a high value on hiring individuals they like and who are similar to themselves in their decision-making style, abilities, motivations, and values. This not only makes the executive group easier to manage but also allows the executives to quickly understand each other and assimilate into the organization. They don't have to waste time on understanding their differences and managing each other differentially based on those differences. This approach is most common among chief executive officers and hiring executives who value organizational clarity and harmony and who dislike ambiguity and interpersonal disagreement.

Third, a standard and narrow executive profile makes the selection process easier because it reduces the complexity of what to look for in an executive. This simplifies the selection decisions and leads everyone to believe that they have made sound choices.

After hearing my explanation of all this, the new chief executive officer questioned whether she wanted to go through the challenge and disruptiveness of identifying a new, diverse, and more heterogeneous executive team. She had to convince herself that she could deliver short-term results while simultaneously reformulating her executive group. She ultimately decided to try to do both, first gaining agreement from the Board of Directors and support from the existing executives on a new strategic direction and structuring and driving the decision-making process to produce noticeable short-term financial results. At the same time she evaluated each executive and assessed each executive's ability to step up to the new direction. It became evident that many of them were not well suited to the new direction; some left on their own, and some were quietly encouraged to leave. Their replacements, combined with those who stayed from the original group, created an executive team that seemed better suited for the direction the chief executive officer wanted to take. The risk for the new chief executive officer was that she would repeat the same mistake made by the previous chief executive officer by hiring everyone to a new single narrowly defined executive profile, which in the long term would not have been an improvement even though it was different from the old one. She had to produce short-term financial improvements while managing the organizational change and building a team that could also deliver on longer-term strategies. She chose this more difficult, complex, and ambiguous path because she became convinced that it was critical to the company's long-term survival.

This is not an unusual dilemma in either older industries or new economy companies. About eight years ago a major telecommunications company faced a very similar challenge. The industry had been deregulated and the company was facing real competition for the first time in its previously protected market. Executive assessments revealed that the 60 corporate executives were remarkably similar to each other in background, experience, leadership style, and ability. They primarily had engineering degrees, careers in operations, and long tenure with the company. Over a number of years this company was distinguished for a solid and predictable financial balance sheet. The narrow executive profile may have been an advantage to the corporation in the previous highly regulated, noncompetitive telephone industry, which had emphasized running physical telephone lines and working on engineering priorities, and where little change had occurred in many years. But now the company was facing strong competition in its once-protected market and had to learn how to compete for customers. However, no one in the executive group knew how to focus on or respond to customers. In getting the executive team aligned the company had promoted a group of executive clones. In this case the simpler approach of hiring to a narrow profile was effective as long as the business challenges remained unchanged. When deregulation, competition, and change finally occurred in the industry the company was largely unprepared for it—and is still struggling to find its new footing and strategic direction.

Predictably, corporations that are most effective in hiring to a single narrow executive profile often get into trouble when they have to deal with significant change in their market or industry. Fidelity to a carefully defined competency model often means having limited executive breadth and few executives in the organization who can actually drive change. Many organizations talk about bringing in change agents as part of the team, but rarely follow through and actually hire them. And if change agents do get hired the organization will often resist their recommendations, leading to their frustration and eventual turnover. Often this gets interpreted as a failure of the change agent—but more frequently it is a failure of the executive group to understand and support the change and to ready the organization to accept the change. The chief executive officer and the executives must fully commit to change and take personal responsibility for preparing the organization for change and for nurturing and championing change in the company.

There are many types of executive failures in organizations. Most of them are kept very quiet—unknown outside the company and frequently unaddressed inside the company.

Executive Failure Is Common and Hidden

Executives occupy the most visible and influential positions in most organizations. They have an enormous impact on the success and effectiveness of the organization. As result they get a lot of attention from both employees and outside business observers. Most organizations place a good deal of emphasis on providing significant rewards for executive contributions and spend a lot of time and resources getting the right people into the right positions.

Despite this effort there has been a rash of executive turnover in recent years. There seems to be an increasing number of senior executives leaving companies under questionable circumstances (Bianco & Lavelle, 2000; Charan & Colvin, 1999). Their departures often get reported as leaving for personal reasons, for personal differences with their immediate manager or the Board of Directors, or for a different career opportunity. Whatever reason gets reported is rarely the complete story and usually covers up many of the actual reasons. Corporations have strong motivation to hide the true underlying reasons for executive turnover so that there will be minimal damage to the company's public reputation and stock price. Similarly departing executives are also motivated to obscure the real issues so their careers and income potential won't be affected. As a result of this quietly shared deception only the most blatant performance failures get reported and known publicly. However, the actual rate of executive ineffectiveness is much higher, perhaps as high as 66 percent (Drucker, 1985; Sorcher, 1985).

Executive success and failure are on a continuum from blatantly disastrous performance outcomes to unquestionable triumph. In between are many degrees of effectiveness and ineffectiveness. Typically the performance of executives that are on either end of this continuum is well known and recognized. The obvious failures are usually addressed because their executive peers will not tolerate having such a clearly ineffective executive in the group. Strong chief executive officers will move these individuals out of their executive role and often out of the company. To avoid firing an ineffective executive for poor performance, however, some chief executive officers have even reorganized the corporate structure so as to eliminate the specific position and as a result to displace the problem executive. This is a face-saving tactic that can fool outside business analysts and most employees, but the executive group usually knows when such intentional displacement is one of the purposes of the reorganization.

The obviously effective executives frequently get additional visibility and compensation for their success even when it does not readily transfer into desired organizational outcomes. Some effective organizations resist rewarding executives when individual achievement has no direct impact on organizational success. Unfortunately, many organizations fail to recognize the need for this contingency. Many of these effective executives also do not recognize or admit the contribution of the organization or the executive team to their own success and conclude it was solely due to their own skills. This only encourages the executive to look for and gain higher-level and more complex executive roles, either internally or externally—and then fail in those roles. Effectiveness is usually due to a combination of individual, group, and organizational factors. Executives who fail to recognize this are much more likely to fail at their next effort than executives who understand the importance of aligning all these factors to achieve success.

Most executives fall somewhere in the middle on the effectiveness continuum. Experience suggests that many of them, perhaps even 50 percent, are ineffective in some of their critical responsibilities—but their deficiencies get overlooked or ignored. Frequently these executives are allowed to fail in place and the rest of the organization gets things done by working around them and often without them. Sometimes these executives are quietly moved or shelved to less critical positions. This may even involve a promotion to more peripheral responsibilities. In the past the position of administrative officer was commonly assigned to someone who was no longer effective or useful in an operational role. It was thought that the executive could not get into too much difficulty overseeing the corporate airplanes or office facilities.

Executive failure is often driven by change. The fast pace of business and organizational change makes executives who cannot or will not adapt less useful to the organization and less effective in their role than are those who can keep up. Change is no longer unexpected and most organizations have now had years to adapt to the faster pace of business change and create adaptive business models and fungible executive teams. But still we have significant executive failure.

A more thorough screening of candidates and more thoughtful selection decisions could have prevented many of these executive failures—and better management, coaching, and development of executives once hired would also help. However, selection of the best-fit executives remains the foundation for building a successful organization, and this can be a rather complex task.

The Complexity of Executive Selection

Making a sound executive selection decision is a critical and challenging task. Many chief executive officers see this as one of their most critical responsibilities. Larry Bossidy, chairman and chief executive officer of Honeywell, believes in spending extensive personal time in screening and hiring business leaders, saying, "There is no way to spend too much time on obtaining and developing the best people" (Bossidy, 2001). Nonetheless, in most organizations executive selection decisions are often poorly made.

Poor executive selection decisions can be due to a number of problems. Here are some that I have personally observed:

- Having little agreement on selection criteria and priorities
- Using a narrow or simplistic selection profile
- Looking only to duplicate the abilities of the predecessor or other current executives
- Using poor interviewing skills and collecting irrelevant data
- Screening candidates sequentially rather than simultaneously
- Poorly coordinating and controlling the screening and selection process
- Collecting insufficient candidate information relevant to selection priorities
- Gathering little input and support from key peers and functions related to the role
- Disagreeing on the interpretation of available candidate information
- Relying on personal biases and intuition that distort the data and the decisions
- Making decisions that are not based on logical reasoning or objective data
- Overvaluing external candidates and undervaluing internal candidates

At the executive level the selection task becomes particularly complex because of the range of considerations that go into matching an individual to an executive position (Carey & Ogden, 2000; DeVries, 1992; Gupta, 1992; Hambrick, 1988; Hollenbeck, 1994; Sessa & Taylor, 2000; Sonnenfeld, 1988). It is not as simple as just matching a candidate to a specific job, which ignores the complex and subtle issues operating at the executive level in an organization. While a *person-position fit* continues to be an important concern at the executive level it is only one of four matching considerations. Several levels of matching need to be considered given the complexity of executive roles (Brady & Helmich, 1984; Kristof, 1996; Schneider, 2001; Werbal & Gilliland, 1999).

Based on experience, I find it useful to look at how well the executive candidate matches the executive role on four different levels:

- The executive position *(person-position fit)*
- The executive group *(person-group fit)*
- The organization *(person-organization fit)*
- The culture of the country *(person-culture fit)*

Person-Position Fit

Matching the Individual to the Current Position

The actual responsibilities of an executive position are important to identify so the organization can be confident that the candidate can handle them effectively and so the candidate has some understanding of the scale and scope of the position's areas of accountability. In some cases this includes very critical and specific tasks such as legal or fiduciary duties. In general, however, executives do not have *jobs*—they have *positions*. A job has a standardized set of duties and responsibilities independent of the person in the job. Typically several or many people have the same job with little opportunity to modify it to better fit their own individual needs, abilities, or preferences. The match between the executive and the fundamental job responsibilities (person-job fit) is an early consideration in the screening process (Edwards, 1991; Silzer & Meyer, 2000). This is a basic selection matching process that has greater usefulness lower in the organization than it does in the leadership ranks.

It is helpful to separate the basic job responsibilities from the unique and person-driven responsibilities. Most, but not all, executive positions have some specific, basic job responsibilities such as delivering accurate, complete, and timely financial information for a chief financial officer or managing the productivity and quality control of operations for a manufacturing general manager. The candidate needs to have the knowledge, skills, and abilities (KSAs) and, in many situations, relevant experience to manage these basic responsibilities. At the executive level candidates would rarely even be considered without these qualifying KSAs and experience. Search firms would surely be told if they referred any unqualified candidates. So only qualified candidates get through the first step of the screening process. Executive candidates at a minimum must be able to handle the basic responsibilities of the job. It is the unique individual qualities of the candidates that distinguish them and that indicate the added value that each candidate brings to the position.

Most executive roles are modified by the person in the role. Even though there is a significant influence of the role and the situation on individual behavior, in the executive suite there is an equally significant influence by the individual on the situation and the role. So the concept of a job with highly structured and standardized duties does not fit very well at the executive level.

The concept of an *executive position* better reflects the uniqueness of each role and the influence on the role by the person in it than an *executive job*. The job responsibilities are important to consider, but they frequently change to accommodate an individual's skills and interests once the person is in the position (Chatman, 1999; Walsh, Craik, & Price, 2000). This is another reason why executive job descriptions are so hard to find. Each executive defines his role differently so there are few standardized duties and common tasks that can be written down. An organization is usually more concerned with performance outcomes than with the way job tasks are handled and gives each executive significant latitude in deciding how to accomplish those outcomes.

The real challenge in determining *person-position fit* is to identify the unique qualities of an individual and determine the likelihood that the candidate can take the position, and the organizational unit reporting to the position, to a new level of effectiveness. Sometimes these unique individual qualities and broader work expectations, such as requiring that a new business strategy drive an organizational unit, can be clearly specified prior to candidate screening. At other times the unique qualities and expectations emerge while interviewing candidates in the selection process. An example would be a chief information officer candidate who can not only deliver state-of-the-art information technology and systems in a timely and cost-effective way as expected, but who can also initiate IT proposals that create new strategic opportunities for the corporation. Initially this may be seen as a unique benefit that only a particular candidate can bring to the organization. However, after one incumbent in the position has successfully accomplished this then it may become part of the basic responsibilities that future candidates for the position must able to achieve in order to be seen as minimally qualified. So what initially is seen as a unique contribution may later come to be expected of all successors.

More frequently the organization does not specify the new unique direction to the executive but is open to considering a range of possibilities depending on the specific skills, interests, and experience of each candidate. For example, one candidate for a chief information officer position may have a broad business view and related strategic thinking skills while another may have significant production experience and a strong interest in IT applications to the manufacturing process. An organization may see each of these candidates as an opportunity to move in a new and often strategic direction. These individual talents are often discovered during the interview process.

When organizations stick to hiring executives by considering only their qualifications to perform the basic responsibilities, they wind up with basic executives who can do the "job" but have limited ability to significantly impact the organization in some new way. The role winds up being limited and the executive rarely rises above a mediocre performance level.

Highly effective executives, on the other hand, typically redefine their role in new ways so they can add value to the organization above and beyond the basic responsibilities. High-performance organizations look for the potential to contribute added value that often distinguishes the outstanding candidate from others. Sometimes the added value may be a strategic contribution to the organization. At other times the executive may have special skills in the contextual performance of the role (Borman & Motowidlo, 1993), such as supporting and collaborating with other business units. So hiring managers need to be open to and interested in discovering these unique talents during the selection process.

The strategic nature of the executive role may also influence the match. Many organizations have filled executive positions by looking for "a man for all seasons" (Sorcher, 1985). However this has often led to a mismatch between the talented executive and the particular business challenge. Some executive positions require the executive to maintain the current level of success and harvest the available financial benefits while other positions require a turnaround and rebuilding of the organizational unit. Each of these positions, harvest versus turnaround, requires an executive with a different set of skills (Gupta, 1988; Gupta & Govindarajan, 1984; Gerstein & Reisman, 1983). Typically a turnaround position requires an individual who can quickly analyze the business, develop a new strategic vision, and take charge of the organization. The executive also needs to be able to clearly communicate the new direction, act decisively, take risks, tolerate ambiguity, and motivate everyone to be fully committed to achieving difficult goals. Alternatively, a harvest role would require an executive to know the business, control costs, and build strong relationships with direct reports and customers. Consequently the strategic mandate of the organizational unit can directly determine some of the critical KSAs to look for during selection.

In addition the performance record and profile of the predecessor in the role can also affect the *person-position fit*. The strengths of a predecessor are often selected for in later executives and the weaknesses are often avoided. For example a new executive might need to build a stronger working relationship with a particular lateral functional group that was ignored by the predecessor in the role, to avoid facing the same criticism of having poor working relationships with the group. As a result it is easier for an executive to follow a weak predecessor where there are lower expectations than a highly effective predecessor who significantly raised the performance expectation bar.

The role expectations of the immediate manager (or the boss, to use a more unfashionable term) also influence the *person-position fit*. Typically the immediate manager has definite ideas about the role priorities that the new executive needs to perform effectively. Sometimes these are based on personal preferences; at other times they may be rooted in past problems and specific incidents. On occasion the expectations of the immediate manager can be very self-serving, such as hiring someone to take on additional responsibilities in order to shore up a personal weakness of the immediate manager or to free the manager up for a promotion or other career moves. More likely the direct manager is looking for an executive to help implement or achieve a new vision and specific strategic goals. Hiring managers frequently have an opinion on which parts of the executive's role are priority areas to accomplish. These work priorities will, in turn, influence the identification and the importance of specific selection factors.

So matching the person to the executive position involves the consideration of several factors:

- The candidate's skills and qualifications to perform the basic job responsibilities
- The candidate's unique talents that can add significant value to the organization
- The strategic mandate of the executive role
- The predecessor's performance record
- The specific expectations of the immediate manager

Matching the Position to the Needs of the Person
The position must also meet the needs of the individual executive (Edwards, 1991; Silzer & Meyer, 2000). An early consideration for most individuals is whether the basic job responsibilities match the person's vocational and career interests (Furnham, 2001; Holland, 1997; Kristof, 1996). This is particularly important for executives who want to stay in specific functional or professional careers (Hambrick & Brandon, 1988). For example, attorneys generally pursue corporate counsel roles because of their strong interest in and identification with the legal profession, while other executives with broader experience may be interested only in general management roles.

Frequently executive candidates want to know whether the role is clearly defined or not. Some executives pursue only clearly defined roles that give them some assurance they will have impact and influence in the organization. They push for clear lines of authority and influence. These individuals worry about future organizational changes or broken promises that might put them on the sidelines of the key decision making. Other executives look for more ambiguously defined roles and see ambiguity as an opportunity to define the role themselves and thereby gain additional influence beyond the basic role. Frequently, an individual's personality, work interests, and self-confidence influence a preference for clarity or ambiguity. Highly confident, adaptive individuals see the influence possibilities in an ambiguous situation while less confident and more structured individuals worry about the loss of influence and control in ambiguous situations. Given the current rapid change in business, executives who can tolerate a great deal of ambiguity are more likely to be effective over the long term than those who depend on clarity and structure.

In addition executives consider the nature of the work when deciding how attractive the opportunity is to them. Is it challenging enough? Is there an opportunity to learn something new? Will there be sufficient resources and support? Will the opportunity expand their skills and broaden their career experience and as a result expand their future career opportunities? A manager who has had responsibility for the financial reporting, auditing, and accounting functions for a corporation may resist taking a controller position that just duplicates previous experience and may prefer a financial transactions position that provides broader experience in mergers and acquisitions. The nature of the work responsibilities can significantly influence the interest of potential candidates in the position. Frequently strong candidates take the opportunity to negotiate the position responsibilities to better suit their interests and abilities. They may even be able to enlarge their responsibilities to gain additional resources and greater involvement in key decisions. If there is some part of the role they are not interested in they might make sure that they can delegate it to a competent direct report.

And, of course, they look closely at the compensation level, both fixed and variable pay and benefits, as Makri and Gomez-Mejia discuss in Chapter 8 of this book. However, their interest often goes beyond being adequately paid. Many candidates pursue pay as a negotiating challenge to see how far they can push for increased compensation. And many corporations respond accordingly if they are very interested in bringing the person into the company. Often candidates even admit privately that the compensation itself is not as important as pushing to see how far the company will go. It becomes a negotiating game and when it is played aggressively the candidate typically comes out ahead of the initial offer. Experienced hiring executives and human resource officers know not only what to offer the candidate but also their own upper compensation limit. They may also start with a lower offer to allow some room for negotiation. So the game gets played out until one party suggests something that reaches or surpasses the other's deal-breaking limits (the upper limits for the organization and the lower limits for the individual). Most likely the two parties then pull back from this and settle on something just inside the expressed limit. It is an interesting game to watch and it seems linked to the personality and drive of each of the negotiating parties, with aggressive, competitive individuals often achieving higher levels of compensation than others.

In matching the position to the needs and interests of the executive the following issues frequently get considered:

- The nature and scope of the work responsibilities
- The clarity of the role
- The level of involvement and influence in decision making
- The compensation level
- The candidate's professional and vocational interests and ambitions

Considering Future Person-Position Fit

Most executive selection decisions focus only on the immediate requirements of the position and the needs of the individual. Frequently, this turns out to be shortsighted because both the role and the individual are likely to change in the future. Sometimes there may be a predictable change in the role due to an anticipated reorganization or an announced merger and consolidation. Or it may be a corporate strategic change that will affect the specific executive position, such as a new commitment to customer focus or a switch from a product orientation to providing services. With a little thought the future impact on the role might be identified and described. This could then be translated into KSAs that will be needed in the future, which may actually be more critical for long-term effectiveness than the KSAs that are needed for immediate short-term performance.

It may be more difficult to predict how the person will change in the future based on their unique profile or in reaction to changes in the position. What is possible is to consider how effectively the individual adapts to change and learns. A constellation of issues can influence a person's ability to change and grow:

- Is the person cognitively bright enough to understand the change?
- Does the person show an interest in learning and a motivation to adapt to new situations?
- Is the person sufficiently flexible, both mentally and behaviorally, to try new approaches?

By getting a good understanding of the individual in these areas, selection decision makers should be able to predict the person's ability and likelihood to change in the future. Some of this will short-term learning (Gabarro, 1988) while other learning will be longer-term and over the course of a career (Graddick & Lane, 1998; Hall and Associates, 1986).

The future direction of the executive role and the adaptability of the executive can be gauged if they are given some thought. Both of these variables can be key to the long-term success of the *person-position fit*. While specific role changes might be difficult to anticipate, the ability of the individual to adapt, to change, or even to drive change can usually be accurately assessed.

So in considering the *person-position fit* over time it is helpful to consider the following points:

- The likely future changes in the executive role
- The ability of the executive to learn, to adapt to change, to deal with ambiguity, and even to drive change

Person-Group Fit

Matching the Person to the Executive Group

With the increased attention to teamwork in corporations (Hoerr, 1989) there has been interest in matching executive candidates to the work group associated with the executive role. The work group includes the immediate manager (to whom the position reports), executive peers, and direct reports. How well the executive fits into this work group can influence the success of the individual and the success of the organization (Guzzo, Salas, & Associates, 1995; Werbal & Gilliland, 1999). This may be particularly true if the executive group is functioning as a true team, as discussed by Spencer, Rivero, and Nadler in Chapter 5 of this book (see also Katzenbach, 1998; Nadler & Spencer, 1998). Teamwork skills at the executive level are likely to include not only typical characteristics of adaptability, shared situational awareness, and regular mutual performance monitoring and feedback (Cannon-Bowers, Tannenbaum, Salas, & Volpe, 1995), but also more complex skills such as trustworthiness (Walton, 1993) and strategic thinking.

One consideration of *person-group fit* is the extent to which the executive has characteristics that are similar to others in the work environment. These characteristics could be interests, values, abilities, attitudes, and so on. Often people perceive themselves as fitting in—and others see them as fitting in—when they are similar to others. Similarity may increase an executive's job satisfaction and organizational tenure (Muchinsky & Monahan, 1987). However, it can also lead to complacency and ultimately to organizational ineffectiveness. The *think alike* syndrome can significantly limit the decision options that get considered. No one is around to challenge the group's assumptions or status quo thinking. So although there may be some positive organizational benefits of cooperation, too much emphasis on similarity can actually be a threat to the organization—primarily through an inability to adapt to or drive change. This was one of the problems faced by the new chief executive officer discussed at the beginning of the chapter. But similarity does help to build interpersonal relationships with others in the work group and contributes to a supportive work environment. The executive team has to interact frequently, rely on each other, and trust one another's judgment, but not be clones of each other. Many executive groups, unfortunately, have a significant number of "norm followers"—individuals who support and advocate for closely shared norms of behavior. Corporations that are structured, hierarchical, and command-and-control oriented actually grow and create executives who are unwilling to challenge others.

The opposite consideration is whether the executive brings characteristics that are different from others in the work group and that make a unique contribution. These characteristics contribute to a complementary *person-group fit* (Muchinsky & Monahan, 1987) and bring added value to the group. Frequently the executive has certain KSAs or values that the group needs, such as a strong customer focus and commitment. Of course the work group needs to have or develop an appreciation for this unique contribution— otherwise the executive may be seen as "not fitting in" or "holding up the team." Complementary balance in the executive group is feasible as long as there is a clear understanding of the mix of skills that are needed and a focus on shared long-term organizational outcomes (Klimoski & Jones, 1995; Muchinsky & Monahan, 1987). Executives who challenge or question the existing norms in the executive group may have a difficult time being accepted or even surviving in the organization. The likelihood of success for change agents in most organizations is relatively low. The match on complementary fit must be gauged so that the unique characteristics are valued enough—at least by the chief executive officer—that the executive can get the support and the resources needed to make a significant contribution and not get quickly rejected.

So in matching the individual to the work group the decision makers should consider the following factors:

- The similarity of the executive to the group
- The complementary fit of the executive to the group
- Support by the chief executive officer for the executive's change efforts

Matching the Work Group to the Executive

In some circumstances organizations need to consider how well the existing work group matches the executive. Usually executives are matched to the current executive peer group and the immediate manager. However, the direct reports to the executive role are often matched to the executive. In the selection process candidates are often asked about changes they would make to their subordinate team. Infrequently do subordinates have much influence over the selection of the new executive—but the executive has considerable influence over the selection of direct reports. This is most evident when a new chief executive officer is hired with a mandate to change the organization. It is not unusual for the chief executive officer's personality, interests, and even work style and habits to be widely noticed and discussed in the organization with the expectation that everyone else will support or endorse these personal idiosyncrasies. The impact of the chief executive officer is far-reaching and the organization is expected to fit to the chief executive officer. This also happens when other senior executives are hired. This adjustment process ensures that the work group matches the executive.

However, effective and self-confident executives often select direct reports with KSAs that complement their own skills and abilities. This is evident in general managers who must manage direct reports in a range of different functional areas. These executives know how to manage different types of individuals and they see the advantage of having a heterogeneous team—at least in terms of functional knowledge and experience—to handle the diversity of responsibilities. They may also hire people very different from themselves to accomplish tasks that the executive is not good at doing or is not interested in doing.

In matching a work group to an executive the considerations include these two issues:

- The similarity of work group characteristics to the executive
- The complementary skills of the work group to the executive

Considering Future Person-Group Fit

How the fit between the person and the executive group evolves over time depends on the characteristics of the person and the group. In most cases a socialization process occurs in which each side accommodates or adopts some characteristics of the other (Ostroff & Kozlowski, 1992).

This process is most visible after the composition of the work group has been decided. The executive first decides which incumbents to keep as part of the direct report group and which ones to replace. The direct reports then decide whether they want to stay in their position reporting to the new executive, to transfer to a different work group, or to leave the organization. A similar but more subtle decision process occurs between the executive and the executive peers and is based not just on perceived effectiveness but also on the level of trust at the executive level. Once the group membership has been determined, then the executive and the work group start learning how to work effectively with each other. This usually leads to some accommodation and adjustment with each side gaining a greater appreciation for the other and even adopting some of the other's values, attitudes, and work approach.

However, sometimes the fit never seems to improve. This may be due to a dominant executive who never builds two-way working relationships with others, is not open to their influence or even their input, and is not willing to adapt to anyone. On occasion a work group may not develop trust or confidence in the new executive and may just wait for the new executive to fail and leave. Senior executives and organizations often create this situation by not sufficiently supporting the new executive against resistant or inflexible direct reports.

To a far lesser extent similar rejections may occur between the executive and the executive peer group. For a while everyone tries to tolerate the apparent differences between the executives—particularly if the chief executive officer has given the new executive a strong mandate for change. But over time the new executive is expected to show some accommodation on at least some issues or attitudes. Sometimes new executives in this situation intentionally resist any accommodation; at other times they may be oblivious to the differences or to the need to accommodate. While it isn't essential to become "one of the guys," it often helps to show some willingness to build a two-way relationship with peers, which usually requires some give-and-take on issues. After a one-year standoff it usually becomes evident that the differences will never get sufficiently bridged. There is a decision point, often in the second year, which results in some executive moves. It takes a year for the new executive to learn the position and the organization. If there is little accommodation during the second annual cycle of meetings and decisions, then it becomes evident that some executive changes need to be made. Few executives can survive the second year of a standoff unless they have the unwavering and open support of the chief executive officer. In these cases the other executives in the peer group may begin to explore external career options when they believe they have lost influence with the chief executive officer. However, greater executive turnover is often linked with lower organizational performance over time (Romanelli & Tushman, 1988).

The degree of socialization and accommodation depends to some extent on the performance track record of the direct reports or the executive peers. Stronger track records can lead to greater resistance to change. Similarly, an executive who comes into the position with a strong performance record or a strong mandate from the chief executive officer to introduce change may be less willing to accommodate the work group. Of course, the personalities and attitudes of the individuals can vary on flexibility and openness to change.

Frequently the organizational strategies and goals may require a strong *person-group fit*, particularly if the executive is in a critical and central role. For other roles the organization may be more tolerant of a mismatch, as when an executive is placed in a role as a short-term rotational development assignment.

In most cases *person-group fit* improves with time, though the executive group itself is likely to change within a few years and part of the socialization process then needs to begin again. These are the key factors that influence *person-group fit* over time:

- The performance record of the executive and the work group
- The flexibility and openness to change of the individuals involved
- The chief executive officer's expectations and support for the fit
- The organizational need for a strong fit

Person-Organization Fit

Matching the Person to the Organization

When matching an executive to an organization there are a number of organizational variables that should be considered (Kristof, 1996; O'Reilly, Chatman, & Caldwell, 1991; Silzer, Jeanneret, & Davis, 1998; Werbal & Gilliland, 1999). The specific variables that are salient will vary across situations and organizations. Organizations differ in a variety of ways—values, social norms, policies and procedures, structure, leadership style, business goals, historical legacies, competitive strengths, and many others. Taken together they might be called the organization's culture and they identify what gets valued and rewarded in the company.

The historical legacies of a company are often connected to the company's reputation and organizational attributes. For example, the company may be well known for having exceptional strength in a particular functional area such as customer service or marketing. Or it may have an innovative product line that is backed up by a strong R&D organization. These legacies may in fact be sacred cows that can't be touched and may dictate some executive selection restraints but also some qualities to look for or avoid in executive candidates.

The business strategies of the organization may also dictate certain qualities to look for in executive candidates. A customer service–driven company will need executives who value and implement that approach by making customers a priority while a low-cost producer will need executives who can tightly manage costs and get things accomplished with minimal resources. These business strategies usually affect everyone in the organization but executives in particular must champion the strategies to others. Executives who disagree with the strategy will need strong leadership and influencing skills if they wish to introduce change to the strategy. Over time, however, they need to actively support the strategy, change the strategy, or consider leaving the company.

Even the organizational structure may be a selection consideration. Flat structures with a broad span of reporting relationships need executives who can handle a broad scope of responsibilities and are effective at delegating to others and coordinating a large team of direct reports. Hierarchical organizations that are more functionally organized need executives with strong interpersonal influence skills who can work across organizational boundaries to get things done.

Similarly the predominant organizational leadership style in the organization should be considered when screening candidates. Some organizations have a command-and-control style that limits the decision authority of an executive and requires a certain amount of restraint and thoughtfulness before taking action. On the other hand, a participative organizational style might expand an executive's decision-making authority and encourage more innovative thinking. The leadership style of the chief executive officer is the most influential on the executives and can significantly alter executives' work approach and leadership influence. Each executive needs to have at least a comfort level with the chief executive officer's style or have a similar personal style. It is not uncommon to find a mismatch between styles that leads to later conflict. An executive with a loose management style who gives direct reports significant decision-making authority is likely to have difficulty reporting to a chief executive officer who is structured, detailed, and controlling and who likes to be involved in most decisions. This leads not just to frustration for the executive and the chief executive officer but to serious work style differences that often can not be easily overcome. The opposite mismatch—a broadly delegating chief executive officer with a structured and controlling executive—is less of a problem but still requires some negotiating if the chief executive officer presses the executive to alter an ingrained command-and-control style. So the match between the leadership styles of the chief executive officer (or immediate manager) and the executive is a particularly important selection consideration.

In the last decade most large corporations have identified and widely communicated a core set of organizational values that serve to guide business decisions and behavior. These value declarations often focus on common themes of integrity and honesty, respect for employees, commitment to customers, and personal accountability. In some cases the values communicate specific rules for personal behavior; at other times the values seem to be used primarily as a marketing tool for company promotion. Executives are often expected to not just adhere to these values but to advocate them to others. Frequently their annual appraisal might even comment on how well they demonstrated the values. Organizations vary a good deal on the clarity of their values, the degree of consensus supporting them, and the intensity to which they are followed (Posner, 1992). It would be important to share the corporate values with candidates for executive positions and even use them to screen the candidates—especially on the values that may affect their daily behavior such as showing respect for others. For example, corporations now have less tolerance for interpersonally abusive executives and frequently will coach or outplace individuals who consistently show this behavior to their employees. It might be easier to screen these individuals out during the selection process. The match between the executive's values and the organizational values can have an impact on organizational outcomes (Edwards, 1991; Hambrick & Brandon, 1988; Posner, 1992; Sorcher, 1985).

Similarly there are unwritten social norms and written policies and procedures that vary quite a bit between companies. Social or behavior norms can distinguish organizational cultures. For example, the level of expected work commitment often varies widely—with some organizations, such as public accounting firms, expecting long hours and a high level of commitment while other organizations, such as some government agencies, have much lower expectations for work hours and work commitment. In the executive suite the work norms might involve regular Saturdays in the office or 7 A.M. breakfast meetings. The norms are usually informal and unwritten and typically reflect the chief executive officer's work habits and expectations. It may take a new executive some time to learn all the informal norms after joining the organization.

Company policies and procedures are designed to standardize and control a range of organizational decisions. The company's degree of decision-making control and the compensation framework are the policy areas that generally have the most impact on an executive. In extreme cases the degree of control exerted by the policies may suggest certain qualities to look for in executives such as norm compliance or a willingness to follow the rules.

As a consequence the organizational culture, broadly defined, is an important consideration when matching an executive to an organization. It is useful to consider the following components of organizational culture when selecting executives:

- Business strategies
- Historical legacies
- Organizational structure
- Organization attributes and competitive advantages
- Dominant leadership style
- Corporate values
- Social norms of behavior
- Policies and procedures
- Chief executive officer expectations

Matching the Organization to the Person

In the past organizations have had an advantage in the selection process because it has been a buyer's market for hiring leadership talent. It has been relatively easy for organizations to identify a substantial list of outside candidates for executive positions, particularly with the help of executive search firms. However, in the last decade—with the strong business economy and the explosion of executive opportunities in technology companies—organizations have found it more difficult to find available and qualified candidates. This has given candidates more leverage in choosing their career opportunities and in negotiating the scope of the position and the associated pay and benefits. In addition, it is not uncommon for executives to move frequently to different companies for new career opportunities. So executive retention in many organizations has become a major strategic issue.

Executive candidates have more career choices now and can be more selective in finding an organization that suits their interests and skills. Their success in finding the right match depends to some degree on their self-awareness of their own skills and interests and on how motivated they are to look for matching opportunities. Most executives are not very good at analyzing and understanding an organization's culture without actually working in it for a while. It is very common for executives to express surprise and disappointment six months after joining a company. This is due not only to poorly reading the culture ahead of time but also to having an inadequate understanding of their own skills, abilities, and work preferences. Many executives do not have a clear sense of how their career interests match to their own skills and abilities. Because candidates have more career choices now they are more likely to express an interest in pursuing an opportunity even though their skills and abilities are unsuited for it. Many executives joined technology start-up companies in the last decade only to discover that they were not entrepreneurs and needed a more structured work routine and greater financial security than these companies have provided. While some stretched themselves and learned new skills during these experiences, many returned to large corporations to find more comfortable and predictable positions.

So executive candidates need to consider many of the same issues that organizations do in order to find the best *person-organization fit:*

- A range of organizational culture issues
- The values of the organization

- Their own skills, abilities, and interests
- The match between their career interests and their skills and abilities

Future Person-Organization Fit

Both individuals and organizations can change. In both cases the particular characteristics of each have a significant influence over how much change is possible. Individuals often get socialized to the organization's culture and norms over time unless they are inflexible or actively resist any accommodation. Similarly, organizations vary on openness to change. Some organizations with strong past success resist change and prefer to stay with approaches that are considered tried and true; other companies with continuing success have learned how to change and adapt.

Though organizations can change the behavior of executives, executives can have substantial influence on the organization as well. These two influences can frequently improve the *person-organization fit*. Executives may get comfortable with a company over time as they adapt to and later internalize the culture. For example, when faced with strong organizational values executives may go through stages of compliance, identification, and then internalization (Posner, 1992), ultimately making the values their own. Similarly the values of executives can have an impact on the organizations they manage and even on their executive peers. An executive with high integrity standards can raise the level of ethical decision making in an organization.

However, if an executive never does more than just comply with the organization's values and culture and the organization only minimally tolerates the executive, then the fit may never improve and, in some cases, will deteriorate. This may become more common as executives move more frequently and have a shorter tenure with any one organization. They may resist adapting to the culture which in turn may only serve to limit their tenure with the organization.

The assimilation of the executive into the organization requires some adjustment by both the executive and the organization (Gabarro, 1987; Silzer & Meyer, 2000). However, the executive is often at risk if the fit does not improve over time, regardless of which side is failing to adapt to the other.

A few key variables may contribute to the *person-organization fit* over time:

- The ability and willingness of the executive to adapt to the organization
- The influencing skills of the executive
- The openness and ability of the organization to accept and support change

Person-Culture Fit

In recent years there has been increased interest in understanding how executives can be effective in different country cultures, as Fulkerson discusses in Chapter 11 of this book (see also Fulkerson, 1998; McCall & Hollenbeck, 2001). The ability to adapt to a culture that is different from the executive's country of origin is a key consideration in successfully placing an executive in an international position.

A wide range of issues need to be considered (Ward & Chang, 1997). For example, the cultural distance between two countries might partially predict an executive's sociocultural adjustment to a new country (Ward & Kennedy, 1993; Parkes, Bochner, & Schneider, 2001). One of the more robust measures of differences in national culture is the individualism-collectivism dimension (Hofstede, 1991; Parkes et al., 2001; Triandis, 1995), which indicates whether individual interests or group interests will be given priority. At the individual level individualists emphasize their independence and autonomy while collectivists see themselves as an interdependent part of a larger group. American executives are individualists by nature and by experience. In the past they have been selected, developed, and rewarded to be independent thinkers and decision makers. So it is no surprise that they fit well in individualist cultures. Many of them have difficulty adjusting to the collectivist cultures frequently found in Asia. Careful thought needs to be given to decisions that place U.S. executives in overseas assignments. However even in the United States many organizations are moving toward a more collectivist, team-oriented culture where the compensation of individual executives is more contingent on group performance than on individual achievements.

Many organizations that have operations in collectivist cultures have had to figure out how to integrate the organization's individualist culture with the country's collectivist culture. This conflict has led to internal tension and many overseas failures because the company insisted on the dominance of its own internal culture over the country culture. Eventually most companies come to see the benefits of accommodating and integrating both cultures so neither one gets wholly rejected (Meglino & Ravlin, 1998).

In some cases a country's culture, particularly as it relates to business, can change and adjust. In fact the globalization of business has brought pressure on local cultures to adapt to globally accepted business practices. So some businesses in Japan have introduced individual performance appraisals that previously were unheard of in that culture. Some businesses in socialist countries are providing executives with stock options in an effort to attract and retain leadership talent. Business in particular has been an important avenue for introducing cultural change in countries. However, individual executives will have limited ability to influence the culture of another country on their own, so the selection process needs to include some evaluation of the match between the executive's values and the values of the country (Fulkerson, 1998; Jackofsky & Slocum, 1988).

The complexity of these issues raises significant selection and placement challenges and has resulted in many overseas placement failures. Organizations would benefit from identifying key selection variables that take a country's culture into account when selecting and screening executives for specific overseas assignments.

Here are some of the variables that contribute to *person-culture fit:*

- A clear understanding of the country culture
- An integration of the country culture and the organizational culture
- The executive's openness to experience and ability to adapt
- The level of adjustment support and coaching available

Addressing a Complex Challenge

Clearly there are a lot of issues to consider when selecting an executive. The task is complex, with a lot of opportunity to make poor decisions. Even if an organization is able to collect extensive and objective candidate data on each critical variable it would be difficult to integrate everything into a clear decision. In addition, executives themselves do a poor job of gauging their fit with an organization and often accept positions that are a poor match for their skills and interests. Sometimes they are driven by their strong ego and lack of self-awareness. Despite these challenges there are ways to increase the likelihood of making the right decisions and increasing the selection success rate. Here are a few suggestions:

Get agreement on the scale and scope of the executive position and the critical success factors. It is essential to settle on the key matching variables that will increase the specific person-position, person-group, person-organization, and *person-culture fit* (see Table 4.1). After reviewing the matching issues that are relevant to the position, identify a limited number of selection factors that seem most directly related to future success in a specific executive position.

Identify valid measures of each of the critical success factors. Consider using a range of evaluation tools including structured interviews, executive assessments, personality inventories, cognitive skill measures, executive simulations, and multisource feedback instruments (for internal candidates) (Jeanneret & Silzer, 1998; Silzer, 1998; Silzer & Hollenbeck, 1992; Silzer & Jeanneret, 1998; Silzer & Meyer, 2000; Silzer, Slider, & Knight, 1994). Develop interview outlines that focus on collecting data on the targeted critical success factors. For each of the success factors consider developing a behaviorally anchored rating scale to evaluate the candidate against specific behaviors and a reliable and standardized measurement scale.

Identify a limited selection team of individuals who will be involved in evaluating the candidates and making the selection decision. Where possible they should represent diverse and critical perspectives and constituencies.

Give each selection team member an interview assignment for collecting data on a specific subset of the success factors. Each success factor should be assigned to several different team members to ensure thorough coverage and a reliable evaluation of the factor.

Structure the selection process to screen candidates early in the process on basic job qualifications and factors that are relatively easy to evaluate. The factors that are harder to measure or that take more time and resources should be assessed later in the process. More senior team members who have extremely busy schedules should also be used later in the process.

Table 4.1. Executive Fit Issues.

Match	Match the Executive to	Match to the Executive	Future Match Issues
Person-Position Fit	*Position* • Executive's skills and characteristics • Executive's unique talents • Strategic mandate of the role • Predecessor's performance record • Expectations of immediate manager	*Position* • Nature and scope of role • Clarity of role • Level of decision making and influence • Compensation level • Executive's vocational interests and ambitions	*Position* • Future change in role • Executive's ability to learn and adapt
Person-Group Fit	*Group* • Similarity of Executive to Group • Complementary fit of executive to group • Support of CEO for Executive's change efforts	*Group* • Similarity of Group to Executive • Complementary skills of Group to Executive	*Group* • Performance record of Executive and Group • Flexibility of Group, Executive • Organizational need for fit

	Organization	Organization	Organization
Person-Organization Fit	• Business strategies • Historical legacies • Structure • Competitive advantages • Leadership style • Corporate values • Social norms • Policies • CEO expectations	• Organizational culture • Executive's skills and interests • Integration of Executive's skills and interests • Organizational values	• Executive's motivation to adapt • Organization's openness to change

	Country Culture
Person-Culture Fit	• Understanding of country culture • Integration of country and organizational culture • Executive's openness to experience • Adjustment support and coaching

After candidate data has been collected have the selection team meet to discuss the candidate against the critical success factors. Rate the candidate on each factor. You might even have team members discuss the factors and then rate them independently to see where there is agreement. List the strengths and development needs of each candidate. Consider a candidate's learning ability and development potential when making the final decision. Make the overall selection decision based on the success factor ratings.

Provide feedback to each candidate on personal strengths and development needs based on the success factors (Meyer, 1998).

Outline an assimilation and development plan that not only familiarizes the hired executive with the organization but also helps them to reach an effective performance level as quickly as possible. Be sure the plan includes steps that will help to strengthen the executive on the critical success factors. It is in everyone's best interests to help the executive be as successful as possible.

After one year review the match between the executive and the role, taking into consideration the fit with the position, the work group, the organization, and the country culture. Look for ways to improve the fit at each level.

Review and adjust the executive selection process based on experience to incorporate new ways of reaching a better fit in future selection decisions. The real goal and challenge becomes helping the hired executive to be successful. In evaluating the success of the selection decision, here are some outcomes to consider:

- Organizational performance
- Executive's individual performance against goals
- Long-term retention of the executive
- Executive's motivation and job satisfaction
- Executive's stress level and physical health
- Executive's adjustment to organization's culture and social norms
- Executive's success in building relationships
- Organizational and work group adjustment to the executive

It is clear that the process of selecting successful executives is complex and difficult. Most organizations do a haphazard or slipshod job of it (Nadler & Nadler, 1998), and the result is a significant number of costly and often visible executive failures. By organizing and structuring the selection process to focus on critical success factors an organization can improve its selection success rate. However, the organization has to see the value of having effective and successful executives.

Some organizations have been very effective at selecting outstanding executives—and they put in the time and resources necessary to achieve that success. Other organizations can be just as successful once they see the importance of selecting the best talent available. They need to see executive talent not only as an organizational goal but also as a competitive advantage.

References

Bianco, A., & Lavelle, L. (2000, December 11). The CEO trap. *Business Week*, pp. 86–92.

Borman, W. C., & Motowidlo, S. J. (1993). Expanding the criterion domain to include elements of contextual performance. In N. Schmitt & W. C. Borman (Eds.), *Personnel selection in organizations*, pp. 71–98. San Francisco: Jossey-Bass.

Bossidy, L. (2001, March). The job no CEO should delegate. *Harvard Business Review*, pp. 46–49.

Brady, G. F., & Helmich, D. L. (1984). *Executive succession: Toward excellence in corporate leadership.* Upper Saddle River, NJ: Prentice Hall.

Cannon-Bowers, J. A., Tannenbaum, S. I., Salas, E., & Volpe, C. E. (1995). Defining competencies and establishing team training requirements. In R. Guzzo, E. Salas, & Associates (Eds.), *Team effectiveness and decision making in organizations*, pp. 330–380. San Francisco: Jossey-Bass.

Carey, D. C., & Ogden, D. (2000). *CEO succession.* Oxford, UK: Oxford University Press.

Charan, R., & Colvin, G. (1999, June 21). Why CEOs fail. *Fortune*, pp. 69–82.

Chatman, J. A. (1989). Improving interactional organizational research: A model of person-organization fit. *Academy of Management Review, 14*(3), 333–349.

DeVries, D. L. (1992). *Executive selection: Why do we know so little about something so important.* Working paper. Greensboro, NC: Center for Creative Leadership.

Drucker, P. (1985, July-August). Getting things done: How people make decisions. *Harvard Business Review*, pp. 22–26.

Edwards, J. E. (1991). Person-job fit: A conceptual integration, literature review, and methodological critique. *International Review of Industrial and Organizational Psychology, 6,* 283–357.

Fulkerson, J. R. (1998). Assessment across cultures. In R. Jeanneret & R. Silzer (Eds.), *Individual psychological assessment: Predicting behavior in organizational settings,* pp. 330–362. San Francisco: Jossey-Bass.

Furnham, A. (2001). Vocational preferences and P-D fit: Reflections on Holland's theory of vocational choice. *Applied Psychology: An International Review, 50*(1), 5–29.

Gabarro, J. J. (1987). *The dynamics of taking charge.* Boston: Harvard Business School Press.

Gabarro, J. J. (1988). Executive leadership and selection: The process of taking charge. In D. C. Hambrick (Ed.), *The executive effect: Concepts and methods for studying top managers,* pp. 237–268. Greenwich, CT: JAI Press.

Gerstein, M., & Reisman, H. (1983). Strategic selection: Matching executives to business conditions. *Sloan Management Review, 19,* 33–49.

Graddick, M. M., & Lane, P. (1998). Evaluating executive performance. In J. W. Smither (Ed.), *Performance appraisal: State of the art in practice,* pp. 370–403. San Francisco: Jossey-Bass.

Gupta, A. K. (1988). Contingency perspectives on strategic leadership: Current knowledge and future research directions. In D. C. Hambrick (Ed.), *The executive effect: Concepts and methods for studying top managers,* pp. 141–178. Greenwich, CT: JAI Press.

Gupta, A. K. (1992). Executive selection: A strategic perspective. *Human Resource Planning, 15,* 47–61.

Gupta, A. K., & Govindarajan, V. J. (1984). Business unit strategy, managerial characteristics, and business unit effectiveness at strategy implementation. *Academy of Management Journal, 7,* 25–41.

Guzzo, R. A., Salas, E., & Associates. (1995). *Team effectiveness and decision making in organizations.* San Francisco: Jossey-Bass.

Hall, D. T., & Associates. (1986). *Career development in organizations.* San Francisco: Jossey-Bass.

Hambrick, D. C. (Ed.). (1988). *The executive effect: Concepts and methods for studying top managers.* Greenwich, CT: JAI Press.

Hambrick, D. C., & Brandon, G. L. (1988). Executive values. In D. C. Hambrick (Ed.), *The executive effect: Concepts and methods for studying top managers,* pp. 3–34. Greenwich, CT: JAI Press.

Hoerr, J. (1989, July 10). The payoff from teamwork. *Business Week,* pp. 56–62.

Hofstede, G. (1991). *Cultures and organizations: Software of the mind.* London: McGraw-Hill.

Holland, J. L. (1997). *Making vocational choices* (3rd ed.). Upper Saddle River, NJ: Prentice Hall.

Hollenbeck, G. P. (1994). *CEO selection: A street-smart review.* Greensboro, NC: Center for Creative Leadership.

Jackofsky, E. F., & Slocum, J. W. (1988). CEO roles across cultures. In D. C. Hambrick (Ed.), *The executive effect: Concepts and methods for studying top managers,* pp. 67–100. Greenwich, CT: JAI Press.

Jeanneret, R., & Silzer, R. F. (Eds.). (1998). *Individual psychological assessment: Predicting behavior in organizational settings.* San Francisco: Jossey-Bass.

Katzenbach, J. R. (1998). *Teams at the top.* Boston: Harvard Business School Press.

Klimoski, R., & Jones, R. G. (1995). Staffing for effective group decision making: Key issues in matching people and teams. In R. A. Guzzo, E. Salas, & Associates (Eds.), *Team effectiveness and decision making in organizations,* pp. 291–332. San Francisco: Jossey-Bass.

Kristof, A. L. (1996). Person-organization fit: An integrative review of its conceptualizations measurement and implications. *Personnel Psychology, 49,* 1–49.

McCall, M., & Hollenbeck, G. (2001). *Frequent flyers: Developing global executives.* Boston: Harvard Business School Press.

Meglino, B. M., & Ravlin, E. C. (1998). Individual values in organizations: Concepts, controversies, and research. *Journal of Management, 24*(3), 351–389.

Meyer, P. (1998). Communicating results for impact. In R. Jeanneret & R. Silzer (Eds.), *Individual psychological assessment: Predicting behavior in organizational settings,* pp. 243–284. San Francisco: Jossey-Bass.

Muchinsky, P. M., & Monahan, C. J. (1987). What is person-environment congruence? Supplementary versus complementary models of fit. *Journal of Vocational Behavior, 31,* 268–277.

Nadler, D. A., & Nadler, M. B. (1998). *Champions of change: How CEOs and their companies are mastering the skills of radical change.* San Francisco: Jossey-Bass.

Nadler, D. A., & Spencer J. L. (1998). *Executive teams.* San Francisco: Jossey-Bass.

O'Reilly, C. A., Chatman, J., & Caldwell, D. F. (1991). People and organizational culture: A profile comparison approach to assessing person-organization fit. *Academy of Management Journal, 3,* 487–516.

Ostroff, C., & Kozlowski, S.W.J. (1992). Organizational socialization as a learning process: The role of information acquisition, *Personnel Psychology, 45,* 849–874.

Parkes, L. P., Bochner, S., & Schneider, S. K. (2001). Person-organization fit across cultures: An empirical investigation of individualism and collectivism. *Applied Psychology: An International Review, 501*(1), 81–108.

Posner, B. Z. (1992). Person-organization values congruence: No support for individual differences as a moderating influence. *Human Relations, 45*(4), 351–362.

Romanelli, E., & Tushman, M. L. (1988). Executive leadership and organizational outcomes: An evolutionary perspective. In D. C. Hambrick (Ed.), *The executive effect: Concepts and methods for studying top managers*, pp. 129–140. Greenwich, CT: JAI Press.

Schneider, B. (2001). Fits about fit. *Applied Psychology: An International Review, 50*(1), 141–152.

Sessa, V. I., & Taylor, J. J. (2000). *Executive selection: Strategies for success.* San Francisco: Jossey-Bass.

Silzer, R. F. (1998). Shaping organizational leadership: The ripple effect of assessment. In R. Jeanneret & R. Silzer (Eds.), *Individual psychological assessment: Predicting behavior in organizational settings*, pp. 391–444. San Francisco: Jossey-Bass.

Silzer, R. F., & Hollenbeck, G. P. (1992, April). Executive assessment. A workshop presented at the annual conference of the Society of Industrial and Organizational Psychology, Montreal.

Silzer, R. F., & Jeanneret, R. (1998). Anticipating the future: Assessment strategies for tomorrow. In R. Jeanneret & R. Silzer (Eds.), *Individual psychological assessment: Predicting behavior in organizational settings*, pp. 445–478. San Francisco: Jossey-Bass.

Silzer, R. F., Jeanneret, R., & Davis, S. (1998, April). Leveraging psychological assessment to accomplish business strategies. A workshop presented at the annual conference of the Society for Industrial and Organizational Psychology, Dallas.

Silzer, R. F., & Meyer, P. (2000, April). Utilizing strategic psychological assessment for executive selection and coaching. A workshop presented at the annual conference of the Society of Industrial and Organizational Psychology, New Orleans.

Silzer, R. F., Slider, R. L., & Knight, M. (1994). *Human Resource development: A study of corporate practices.* Atlanta: BellSouth and Anheuser-Busch.

Sonnenfeld, J. (1988). *The hero's farewell: What happens when CEOs retire.* New York: Oxford University Press.

Sorcher, M. (1985). *Predicting executive success: What it takes to make it to senior management.* New York: Wiley.

Triandis, H. C. (1995). *Individualism and collectivism.* Boulder, CO: Westview.

Walsh, W. B., Craik, K. H., & Price, R. H. (Eds.). (2000). *Person-environment psychology: Models and perspectives.* Mahwah, NJ: Erlbaum.

Walton, A. E. (1993). The importance of trust. In D. Nadler & J. L. Spencer (Eds.), *Executive teams,* pp. 135–148. San Francisco: Jossey-Bass.

Ward, C., & Chang, W. C. (1997). "Cultural fit": A new perspective on personality and sojourner adjustment. *International Journal of Intercultural Relations, 21*(4), 525–533.

Ward, C., & Kennedy, A. (1993). Where's the culture in cross-cultural transition? Comparative studies of sojourner adjustment. *Journal of Cross-Cultural Psychology, 24,* 221–249.

Werbal, J. D., & Gilliland, S. W. (1999). Person-environment fit in the selection process. *Research in Personnel and Human Resources Management, 17,* 209–243.

CHAPTER 5

Leveraging Executive Teams
What's New (and What's Not) in the Strategic Enterprise
Janet L. Spencer, J. Carlos Rivero, David A. Nadler

Today's business leaders stand at a crossroads: the models and frameworks that shaped leading organizations from the end of the Second World War through the conclusion of the Cold War have been rendered obsolete by a new era of digital business, perpetual innovation, and global competition. The design and leadership of complex enterprises capable of creating and sustaining value over the long term requires an entirely new way of thinking about organizations. We believe the answer lies in an emerging pattern of organization architecture: the Strategic Enterprise ("The Strategic Enterprise," 2000).

In our view, the Strategic Enterprise will take its place as the third modern paradigm of organization design. From the late 1940s through the early 1960s, the dominant model was the integrated operating company—a tight collection of closely related operating units characterized by similar business designs and closely linked by consistent patterns of management structures and processes. Then came the conglomerates, portfolio holding companies consisting of widely varying businesses loosely linked through a common financial pool. The Strategic Enterprise, in contrast with its predecessors, combines strategically aligned businesses employing a wide variety of business models, linked closely where there are opportunities to create value by leveraging shared capabilities but only loosely where the greater value lies in differentiated focus. Figure 5.1 diagrams the pattern.

The emergence of digital technology and the Internet have, in large part, driven this phenomenon, as they spawned the radically different online business designs that have begun to spring up alongside traditional businesses. The challenge of combining these models under one corporate umbrella is twofold: how best to link the businesses where leverage creates value and how best to govern the different models in ways that maximize the potential of each while contributing to the success of the whole. The solution lies in "designed divergence"—the creation of structures that not only allow but nurture differences in unit-operating models in order to maximize independent success and enterprise performance. Rather than congruence or uniformity among operating

Figure 5.1. The Strategic Enterprise.

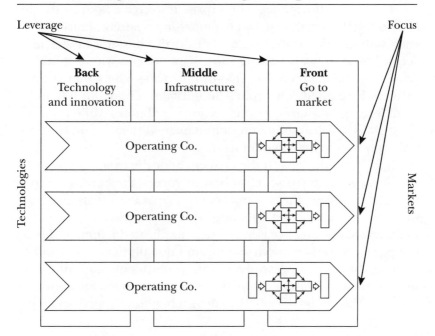

models, the ultimate goal becomes coherence within the overall corporate strategy.

The key to understanding the Strategic Enterprise lies in balancing the dual objectives of focus and leverage. At the most basic level, businesses can be defined as collections of people who seek profitable ways to marry core technologies with markets. In recent years, the concept of the value chain has come to represent the series of processes—research, product development, production, distribution, sales, and support—that are required to convert technologies into profitable offerings. The best way to achieve maximum focus within an organization is to concentrate on translating a single core technology into a set of offerings targeted at a specific market—the model normally found in small start-ups. More complex organizations seek focus through the creation of business units, each with its own internal value chain. However, at a certain point, a single-minded emphasis on focus causes the organization to miss out on the potential benefits of leverage such as economies of scale, pooled research capacity, and shared distribution channels. There is latent value that can be realized from common ownership and management.

The goal of the Strategic Enterprise is to create both focus and leverage. It does that, first, by encompassing a variety of businesses, each with its own value chain and distinctive business model, and second by selectively linking those value chains where it makes sense, and linking them loosely—or not at all—where there's little value to be gained. The goal is to derive the maximum benefit from leveraging shared resources and capabilities while keeping those links to the absolute minimum needed to maintain focus in a sharply fragmented marketplace.

Implicit in this goal is the challenge for the executive team in the Strategic Enterprise: How best to govern the enterprise in a way that maximizes the potential of each separate and distinct business while simultaneously creating value by providing the glue that maintains corporate cohesion? The complicated patterns of processes, structures, and policies that traditionally maintained cohesion in the old integrated operating company can stifle the divergence and internal competition so critical to the Strategic Enterprise. The key is for leaders to determine the minimal "glue" required to maintain organizational coherence and to design the appropriate governance structures accordingly.

For many of today's large, complex organizations, answering the analysts' question—What purpose does common ownership of these assets serve?—becomes more and more difficult. Defining and providing the corporate coherence that will hold the companies together and make the whole greater than the sum of the various parts becomes one of the executive team's most significant roles.

Executive Teams in the Strategic Enterprise: What's New

As we have written elsewhere ("The Strategic Enterprise," 2000; Nadler & Spencer, 1998), we believe that it is virtually impossible for a chief executive officer, no matter how wise or talented, to successfully balance all the monumental challenges of making a Strategic Enterprise operate effectively. The executive team is a linchpin of corporate governance and a critical element in the ultimate success of the enterprise. New leadership demands are being created by the emergence of the Strategic Enterprise, and the executive team is the only group of individuals in a position to provide the enterprise-wide perspective that will ultimately be the source of corporate cohesion. Designing the team's work process in such a way as to maximize the potential for high performance becomes a critical activity for the chief executive officer.

The task of designing and implementing the right work process for an executive team is frequently called *team building*. We use the framework illustrated in Figure 5.2 with our chief executive officer clients to ensure that all critical elements are attended to in this process.

We will not review each component of this framework in depth as more detailed discussion can be found elsewhere (Nadler & Spencer, 1998; "Teamwork at the Top," 1998); however, we will elaborate on aspects of the framework that pose particular challenges in the Strategic Enterprise.

The starting point for building the executive team is to clarify the context and charter for team members so that they have a

Figure 5.2. Team-Building Framework.

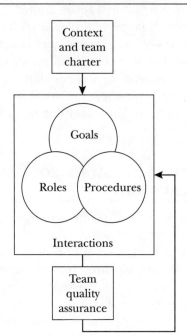

shared understanding of the elements surrounding and defining the team's work process. In the Strategic Enterprise, the vision for the enterprise and the choices regarding where and how to link the disparate businesses under the corporate umbrella provide this context. Ideally, the executive team will have been involved in the crafting of this vision and the choices regarding architecture (for example, the balance of focus and leverage among the businesses). Explicit discussion of these issues should provide the backdrop against which decisions regarding team building can then be made.

At the core of this framework are four elements that provide leverage points for designing how an executive team functions: goals, roles, procedures, and interactions. Perhaps the most important of these in the context of the Strategic Enterprise, and the one which should be addressed first, is goals.

Goals: The Value-Added Work of the Executive Team

The fundamental issue to be addressed here is defining the value-added work of the executive team—the work they engage in that contributes to the management of a mixed-model enterprise, providing the cohesive glue among and between businesses *only where it is needed and adds value.* In the Strategic Enterprise, this concept goes beyond deciding how the team will spend its time—it defines the central issue regarding corporate coherence. The activities that the executive team chooses to engage in collectively must be aligned with choices it makes regarding how the Strategic Enterprise will be organized and managed.

The Strategic Enterprise structure theoretically unlocks the potential for each business by allowing access to the resources of the corporation where (and only where) they will provide value. Lack of clarity on what this means or how it translates directly into the management of the business is often the factor limiting enterprise performance. Without clear alignment on how and where to add value from the top, the executive team can collectively spin its wheels, neglecting certain critical activities that should be leveraged from the top or even imposing constraints on businesses through unnecessary corporate involvement. Therefore, it becomes critical that the executive team make conscious decisions regarding how best to govern the enterprise—in colloquial terms, determining the appropriate balance between federal (corporate) and states' (individual business) rights.

As a starting point, there are several domains—potential sources of value creation—for the executive team. The challenge is to determine the degree and nature of executive team oversight and involvement within each category. In our work with chief executive officers and their direct reports we have used the list shown in Exhibit 5.1 to prompt their thinking and discussion regarding these challenges.

Exhibit 5.1, while not complete for any given company in its generic form, represents the majority of activities that must be managed in a complex company with multiple lines of business. The value in the list lies not in its completeness but in the dialogue

**Exhibit 5.1. Potential Sources of
Executive Team Value Creation.**

Strategy

Establish and manage portfolios.

Establish successful alliances and joint ventures.

Make decisions on key strategic issues facing company (for example, market entry, acquisitions).

Periodically review business strategies to ensure organization anticipates and responds to changing business conditions.

Set strategic marketing direction.

Define and protect brand integrity.

Communicate and build commitment to corporate strategic direction among internal and external constituents.

Set tone and direction for relations with key external constituents (clients, shareholders, analysts, and so on).

Organization

Establish organizational structure.

Define desired corporate philosophy, values, and operating environment.

Define core business processes.

Policy

Translate corporate vision and strategy into organizational policies, directives, and procedures.

Communicate and build commitment to organizational policies, directives, and procedures among key internal and external constituents.

Ensure effective implementation of policies, directives, and procedures.

Performance Management

Translate and deploy corporate vision, strategy, and performance targets into business unit plans and financial performance targets.

Review and approve business unit strategies.

Review business unit process performance against world-class criteria (such as the Baldrige Award standards).

Exhibit 5.1. Potential Sources of
Executive Team Value Creation, Cont'd.

Performance Management, Cont'd.

Manage infrastructure required to support operating units.

Manage IT activities and resources.

Manage procurement activities and resources.

Process Management

Ensure that core business processes are in place and working effectively.

Ensure effective management processes (such as decision making and conflict resolution) are in place at all levels.

Ensure quality tools and methods are used in managing the business.

People Management

Ensure the right leadership is in place (through recruiting, selection, and succession planning).

Develop top leadership through education, training, coaching, and reinforcement.

Ensure appropriate recognition and rewards for performance.

Innovation

Establish priorities and resource allocation for R&D.

Review and monitor innovation pipeline.

Special Initiatives

Diversity.

Six Sigma.

Other special ad hoc initiatives that address issues requiring attention in a company.

it stimulates in an executive team and the choices it forces the team to make with regard to how these activities will be handled. For teams that are engaged in implementing fundamental changes to their company (which arguably describes most teams today), being clear about the management of these activities is critical. Talking through this list tends to elicit very different individual assumptions about how the enterprise should be managed from the top. And even when the vision for the company's direction and change is clear to all, translating the vision into day-to-day activity is much less certain and requires thorough discussion.

In the Strategic Enterprise, it is not immediately evident where the team can best add value from the top. Indeed, many executive teams can get bogged down in lack of agreement on where to spend their time, which often contributes to their collective dissatisfaction with executive team meetings as these forums do not satisfy anyone. The truth is that there is no right answer, or right model, that fits each business. However, the model that is driven by decisions regarding architecture (where to link the businesses and where to focus them) is the one most likely to be effective. The process that is used to arrive at the most appropriate model is equally as important as the final determination of how activities will be handled. The team that decides, together, how to run the enterprise will be more committed to the final model and its implementation.

To be clear, it is often quite difficult to engage senior executives in these conversations. The truth is that ambiguity around these matters allows strong-willed individuals to act as they'd like. Lack of clarity regarding who owns which decisions works for those who prefer to behave independently and take action on their own, without having to first test those actions against an agreed-upon model for running the enterprise. And, unfortunately, this model also works for the chief executive officer who does not want to put potentially contentious issues on the table for discussion with his team—particularly when those discussions may elicit differences of opinion that cannot be resolved through a consensus-based model. More than one chief executive officer we have worked with resisted dealing with this issue of decision rights openly with his team, adopting a stance of "we'll figure it out as we go along" only to run into very difficult situations later on.

When working through the list in Exhibit 5.1 and making choices about how the enterprise will be governed, we find it useful to think about four potential choices for each activity. Essentially, these activities can be done in four ways:

- *Centrally:* Managed by corporate and conducted the same way in each business or function.
- *In Common:* Managed by each business or function, but done the same way throughout the company.
- *Differentially:* Managed by each business or function, and done however the leaders choose. (That is, participation is required, but symmetry is not.)
- *Optionally:* Participation is not required by any unit.

It is possible to illustrate examples of each of these approaches. In certain companies where projected growth of the enterprise is driven largely by acquisition and alliances, activities relating to the selection of potential strategic partners are managed centrally. This is done to take advantage of expertise in deal making, and to ensure that the executive team has instant access to ever-changing information that will affect the company's growth rate. In other companies with portfolios of vastly different business models, where growth may be the goal but the means to that end varies by business, acquisition and alliance activities may be highly decentralized and managed differentially. A third example involves companies in which certain standard processes or common procedures may be required of each business, while corporate plays a very minimal role, from a distance.

It is important to note here that there are numerous models and examples illustrating how companies can handle these activities. In the Strategic Enterprise, it is critical that the executive team give careful thought to how each activity should be managed, and where the executive team (and corporate) can best add value in the context of the company's vision and requisite balance of focus and leverage among the businesses. Their goals—their value-added work as they define it—will provide the cohesive glue for the corporation and will tangibly determine the value of common ownership of the assets that exist within the enterprise.

Roles: Expectations of Individuals

The fundamental issue to be addressed here has to do with individual team members' roles on the team—what is required of them, and how they are expected to contribute to enterprise governance. In many ways defining appropriate roles on the executive team is no different today than at any other time. There are still questions concerning who has the real power or the most voting rights, what latitude each member has in questioning or challenging others' areas of responsibility or expertise, how specialized roles (for example, the chief executive officer's) will be defined, and so on. Role clarity will always be essential to a high-performing executive team. Yet there are some unique challenges presented to role definition on the executive team within the Strategic Enterprise.

The most important of these has to do with the inherent lack of equality that, by definition, exists among the businesses—and therefore among the business leaders. While it is true that there have always been power differentials at the table (line executives tend to be more powerful than staff executives, for example), in the Strategic Enterprise traditional notions of symmetry, consistency, and uniform treatment no longer apply. The goal is not to achieve balance and harmony but enterprise coherence, and this does not automatically translate into a team of equals at the table. The value proposition of why different businesses should exist under a single corporate umbrella without consistent or symmetrical structures and processes requires a new definition of fairness, as it relates to both businesses and individuals. One size no longer fits all for several important reasons:

- Performance metrics will vary from business to business, and from team member to team member.
- Some executives will have almost complete latitude to run their businesses, others will be under constant scrutiny.
- Even among line peers running businesses of equal size, some will be required to continually answer to Wall Street while others play a quieter behind-the-scenes role.
- Compensation and benefits may vary among executives, as some have responsibility for launching new (often digital) ven-

tures while others manage the company's traditional and perhaps more mature businesses.

All these variations, and more, are essential if the executive team is to manage a broad range of business models effectively at the enterprise level. Clearly, this marks a radical departure from traditional management practices and will challenge corporate and even personal values. What will be required to make such asymmetry work at the senior-most level in the company is strong chief executive officer leadership and open, candid dialogue within the team regarding roles and related expectations of individuals.

One of our chief executive officer clients, in charge of a Strategic Enterprise, took this responsibility very seriously as he took over the reins of the company. Prior to the announcement of his appointment, he invested a great deal of time thinking through the individual strengths, development challenges, and expectations he held of each member of his team. He wrote his perspectives on each in personal memos, then delivered these in one-on-one conversations with each direct report. Given the mixed-model nature of his company (and also the very diverse talent on his team), he wanted to ensure that each key player understood how he saw the executive's performance, and what he expected of each executive going forward. While the team still faces many of the challenges inherent in leadership of a Strategic Enterprise, the members are starting their tenure as an executive team with absolute clarity regarding their roles and the chief executive officer's expectations.

Procedures: How the Team Will Carry Out Its Work

Once decisions have been made regarding the value-added work to be done by the executive team and the roles of individual players, attention must be turned to establishing the appropriate operating practices—in essence, defining *how* the team will do its work together. Led by the chief executive officer, the team must consciously design the following mechanisms by which it will do its work:

- The structure of the meetings and work sessions (where, when, and why to meet)

- The management of team agendas (who will compile topics and run the meetings)
- The management of information flow to and from the team (for example, how will the team communicate and what will the norms be regarding distribution of pre- and post-meeting materials)
- The process the team will use to make decisions (for example, what will be brought to the team for decision, and how the team will decide—by consensus, majority rule, input to chief executive officer)
- The output of the team (how it will be captured and distributed, and to whom)

While these may sound like rather mundane and trivial logistical issues, they are often the details that prove to be roadblocks to executive team performance. Two forces exist in the Strategic Enterprise that serve to heighten the challenges in this aspect of team design: the need to operate with ever increasing rates of speed, and the disparate nature of the business models that exist under the corporate umbrella.

The need for increased strategic clock speed to deal with hypercompetition combined with abbreviated product life cycles and pressure to reshape portfolios faster through acquisitions, mergers, divestitures, and strategic alliances creates a volatile atmosphere for many executives. The pressure to deliver today's goods while simultaneously planning for tomorrow's challenges leaves no room for failure—and no time for frivolous meetings that are not directly related to business performance. The forces driving the pace of business and the rate of change cause a centrifugal force that pulls executive team members in separate directions and exacerbates the ever-present tension around how often to get together and how best to spend one's time. Add to this the different nature and requirements of the business models that exist within the enterprise, and you begin to build a very compelling argument for designing procedures that minimize the time the team should spend together.

A recent quick poll of six of our current client organizations revealed that, on average, the executive team spent between 15 percent and 30 percent of its time engaged in corporate-related or corporate-driven activities:

- Executive team meetings including chief executive officer offsites
- Senior management meetings engaging the top 200–300 leaders
- Board and analyst meetings and the requisite preparation time
- Strategy and business reviews

With more attention to important mechanics and better management of these processes, an executive team could reduce the amount of time it spends on these activities—but it is not realistic, or even desirable, to eliminate or reduce them beyond a certain point.

The activities that usually draw the most criticism from executive team members are the team meetings and offsites. This is usually due, in part, to the natural tension felt by team members as they consider other ways they could be spending their precious time. The difficulty inherent in running an enterprise with an executive team is that the intangibles of building team ownership and commitment, while not always as *evident,* are just as important as sales meetings with customers, earnings presentations to analysts, and technology reviews with key R&D talent. Our experience with more than 100 executive teams, over 20 years, supports this assertion: true executive teams—what Warren Bennis calls "great groups"—who are collectively committed to providing leadership for the entire enterprise provide a true competitive advantage. But these teams are difficult to lead and take *time* to create.

In the Strategic Enterprise, it is critical that the executive team members devote time together to build a shared approach to running the enterprise, develop in-depth understanding of one another (thereby fostering trust), and create greater collective comfort with operating more quickly, utilizing less data, and making fewer consensus-based decisions. In her insightful article *Strategy as Strategic Decision Making* (1999), Kathleen Eisenhardt terms this process "building collective intuition" and cites it as one of the most important hallmarks of effective strategic decision makers. "Must attend" meetings and the sharing of real-time information foster intense interaction, which helps to promote "familiarity and friendship [which] make frank conversation easier because people are less constrained by politeness and more willing to express diverse views." Building collective intuition allows executives to "move quickly and accurately as opportunities arise. Most important, when intense interaction focuses on the operating metrics of today's businesses, a deep intuition, or 'gut feeling,' is created, giving managers a superior grasp of changing competitive dynamics. . . . This intuition gives managers a head start in recognizing and understanding strategic issues." Building collective intuition may be one of the most important things an executive team does to lead a Strategic Enterprise.

There is one more vital reason to develop this way of operating together: When the inevitable crisis hits (and in today's environment, it is wise to depend on this happening at least once in the life span of the team), the ability to act quickly, decisively, and with one voice will be invaluable.

One new executive team we are working with, which is comprised of senior executives from three different companies (coming together through a series of mergers and acquisitions), spends a great deal of time together focusing on immediate merger-related challenges while simultaneously developing greater understanding of one another. Their biweekly in-person meetings last at least four to six hours and cover a range of topics, many relating to performance of the very different businesses represented at the table. One could argue that their time could be better spent out in their respective businesses, since there is relatively little leverage to be gained from tight integration and management. Indeed, over time, it is likely that the team will need less time together as the members become clearer on where they can collectively add value to the institution, but this initial stage in their development is proving invaluable as they develop their collective intuition and focus on defining the best governance model possible for the newly combined entity that they lead.

Interactions: Required Behaviors and Team Norms

The fourth core element to consider in defining how the executive team will function concerns the team's interactions: The members' pattern of behavior with one another, in and outside of team meetings, as well as norms regarding how they will interact with others in the organization in carrying out their work. Defining this aspect of executive teams typically involves working with them to develop a set of "rules of the road" that the team can use as guidelines for their actions. These rules are often posted during meetings or periodically reviewed at the close of sessions as ways to be able to legitimately call each other on behavior that is out of line.

Defining desired behaviors and embedding them in the appropriate performance management processes is not something new to executive team management and, indeed, some desired operating principles endure for executive teams even in the face of a new organization architecture. Here are some examples:

- Implementing timely decisions with one voice
- Communicating openly and directly, avoiding grandstanding, speech-making, or politically correct statements
- Operating with an enterprise perspective in mind, avoiding parochial viewpoints

But the Strategic Enterprise poses some *new* challenges as well—challenges that point to the need for discussion among team members of how they can best deal with these issues.

First, as stated earlier, both the need to operate with speed and the complexity of having multiple business models under one corporate roof affect executive team interactions within the Strategic Enterprise. Both contribute to an environment that can be characterized by high degrees of ambiguity and uncertainty—working as an executive team under these types of circumstances calls for behavior that supports exceptionally open, direct communication, as well as behavior that "assumes beneficial intent" on the part of others. During tense and ambiguous times, it is important that executive team members avoid misattribution. It is all too easy for extremely busy executives charged with leading very different businesses or functions to leap to conclusions when they do not fully understand one another's actions, attributing motives based on mistaken assumptions, incomplete information, or erroneous hypotheses. To counteract this phenomenon, executive team members need to ensure that they take the time to have candid discussions that balance advocacy and inquiry, with each person expressing a point of view while simultaneously exploring others' perspectives and the reasoning behind them. While each team needs to develop its own set of norms and behaviors in this regard, what is important is that the members explicitly discuss how they will deal with the inevitable event where misattributions are made and tensions escalate—before the event occurs.

Second, the Strategic Enterprise will, by definition, foster conflict and internal competition. That is the nature of asymmetry, and the unfortunate truth is that few organizations are equipped to deal with the magnitude of conflict that can come from managing disparate business models. The new demands of the Strategic Enterprise often clash with well-established social systems that were designed to create harmony, symmetry, and balance, forcing leaders to question their own notions of what constitutes good management. For example, the widely embraced concept of synergy—the idea that all components of a business should unite and progress together—is at best questionable in an era when success may well depend on cannibalization of existing channels or even whole businesses. The Strategic Enterprise represents the diametric opposite of synergy—internal competition is essential, even if businesses end up duplicating efforts or resenting each other. The result at the executive team level can be hostile, destructive, and even manipulative behavior, if team members are not able to channel their competitive feelings in healthy ways, either toward outside competition or by fighting fair with one another. Again, it is important for the team to develop norms and ways of interacting that support team members' ability to put contentious issues on the table and discuss them directly and effectively—and to discuss these norms in advance of conflicts that will inevitably arise.

Finally, the Strategic Enterprise is, by definition, global in nature and this will affect the executive team's interactions. More often than not these days members of executive teams are spending a great deal of their time traveling around the world and on any given day there may be tens of thousands of miles between them. The days of walking down the hall to bump into your executive team counterpart are nearing their end, even while the majority of executive teams are still "co-located" in one building complex. This means that the team will need to develop operating norms that take into account multiple time zones, long-distance travel, and the use of advanced technology to stay connected between meetings. Videoconferences, voice mail, and e-mail traffic tend to be the glue for between-meeting interactions, and establishing explicit, common norms regarding use of these technologies can greatly facilitate team members' sharing of information and staying connected.

Team Quality Assurance

The last element of the team-building framework involves developing a feedback loop that enables the team to be self-corrective, preventing errors and promoting continuous improvement. There are several ways to consider building such a process into the work of the team:

- Investing initial time at the launch of the team to focus on each element of the model
- Having the team review each meeting agenda and discuss, briefly, how the work will be done
- Having the team debrief each meeting, touching on what worked and what didn't, in an effort to develop its own capacity to learn and to improve its work process
- Building in periodic formal reviews of how the team is working together

For the executive team in the Strategic Enterprise, any or all of these are options—what is *not* an option is to opt out of this part of the process under the guise of needing to move quickly, or not being able to take the time for such process luxuries. In an era driven by the pressing imperative of web speed, one thing that is still more essential than doing things quickly is doing them right—even if that takes a bit of time. Often, what looks like a time-saving device (for example, removing or bypassing a process) actually ends up *costing* time—and effectiveness—down the road. Eliminating the quality assurance step is one guaranteed way to ensure that you will need to revisit the team's performance before long.

Executive Teams in the Strategic Enterprise: Implications for the HR Leader

Many of the opportunities and challenges discussed thus far speak directly to the role of the HR leader. This role is critical to the overall success of the Strategic Enterprise, and our work with chief executive officers and their teams tells us there is a strong and growing recognition of the strategic nature of HR. Many of the Strategic Enterprises we currently work with have highly talented and personally strong HR leaders sitting at the executive team table as full and equal players. Working closely with these individuals, we have identified four aspects of the role they play:

- Coach to the chief executive officer
- Facilitator of change
- Supporter of change
- Administrator

We'll discuss each of those here in the context of things they do that enable leadership effectiveness—their own, as well as that of the chief executive officer and other members of the executive team. Each aspect of their role is uniquely critical but all are necessary for success.

Coach to the Chief Executive Officer

As in any organization, be it a mono-line company or a Strategic Enterprise, the HR leader's connection to the chief executive officer can be an invaluable source of leverage in the leadership equation. As a sounding board, a confidant, and an informed and objective source of input, the HR leader can play a role no other executive team member can play. In the Strategic Enterprise, where conflict, ambiguity, and ever-escalating performance pressures are simply part of everyday life, a relationship with HR founded on trust and respect can help alleviate stress, keep the chief executive officer from becoming disconnected, and facilitate problem solving. Indeed, in this type of environment, open channels of dialogue become even more important—the HR executive who provides the chief executive officer with feedback no one else will (or can) is critically important to the organization.

Facilitator of Change

As a full team player, with no agenda aligned with any one business in the enterprise, the HR leader is uniquely positioned to act as a catalyst in putting cross-business imperatives on the table for discussion. As champion of the "people agenda," the HR leader can objectively jump-start discussions that raise issues needing to be resolved, without being seen as biased toward one business or another. This is of vital importance in a mixed-model enterprise where people issues relating to reallocation of resources can be contentious, as businesses may be in competition with one another.

Supporter of Change

Also as champion of the people agenda the HR leader can exert great influence in the areas of culture and leadership development. Leaders of most Strategic Enterprises will find it difficult to grapple with these topics, as they search for the dynamic balance between what is defined "the same way for everyone" and what is defined at a business (or even functional) level. HR leaders can both facilitate this dialogue with the team and also develop processes to implement the final decisions made. In their neutral position, they wield tremendous potential power in being able to create the environment and develop the leadership skills necessary for the future success of the business.

Administrator

Finally, the most transactional element of the HR leader's role is also critical in the context of the Strategic Enterprise. Acting as the corporate conscience and enforcing compliance in certain arenas represents a challenge across multiple business models. The area in which this is most evident these days is in compensation; designing and implementing asymmetric compensation systems that reward performance equitably while remaining grounded in marketplace dynamics *and* still facilitating movement of resources across businesses is a very big challenge.

Playing this role well brings its own set of unique challenges. Perhaps the most difficult one is walking the tightrope with executive team peers—winning their acceptance and support even while playing a major role as catalyst for change. This involves building relationships with peers in ways that allow you to exert your own voice while also preserving and strengthening your relationship to the chief executive officer. Here are five pieces of advice we give to HR leaders in Strategic Enterprises:

- Demonstrate that the right issues are being addressed, and that tangible progress is being made, by grounding all that you do in data—act as the bridge between the employees (and the organization) and the executive team on people issues
- Push back when appropriate, both in team meetings and individually, to demonstrate your own independence
- Provide candid, confidential advice to members of the team and be available to them
- Remember that you work for the chief executive officer, not the team. In that context, however, resist the urge to play to the chief executive officer, invoke the chief executive officer's name as a reason why people should talk or deal with you, or be a message carrier—any of this will undermine your credibility
- Never do anything that could be construed as undermining the chief executive officer's position—and always be conscious of the power of your role, with the advantages and the responsibility that brings

Executive Teams in the Strategic Enterprise: What's *Not* New

As stated several times in this chapter, there are certain challenges to running a Strategic Enterprise as an executive team. Having said that, it is important to note that the essence of the business organization has not changed. It's still all about "people coming together to get work done." At the heart of business success is the ability to understand and predict patterns of organizational behavior and performance—at the executive team level and throughout the organization.

Designing an effective executive team by attending to its charter, goals, roles, procedures, interactions, and quality assurance is a complex process that is actually much more than the sum of each individual step that must be taken. By going through this process in a fast-paced, complicated Strategic Enterprise, a chief executive officer reinforces the following:

- The need to engage the team in collectively building its own work process, thereby engendering commitment to what is created

- The importance of being thorough, thoughtful, and explicit in establishing norms and ways of operating, working to build an intuitive, shared understanding of how to run the enterprise that will save time and increase effectiveness down the road
- The need for open communication, and full sharing of perspectives, even on contentious issues, or on topics not directly related to the immediate running of the business
- The importance of collective and individual accountability for making difficult, enterprise-wide decisions, being committed and following through
- The need to ensure process discipline, and to stop the clock on important things even while recognizing the need for urgency and speed
- The importance of running the enterprise with a team of individuals who collectively contribute more than they do individually

Summary

The evolution of information technologies and the Internet will continue to drive change of immense magnitude, making it impossible for businesses to hold onto the architecture of the past. The Strategic Enterprise offers a way for leaders to reconfigure their organizations to meet both the threats and the opportunities presented by this new digital environment. At the same time, however, the Strategic Enterprise poses a new set of challenges for the chief executive officer and the executive team. The complex balancing act implicit in leading the Strategic Enterprise is, frankly, too much for any one individual, no matter how gifted, to coordinate. Accordingly, the development of a strong executive team and organizational governance models become a paramount concern. As we have shown through our team-building framework, a key to business success is consciously designing an executive team—clearly defining what the team does, how it does it, the role of the leader, and how to ensure quality in the team's functioning. With the help of this "great group," the chief executive officer will be equipped to rise to the unprecedented demands of leading an organization capable of harnessing conflict and competition within itself as a potent competitive advantage. Organizations that fail to develop this leadership resource will most likely fall prey to the relentless demands of speed, complexity, and conflict that are the inescapable hallmarks of the digital age.

References

Eisenhardt, K. (1999, Spring). "Strategy as strategic decision making." *Sloan Management Review, 40*(3), 65–73.

Nadler, D. A., & Spencer, J. L. *Executive teams.* (1998). San Francisco: Jossey-Bass.

"Teamwork at the top: Designing and leading executive teams." (1998). New York: Mercer Delta Consulting, LLC.

"The Strategic Enterprise: Organization architecture in the digital age." (2000). New York: Mercer Delta Consulting, LLC.

CHAPTER 6

Coaching Executives
Individual Leader Development
George P. Hollenbeck

Executive coaching has become the leadership development method of choice in many organizations. "Get him (or her) a coach" has replaced "Get him some training" or "send him to Harvard" as an all-purpose solution for enhancing executive performance. Although executive coaching itself has a long history, in recent years the coaching phenomenon has blossomed to the point of meriting articles in most of the business press and newspapers, a steady stream of books about coaching, and a circuit of workshops and programs by consultants displaying their wares and their experiences. A recent article describes the state of the art: "Coaches are everywhere these days"; "Coaching really is the Wild West of HR" (Morris, 2000, pp. 145, 152).

With the widespread use of coaches, with coaching everywhere in a free- (or not so free-) for-all market, with every consultant a coach, it seems useful to identify and discuss the issues and trends in executive coaching. But how do companies use executive coaching? Where did executive coaching come from and why is it so popular? What makes it so attractive as a general-purpose leader development tool? What do executive coaches do? How does *executive*

Note: The discussion of the selection of executive coaches and their matching with individual executives has been informed by conversations with Raymond Flautt at Chase Manhattan Bank, Steve Hrop and Cynthia Lowden at The Prudential Insurance Company, and Doug McKenna at Microsoft Corporation.

coaching differ from lifestyle coaching, personal coaching, and psychotherapy? Does executive coaching work? What are the dangers and downsides? What steps can organizations and executives take to make the best use of coaches and coaching? What is the future of executive coaching?

This is more a chapter about coaching executives than about *how to* coach them. It is designed for human resources executives with responsibility for coaching, as well as for executives interested in learning more about coaching as a leadership development tool.

How Do Organizations Use Executive Coaches?

Organizations use executive coaches for a wide range of leadership development activities, to address both individual issues and organization-wide ones. One of the early uses was fix-it—bringing in an executive coach to work with a problem executive who was in danger of derailing. Today, using coaches goes well beyond the fix-its to *upside coaching*—working to enhance already good performance, or to help develop executive skills that are needed in a new job. Candidates for chief executive officer may be offered a coach to help groom them in specific areas that will be required in their new roles. High-potentials may be assigned a coach to accelerate their development, with the related benefit of making them feel important and well taken care of.

With 360-degree feedback so prevalent, coaches are frequently employed to help executives understand the (sometimes complicated) feedback and to help them craft individual development plans. In HR- or corporate-driven programs, executives may be offered a coach to assist with putting the development plan into action. Most leadership development programs today provide 360-degree feedback as a part of the program, with coaches to help the executives make meaning of the data.

New companies (for example, Dell Computer) without a long history of leadership development may use executive coaching as their primary executive development strategy to help technically oriented executives learn the leadership lessons required to grow. Older companies (for example, Abbott Laboratories) seeking to change their leadership model from the old command-and-control style to manager-as-coach may use executive coaches with all their executives to help make that transition. Leadership development may be seen as an important lever for organization change, and the organization's leader-of-the-future competencies may be communicated via some assessment against those competencies, with a coach to help leaders develop the new competencies. When organizations change through merger, coaches may be used to help executives lead the change and adapt to the new organization with its new players and new working style.

Coaching has burst upon the scene so quickly and has grown so rapidly that we sometimes forget that executive coaching has a long history.

Executive Coaching in Context

What are the roots of executive coaching? "Consultant to the King" no doubt has as long a history as organizations themselves. Whether Joseph interpreting dreams for Pharaoh or Circe advising Odysseus, throughout human history executives who were trying to make sense of a changing world have called upon sages and gurus with specialized knowledge to help them (Groder's 1991 [1982] classic describes the Grand Vizier role).

After World War II, a small group from the emerging profession of psychology began advising business executives about the perplexing problems of managing and working with the executives in their companies. Primarily clinical and counseling psychologists, these early coaches found that their understanding of the psychological dynamics of behavior provided a useful base for advising. Derisively called "hand holders" by their more scientific colleagues, by the 1960s and 1970s they were joined by a growing number of colleagues from industrial/organizational psychology who found that their skills and understanding of organizations were also applicable in the executive suite, and that the rewards—both psychological (described by Thompson in 1991 as "absolutely exhilarating") and financial—were often greater working with executives than in more traditional activities such as developing selection procedures, training employees to do performance appraisals, and conducting attitude surveys. They were being asked to fix executives who needed help, and by the 1980s the growing industrial psychology consulting firms were offering executive coaching, usually by names like "individual executive development."

During the same period, consultants from the growing field of organization development, coming primarily from corporate training functions, found that succeeding in their consulting depended as often on helping *executives* develop as it did on helping *organizations;* they, too, began coaching. Also at this time, schools of social work and education began turning out increasing numbers of graduates, not specifically trained as coaches but with a helping orientation, and the increasing numbers of MBA graduates included many who were more interested in people than in business careers per se. All these provided a ready supply of consultants who were trained in behavior in organizations or were crossover professionals from other fields; many of these were eager to work in companies. The base was in place for the new profession of coaching.

The rise of coaching was not primarily supply driven, however, no matter how many potential coaches might have been waiting in the wings. Without the dramatic changes in society and the world of business in the 1960s, 70s, 80s, and 90s, that small cadre of psychologists who coached executives might have remained a small and little-known group. Instead, a new workforce with new wants and desires, operating within new social and economic arrangements in a world characterized by technological change and increasing globalization, required that business and people be managed differently. *Leadership*, in addition to management, was needed, John Kotter (1990) convincingly argued, in order to make our way in the face of change. The manager's job changed from managing processes to leading people; managers with a new workforce were called upon to provide coaching rather than continue their old command-and-control style (Peters & Austin, 1985).

New organization forms, downsizing, and the new career contract—with companies no longer promising lifetime employment and employees no longer promising loyalty and obedience—were the order of the day in the 1980s and 1990s. The attendant restructuring required workforce reductions, giving impetus and legitimacy to outplacement; outplacement counselors, a previously little-known occupation, were in great demand.

With globalization and IT moving from a foothold to a stranglehold in the 1990s, and a changing workforce and Internet speed, organization leaders at the turn of the 21st century would almost universally endorse "all the help I can get, from wherever I can get it." Managers were often changing jobs more frequently than in the past, giving them little opportunity to develop leadership skills. An economic expansion of historic proportions created great wealth and prosperity so that by the year 2000, issues of work and family, diversity, and quality of life had become important issues. "Get a life" replaced "get a job" as a central theme for large portions of the workforce. (See Biederman, 2000, for a recent *LA Times* article on getting a coach to deal with life dissatisfaction.)

Coaching offers to provide that help. In a recent *Fortune* article (Morris, 2000), John Kotter of the Harvard Business School comments on the changes behind the growth of coaching: "As we move from 30 miles an hour to 70 to 120 to 180 . . . as we go from driving straight down the road to making right turns and left turns, to abandoning cars and getting on motorcycles . . . the whole game changes, and a lot of people are trying to keep up, learn how, not fall off" (p. 146). Given the demand (and the supply) it may be small wonder that the coaching game has grown so fast. Small wonder that the International Coaching Federation has 2,000+ members, but estimates that there are more than 10,000 coaches in the business (p. 146).

Executive coaching is a small subset of this more general coaching phenomenon. It draws heavily on well-established principles of consulting, psychology, and organization and individual change. It focuses specifically on executives and their performance in organizations. It is attractive as a leadership development tool because it offers both the executive and the organization a convenient, flexible way to help cope with new demands. It can be targeted where the need is, rather than the one-size-fits-all programs of lectures and cases applied to a group of executives, whether they need it or not. Unlike action learning models, which are criticized for the great amounts of time they require, coaching can be applied in small or large doses and adapted to the schedule of the busier executive. With the demise of lifetime careers and mentors along with the stable, hierarchical organizations of which they were a part, executive coaching can fill the need for someone to turn to when the executive faces a new situation, is attempting to recover from failure, or simply wants to grow new skills.

This brief historical review of its growth illustrates that coaching has indeed come a long way from the 1500s—when the word *coach* was first used to mean a conveyance for a valued person from where he is to where he *wants to be* (Evered & Selman, 1989).

What Is Executive Coaching?

Despite the widespread interest in and use of coaching as a process, defining executive coaching eludes most of those who discuss it. Books about executive coaching (for example, see Dottlich & Cairo, 1999, for a systematic approach) may not define it at all, and books about coaching in general (for example, Flaherty, 1999) may define it but fail to differentiate how it applies to executives. Others (for example, Witherspoon & White, 1997) describe the role coaches play and what they try to do.

I have elsewhere attempted to define coaching: "Executive Coaching is a personal, one-on-one helping relationship between an executive and a coach with the purpose of enhancing the executive's performance and, in turn, organization performance. . . . It is an interaction of personal and business counseling that focuses on the executive's talents, abilities, and motivations as they apply to the business situations at hand" (Hollenbeck, 1996).

Similarly, "Coaching is meant to be a practical, goal-focused form of personal, one-on-one learning for busy executives and may be used to improve performance or executive behavior, enhance a career or prevent derailment, and work through organizational issues or change initiatives" (Hall, Otazo, & Hollenbeck, 1999).

Both these definitions and the descriptions of roles of coaches have several common elements:

• *The executive:* Executive coaching involves an individual who is either in or aspiring to an executive job. Few organizations escape labeling the top positions as executive positions, often defining them as those including some level of responsibility (a major line of business or functional area) with the incumbents typically included in the organization's executive pay package. (See the Preface for a discussion of who is an executive.) Although the line may be fuzzy, it is possible to differentiate executives from other employees.

• *The executive coach:* The executive coach is the individual consultant who is working with the executive; the executive coach has credibility (more on credibility later) in working with the executive, and is able to engage the executive in a process of individual change.

- *Helping and consulting relationship:* The executive and the executive coach participate in a helping relationship; the coach is attempting through the coaching process to help the executive change. Both the executive and the coach must buy into this relationship, its goals, loyalties, and limits. The relationship is usually time-limited, often for six months or a year, but sometimes as short as a meeting or two. (One wag described very short-term coaching as "drive-by coaching.")

- *The organization or company:* There is a more-or-less silent third partner in the relationship, the organization, or company that employs the executive and, directly or indirectly, the coach. Given the performance focus assigned to executive coaching, the organization has an important role to play. Executive coaching can run aground if the relationships among the players are not clear.

- *The process:* The coaching process is the set of activities that the executive and the coach engage in with the aim of helping the executive to change. The process usually proceeds through several stages: contracting and problem definition, assessment, feedback, action planning, implementation, and follow-up; at any stage in the process, new data may result in a looping back to an earlier stage—for example, data gathered during the assessment stage may trigger a redefinition of the problem and a new agreement of what needs to be done. Executive coaches have a range of tools that they may employ in each stage, and different coaches may specialize in certain tools. In almost all executive coaching, however, feedback to the executive is a critical element that helps to define how the executive needs to change and to motivate the executive.

- *Performance focus:* The purpose of executive coaching is to enhance executive performance and, in turn, organization performance. Although the executive may well have personal as well as job-related goals, the focus is on the job. This focus is one of the key factors that distinguishes executive coaching from other forms of coaching and psychotherapy. I once talked with an executive after six months of coaching, who said, "I may be doing better at my job, but I am still not happy." I pointed out that *happiness* per se was not the goal of the coaching, but that I could help the executive find a psychotherapist who might more directly address the happiness issue if he so desired. He did, and I did, and six months later he was a happier as well as better-performing executive.

The Uniqueness of Executive Coaching

Definitions of executive coaching and a breakdown into elements inevitably lose the reality and excitement of what executive coaching is and what executive coaches do. What makes executive coaching unique? Primarily, the nature of executives and executive jobs. Every case is different; there is no one way to do an executive job. No matter how detailed an organization's competency model, the model cannot capture the entirety of being an executive—there is no one way to lead, no specific set of skills or competencies that will ensure success.

The excitement of executive jobs comes—at least in part—from the fact that success or failure depends on an individual applying her unique capabilities, developed and developing, in unique ways to the situation at hand; there is no formula. As a result, executives come in all shapes and sizes, with widely differing talents and interests. There are common denominators, however, of success in the executive ranks; such a list would include bright, fast learners, focused and intense, results-oriented, ambitious, very good at some things, self-confident and independent, able to use the talents of others, able to learn from experience.

Executive positions have disproportionate impact and rewards in the organization. These positions often make seemingly infinite demands on those who fill them. Results are usually slow in coming, impact is indirect and difficult to measure, and they are never completed—there is always more that could be done. These jobs usually encompass geographically widespread responsibilities, with the result that those doing them may be difficult to access and meet with. These jobs and the executives who hold them are highly visible in political organizations where neither the incumbent nor the organization may be eager to admit weakness or need for improvement. With bosses, if any, who are as busy as they are, the jobs offer the executive little feedback and little support for anything but getting results.

Given the ambiguity of executive job requirements and the demands on the people who fill them, it is no surprise that executive coaching reflects those demands. The coaching process is subject to the same demands as the executive job and is unlikely to follow a well-ordered plan; no one model of executive coaching will fit all cases and all situations—cookie-cutter approaches won't work. There is a premium on value added and savvy tips that can be immediately applied on the job. The best executive coaches, like any top-quality professionals, must adapt to the executive and be flexible in adapting their methods, and must have a wide repertoire yet be sensitive to the limits of their expertise.

What Do Executive Coaches Do?

Although an agreed-upon definition of executive coaching may be elusive, most coaches would agree on the stages of the coaching process, a process that follows quite closely the more general stages of a consulting agreement. Block (1999) provides a description of general consulting; Witherspoon and White (1997) describe executive coaching, and Flaherty (1999) focuses on the more general interpersonal coaching. Drawing from all of these, I describe a six-step executive coaching process:

1. *Contracting and purpose.* At this initial stage the terms of the engagement are spelled out, exactly who is the client is clarified, and at least the broad purpose and goals of the coaching are spelled out. This step also includes the development of rapport between the executive and coach—chemistry is important, as executive coaching is more personal than most types of consulting. In many ways this step is the most critical part of the process—Block (1999) relates that when consultants talk about their disasters, they usually conclude that the fault began at this stage. Coaching fits that model, also.
2. *Data gathering.* The executive, the coach, and the organization decide (and go about collecting) the data needed to examine where the executive *is now* and where he or she *needs to go.* For leadership performance coaching, that data includes several perspectives on the executive's leadership, usually including the executive's boss, peers, and direct reports.
3. *Feedback.* This step, a critical one in the coaching process, provides the feedback data to the executive, usually in an anonymous

form. The feedback process—sometimes emotional, always sensitive—provides the directions for needed change and often the motivation for change, also. Nothing is so motivational to competitive executives as feedback indicating that they lag behind their peers in leadership skills.

4. *Action planning.* Development planning, based on the issues identified in feedback, may be more or less formal, but it provides the detailed outline for the road ahead—the specific goals of coaching, how they will be met, who will do what and how—and it sets milestones for progress.

5. *Implementation.* If success in Step 1 avoids disaster, then success in Step 5 is the essence of executive change. Failure at this stage usually comes not with a bang but a whimper—one more well-intentioned development plan that never gets implemented. Particularly at this stage, the expertise of the coach is critical in helping the executive learn new ways that pay off in performance.

6. *Follow-up and maintenance.* All three partners, the executive, the coach, and the organization, have a stake in evaluating the effectiveness of the process; for the executive, few real changes take place without booster shots—thoughtful reviews of what's happening—to maintain the changes.

Within this six-step framework, executive coaching may proceed on several tracks, depending on the needs of the organization and the executive. One track involves a number of coaches in a large-scale executive or organization development effort. For example, the organization pursuing a new set of competencies may ask coaches to assist with 360-degree feedback and development plans for all its executives. Executives in these programs may participate in extended coaching (often lasting six months) after the feedback process. Another track is more individual, with coaching designed to help executives develop new skills in a new level of position, to help high-potentials develop executive-level skills, or to help executives remedy weaknesses and deal with blind spots.

Witherspoon and White (1997) organize executive coaching into four roles or functions to describe different types of coaching that may take place:

- *Coaching for skills,* where the learning is sharply focused on a person's current tasks
- *Coaching for performance,* where the learning is focused more broadly on an executive's present job
- *Coaching for development,* where the focus is primarily on a future job
- *Coaching for the executive's agenda,* where the learning is focused in a broad sense on helping the executive lead a business or major function

With different aims, each of these types of coaching involves different time frames, techniques, resources, and results. These differences emphasize the importance of a clear understanding on the part of the executive, the coach, and the organization about what the coaching will be.

Whatever the coaching that takes place, providing feedback (Step 3 in the process)—often brutally honest, sometimes for the first time—is a major function of the coach. A follow-up study of executives who had been coached found that a primary factor in good coaching was "honest reliable feedback" (Hall, Otazo, & Hollenbeck, 1999). In whatever way the feedback data is gathered (Step 2), whether via a survey instrument, interviews, or the coach's observations, a key skill of the coach is presenting the feedback in a way that will motivate the executive and provide guidelines for change.

What feedback is gathered depends on the purpose of the coaching. The typical 360-degree feedback instrument may easily support coaching for the task at hand or the current job, but 360-degree data is not likely to be sufficient for agenda coaching. Executive coaching aimed at changing the fundamental character of the person requires a great deal of very personal feedback. Kaplan (1998) describes a coaching process designed to achieve such major change in an executive, with feedback that may include interviews with 30 or more individuals who know the executive and several days of feedback of verbatim comments delivered by two psychologists.

Whether or not coaching works depends on effective action planning and implementation. Action planning is a process of analyzing gaps between where the executive is and where he wants to be (see Peterson & Hicks, 1996) and developing specific steps for closing the gaps. What do coaches do? The coach guides the gap analysis process and serves as a resource for action planning. Effective executive coaching requires expertise in interpersonal change. The ability to offer good action ideas or pointers was one of the primary factors listed by executives as contributing to good coaching (Hall, Otazo, & Hollenbeck, 1999).

Implementation is where executive change typically derails— change inevitably requires giving up the old and bringing in the new, is usually uncomfortable, and is too easily put aside in a busy workday; corporate HR files are filled with executive development plans that were never acted upon! An executive coach specializes in making sure that development plans do get acted upon. The coach serves as a motivator, a monitor, an enforcer to keep the executive on track. The coach may provide detailed exercises (Flaherty, 1999), such as regular reflection on lessons learned, consciously withholding judgment, or practice in listening, that help the executive develop new perspectives, skills, and approaches.

Executive coaches may be viewed as learning managers and consultants in a very specific area—executive performance. They may play a number of roles and use a number of tools; like master teachers, they may be truth tellers, nudges, cops, motivators, resource providers, even gofers. Sometimes this will be very hands-on, as with role-playing specific situations; sometimes it will be indirect, perhaps finding a time management specialist, a presentation specialist, an executive shopper, a physical fitness trainer. As learning managers, coaches may need to interface with other learning resources available inside and outside the organization.

How Does Executive Coaching Differ From Other Forms of Coaching and Psychotherapy?

One frequently expressed concern is the difference between executive coaching and psychotherapy. As Dottlich and Cairo (1999) point out, some people "view any type of coaching as psychotherapy, and they don't believe therapy has any place or purpose in business" (p. 136). I see executive coaching as distinct from psychotherapy as well as other types of coaching. The primary distinction is in terms of the overarching goal or outcome: the goal of executive coaching is better job performance for the executive and the organization. In contrast, the goal of psychotherapy is a more fully functioning person.

Executive coaching *may* make the person more self-aware, less anxious, happier, and better functioning, but these outcomes occur, if they occur at all, as *means* not *ends* of the coaching process. Even in the intensive coaching described by Kaplan (1998) that attempts to bring about fundamental changes in the character of the executive, the end sought is better performance. In describing their coaching model, Dottlich and Cairo (1999) emphasize that self-awareness leads to performance improvement and organizational transformation. They also point out that the coach needs "to allay these concerns [about therapy] by maintaining a focus on business results" (p. 2).

This outcome distinction is fundamental. Psychotherapy may make one a better executive, but that is not its goal. Golf coaching may enhance an executive's career, but the goal of the golf coach, and his expertise, is golf. Likewise, speech coaches show remarkable success at helping executives make better speeches, but speech making is only part of the executive's job. Lifestyle and personal coaching may succeed in their endeavors, but seldom is the purpose of the coaching or the expertise of the coaches in the area of executive performance.

As the golf coaching example indicates, the factors that contribute to and enhance executive performance may cover a broad range. Executives' personal lives and work lives overlap—many chief executive officers would say that there is no way to separate the two—despite our efforts to reduce performance to a finite set of competencies and piece parts. That overlap, in fact, may be even greater today than in the past as executives work longer hours and work-family-life balance seems more valued and more difficult to find. New-form, high-tech organizations are even designing the workplace as living rather than solely as working places, described in *Fortune's* "Best Companies to Work For" issue as "the new company town" (Useem, 2000, p. 62).

Because one's work is embedded in one's larger life, during the course of coaching the executive coach may be called upon to deal with concerns well beyond the executive's job and career. As the executive's learning consultant, the coach must be prepared to find appropriate resources. Executive coaches may be that resource themselves (conceivably even to helping with putting and driving!), but the coaches must not forget that their fundamental expertise is executive job performance. When *Fortune* describes coaching as the "Wild West of HR practice," it is referring to practices and purposes well outside what this chapter advocates. A glance at the web site of the International Coaching Federation will clarify that their 2,000 members may all call themselves *coaches,* offering expertise in an extraordinary range of topics, but few offer expertise in executive coaching or would call themselves *executive coaches.* They seem to be part of the larger self-help movement that has become a major industry, even including an entry from the Harvard Business School Press (Zander & Zander, 2000).

It is also useful to distinguish between executive coaches and coaching executives, or managers who coach their direct reports or associates. The manager-as-coach, as much a style of management as a method (Peters & Austin, 1985; Evered & Selman, 1989), differs from the executive coach in terms of power and influence. Executive coaches "have little or no direct influence—much less control—over the outcome. To have direct control is to manage, not to coach" (Witherspoon & White, 1997, p. 2).

Another distinction between executive coaches and coaching executives is who is involved in determining the specific coaching goals and how the coaching process is managed. In executive coaching, the executive and the coach set goals in conjunction with the organization (the boss, HR, and others); like it or not, unlike psychotherapy, the organization is a partner in the coaching. Although organizations admit and accept that personal as well as organization issues may arise, most want to ensure that the organization's focus—performance—is paramount.

One of the characteristics of coaches, whatever the specialty—executive or golf or voice—is that their goals include not just better performance during the coaching engagement, but also that the executives will leave coaching able to evaluate their own performance, to take corrective action on their own, and even to find new approaches on their own after leaving the coaching. "Well-coached clients can observe when they are performing well and when they are not and will make any necessary adjustments independently of the coach" and they know that performance can always improve "and will continually find ways on their own to do so" (Flaherty, 1999, p. 4).

To the chagrin of some, I distinguish between executive coaching and working with an executive team. Although team performance may be central to executive and organization performance, team building is different from executive coaching, it has a different set of clients, different loyalties, and different purposes than individual executive coaching does. Team builders may well coach individual team members on their teaming skills and deficits, but serving as the executive coach to different executives and their boss invites conflicts of interest for the coach, and it limits the coach's ability to work with undivided loyalty with the individual executives. Especially near the top of an organization, the power and political relationships among the executives and their peers and bosses can be central to the coaching agenda.

Does Executive Coaching Work?

Asking whether coaching works is a little like asking whether training works. When you view the executive coach as a learning consultant, the question becomes, Has the executive learned and are the results in place to prove it? Although the question can be convincingly answered for individual cases, general answers based on systematic research are very difficult to find. Executive coaching is so varied in terms of approach, process, goals, and outcomes that most evaluations resort to surveys and anecdotes and case studies. Based on the results to date, about the best anyone can say is that executive coaching *can* work, leaving it open to define the conditions under which it does. The answer becomes, "Yes, executive coaching does work if the right coach is used for the right executive in the right situation with the right goals."

Efforts at describing whether coaching works vary from anecdotes and market research to more serious efforts at systematic behavioral research. Anecdotes and promises typically accompany popular press articles—a recent article quoted one coach to the effect that 100 percent of his clients improved, another that only 2 of 50 who had been through the process had not changed. Despite the doubts that statements like this leave in the mind, the descriptions of changes, even in the popular press, leave little doubt that executives *believe* that their coaching has been worthwhile.

In addition to personal success stories, a number of follow-up studies have examined coaching effectiveness. In a study of executives from several companies who had participated in executive coaching, Hall, Otazo, and Hollenbeck (1999) report that executives typically rated the overall effectiveness of their experience 4 (very satisfactory) on a 5-point scale; the executives reported that the coaching process produced specific value added. Edelstein and Armstrong (1993) found that participants in a coaching-based executive development program rated the process very valuable (3.95 out of 5) and producing consistent changes (4.07 on a 5 point scale); 68 percent of their participants said they demonstrated at least occasional changes. These kinds of changes were reported:

- Improved interpersonal skills
- Became more team-oriented, cooperative
- Improved listening to others' ideas
- Became less defensive, more open to criticism
- Used more coaching and showed respect for subordinates
- Acted more assertively, was less intimidating
- Became more results oriented

Interestingly enough, Peterson (1993), in a follow-up study of targeted coaching, found similar results; when 370 participants rated how much they had changed due to their coaching they gave a rating of 3.8 on a 5-point scale. (For the serious evaluator, Peterson's paper also presents an excellent discussion of the difficulties and dilemmas in the methodology of systematically measuring behavior change.) Peterson was also kind enough to share the results from an unpublished follow-up study of executive coaching with one client company's high-potentials; 70 percent of the high-potentials demonstrated substantial to moderate development during the coaching, and participants gave a rating of 5 out of 7 to changes in the specific behaviors that had been targeted for coaching. In a quite different setting, McCauley and Hughes-James (1994) evaluated a program for school superintendents that included 360-degree feedback, development planning, and a year of support and follow-up. They report that 58 percent of participants showed behavior change following the development program.

The consistency of these results across studies (4 out of 5 rating, 60–70 percent had changed), whether consistent because of similar methodology or indeed actual changes, suggests at least a broad guideline for success in the coaching process.

McCauley and Hughes-James went one step further and asked which of their school superintendents changed and which did not. They found that the 29 percent who changed very little were quite experienced, were already doing well, and had stable back-home environments. An additional 13 percent who showed almost no change had deep-seated issues, often trait-based, and went back to difficult, if not hostile, work environments. In the study shared by Peterson, although 70 percent of high-potentials changed, only 20 percent of participants judged to be derailment risks showed the expected level of improvement. Both of these studies emphasize something that every experienced coach has learned along the way, that not every executive is equally likely to change from coaching.

A series of articles in a special issue of the *Consulting Psychology Journal* devoted to executive coaching presents numerous case studies of the coaching process. A case study by Peterson (1996, p. 82) illustrates the impact that executives may experience from their coaching, in this case an IT executive at an electronics firm: "I feel like a fundamentally different person. I do things differently. I respond to situations differently. I'm more confident about what I'm doing. I listen more. I'm more comfortable with conflict. I'm more strategic and more proactive. My relationship with my manager has changed dramatically."

Not surprisingly, with this type of change reported, the executive's increased effectiveness may spill over into family life and out-of-work relationships. Peterson's unpublished study cites instances of marriages saved and relationships with children dramatically improved by using new communication skills.

Books about executive coaching include tools to help the coaches evaluate their own work. Dottlich and Cairo (1999), while recognizing the particularity of coaching success in any given coaching situation, present an evaluation tool that illustrates the type of evaluation that the executive coach should be doing. These are the questions that make up their evaluation tool:

1. Has your client achieved the targeted goal?
2. What specific changes in behavior and attitude indicate that this goal level has been reached?
3. If you believe the goal has been reached, specify why these changes are sufficient to meet the criteria of the goal level.
4. Does the client feel the goal has been reached? Does this achievement help meet his or her job and career objectives?
5. How does the client believe job and career objectives have been met?
6. What motivated the person to achieve these objectives? Will this motivation continue to keep the person on track?
7. Do others in the organization (boss, HR, peers, direct reports, customers) believe the client has met key organizational requirements?
8. How do they describe the changes showing that the requirements have been met?
9. If the requirements have not been met, where do they believe the client has gone off track? [p. 79].

Companies, of course, have their own interests in the effectiveness of the particular coach as well as whether the coaching worked. An example of that is the follow-up that takes place after executive coaching at The Prudential Insurance Company of America; both the executive who has been coached and the business unit HR consultant complete an evaluation form that includes questions about the process and its effectiveness—and that of the coach. The evaluation form shown in Exhibit 6.1 asks the executive to rate the questions on a 1 to 5 scale.

These items could, in fact, serve as an outline for the skill requirements of an effective coach. The areas of competence emphasize how much the effectiveness of executive coaching depends on the right combination of executive, coach, and situation.

The evaluation sought from the business unit HR consultant (Exhibit 6.2) uses an open-ended format and reflects the type of information companies need to administer coaching effectively. Executive coaching is subject to the same pressures for evaluation that exist for other executive development tools, such as training programs. The individuality of the process makes systematic evaluation difficult. Despite the difficulties, however, the widespread use of executive coaching will encourage systematic evaluation that

**Exhibit 6.1. Prudential Coaching Evaluation Form—
Participant's Version.**

The Coach:

- Had the expertise in the areas that I wanted to address and change.
- Created a comfortable environment.
- Showed respect and was nonjudgmental.
- Understood Prudential's organizational culture.
- Was able to truly listen and give honest, direct feedback.
- Had the insight and strength to guide me toward productive, self-directed change.
- Was sensitive, open, and truly interested in me as a client.
- Maintained confidentiality.
- Effectively taught me how to develop myself to move on after coaching relationship.

Results:

- I made a positive change as a result of this coaching experience.
- Others have noticed a positive change in my behavior.
- I would recommend this coach to others.

Overall Rating:

---

should provide useful data concerning what works and what doesn't. In the meantime, experience with the process has provided much that can be said about what makes executive coaching more and less effective.

How Do Organizations Select Coaches and Match Them with Executives?

The practice of executive coaching varies so widely that no single set of parameters or administrative guidelines fits. This section raises some generic issues and gives examples of how very different companies are handling them. Recognizing that these processes

**Exhibit 6.2. Prudential Coaching Evaluation Form—
HR Consultant's Version.**

- What feedback about the coach did you receive from the coachee?
- What feedback did you receive from the manager of the coachee? Did they perceive a positive change in the individual as a result of the coaching experience?
- How long did the coach work with the coachee? Did the timing follow as planned? If not, why not?
- How was the coach to deal with on the business end (billing, sticking to pricing agreements, communications)?
- Would you recommend the coach to others? If yes, why? If not, why not?

and organizations change so rapidly that none of them is likely to be precisely in place at the time this is read, I nonetheless offer them as examples of ways to handle the issues.

The Competent Executive Coach

Competent coaching requires knowledge of the field of endeavor and an understanding of how people change. No one would think of hiring a golf coach who didn't know golf or a Spanish language coach who didn't know Spanish. In the same way, an executive coach must know the ways of executives and organizations. Credibility, as defined by the field of communication, fits the need for judging coaches also: credibility is based on having expertise, being trustworthy, and being dynamic. These three components make up the competent coach:

- *Trustworthiness:* Absolute integrity is the foundation for executive coaching. It is the coin of the coaches' trade. The ability to maintain complete confidentiality, meet commitments, and balance the interests of the executive and the organization are key ingredients. See the "Dangers and Downsides" section later in this chapter for more on the issue of trust.
- *Expertise:* Two sets of expertise are required—knowledge of business and how business operates, and knowledge of behav-

ior change. Either alone is not enough. An HR executive related to us his company's experience that perhaps the largest groups of wannabe coaches were on one hand former executives with no knowledge of behavior change, and on the other psychologists with no knowledge of business. In addition to these broad knowledge areas, special situations may require special competencies—for example, knowledge of a different culture or language, or knowledge of nonprofit organizations.

- *Dynamism:* Personal dynamism is the third of the factors that contribute to credibility among communicators and is a key element in the credibility of the coach. This does not mean that coaches must have personal charisma or charm. In the coaching relationship, dynamism may be interpreted as the interpersonal skills to engage the coachee in a process of change, whether it requires persuasion, feedback, cheerleading, or encouragement. Unless the coach has the dynamism to engage the executive, a crucial element in the change process will be missing.

As simple as this credibility model is, we argue that selecting an executive coach is a process of evaluating credibility.

Selecting an Executive Coach

The organization's HR function usually serves as the gatekeeper in selecting executive coaches. This role is especially important with executive coaches, as opposed to other consultants, because, surprisingly enough, executives seem to assume that the coaches referred to them are competent (Hall, Otazo, & Hollenbeck, 1999). The particular process the organization uses for selection, how formal and how well developed, depends on how widely coaching is being used and how the organization has been using coaches. The examples that follow cover a wide range of uses.

A relatively large, formal, and long-lasting executive coaching process is in place at Chase Manhattan Bank. The bank's corporate human resources function includes a manager of the executive coaching process who serves as a broker between 70–75 executive coaches and the various line HR and line of business organizations. Chase is well known for using coaching, so executive coaches find Chase—it seldom has to go looking. The screening of new coaches typically begins with a review of the résumé of the coach, a two-hour interview, and follow-up reference checks of the coach's previous clients. Topics covered in the interview include the coach's definition of coaching and approach to coaching, the types of assignments the coach accepts and refuses, the coach's orientation toward business rather than therapy, and the flexibility of the coach to work within the well-developed Chase Coaching Process. A coach candidate who is judged an appropriate addition to the roster of coaches will then be offered training in the Chase Coaching Process, Chase's Competency Model and 360-degree feedback process, and its Diversity initiatives. The coach coordinator may then include the coach's profile along with those of other coaches in referrals to the business units for selecting coaches for specific assignments.

Another large organization, The Prudential Insurance Company, is in an earlier stage of using executive coaches and consequently has a less-developed process, though similar to the one used at Chase. Prudential asks potential coaches to complete for their firms (or for themselves) an extensive coaching survey that serves as the basis for an interview with the corporate coaching coordinator. In addition to basic administrative data (fee structure and so on) the coaching survey (shown in Exhibit 6.3) asks a number of very specific coaching questions that touch on key areas of the coaching relationship.

Microsoft Corporation is a much different company from Chase Manhattan or Prudential; as might be expected, it handles the use and selection of executive coaches quite differently. In one use of coaches, several hundred managers and executives are offered 360-degree feedback each year and the feedback is facilitated by a cadre of former management development employees. Executive coaching—a more extensive process (usually six months)—is reserved for a few very high-potential managers who are about to step into executive positions. A small number of executive coaches have been carefully selected to do that coaching. The selection process, like those at Chase Manhattan and Prudential, is much concerned with the fit of the coach with the organization as well as the competence of the coach candidate.

Exhibit 6.3. Prudential Human Resources
Coaching Survey.

- What are your credentials? (Degrees and Designations)
- What are your professional and life experiences?
- What approaches or behavioral models do you use? What is your coaching philosophy?
- Please indicate your role: mentor, motivator, confidant, sounding board, consultant?
- How does what you do differ from counseling, clinical psychology, or psychotherapy?
- How do you decide what is to be addressed and accomplished with the client?
- How do you establish a good rapport with the client? What do you do if you and the client cannot establish good rapport?
- When you meet in person, where do you meet?
- Do you meet on a schedule or an as-needed basis?
- Describe the structure and content of a typical coaching session.
- What coaching or development tools do you use?
- Describe a case and how you handled it from beginning to end. What type of problems were addressed and how did you approach them? What was the outcome?
- What types of people do you relate to best? Least? What type of people relate best to you? Not as well?
- What type of people do you prefer not to coach?
- How do you assess the client's development on the issues being addressed?
- How do you assess the client's ongoing satisfaction with you as a coach?
- In your opinion, when does coaching not work?
- How do you handle confidentiality between you and the client?
- What contact do you have with the client's boss or other organizational representatives? What information do you share with them?
- How do you help the client move off the coaching relationship?

The selection process at Microsoft began with collecting résumés from 30 potential coaches; half of these were asked to visit the company to make a coaching presentation that included the coaches' philosophy of coaching and the psychological content of their approach; how they assessed coachees and the dimensions used; their views of leadership and management and what they saw as the levers for change; how they managed the coaching process to ensure that all the stakeholders were aligned; and how they combined both business and psychological perspectives. The team of assessors that evaluated the coach presentation included key Microsoft employees in management development and the high-potential program, senior line HR directors, and organization consultants who do internal coaching.

All three organizations place a high premium on their coaches' having an understanding of business and leadership. Expertise in helping people change, taken by itself, is not enough.

Matching the Executive Coach and the Executive

Whether based on chemistry or trust, or both, a good match—getting the right coach with the right executive—is the factor most practitioners emphasize. Most coaching coordinators can list coaching failures based on a bad match. The right match can be defined in terms of area of expertise, but also in terms of style—one executive complained to the HR rep that the coach referred to him "had no pulse." Finding the right match is a subjective process where the broker (usually the HR representative) assesses the coach's approach and qualities, first for fit with the organization (for example, Chase or Microsoft or Prudential) and then for fit with the particular executive in mind. A common tactic used to help get a good match is to give the executive several coaches to choose among in a process that coaches often refer to as a "beauty contest." Whether "selecting my own" is itself the factor that ensures a match between the executive and the coach, the common wisdom is that allowing executives to choose their own coach helps ensure a good fit. There is no known research that prescribes a more scientific process.

During the selection process, executive coaches are, of course, making their own assessments of whether they match with the organization and its executives. In a kind of ROI analysis, the coach should be asking, "Am I likely to work well with this organization? This executive? Does the executive need what I have? Can I relate to this executive? Is the executive likely to change? Does the organization support this or is it a 'last ditch' effort to save the executive?"

Dangers and Downsides of Executive Coaching

While most organizations pay attention to the dollars spent paying the executive coaching fees (fees as much as $20,000 to $100,000 or more for a six-month assignment), the biggest cost is probably the time spent on the effort by the executives, their bosses, and others in the organization. Other than the time and money wasted when coaching doesn't work, executive coaching seems to have few downsides. Gone are the days when having a coach meant that the executive was suspect; more likely today, having a coach means that the executive is a valued commodity; a coach may, in fact, be a status symbol rather than a stigma. My informal survey found no stories of executives whose performance actually declined as a result of coaching.

Coaching is not without its dangers, however, for both the coached executives and the organization. Those dangers for the most part result from failure, intentional or inadvertent, on the part of the coach. To be effective, coaches must work as a part of the organization system; they are dependent on the system for data and understanding, but at the same time they must guard against being co-opted by the system to the detriment of the person they are coaching.

In my experience, the most common problem for the coach is being caught between different interests within the organization— the interests of the executive being coached, another executive or coach, the boss, the HR person. To avoid these conflicts, the coach and those in the organization must be diligent in framing Step 1 of the coaching process—a clear contract of where the coach's loyalties lie. Thereafter, the coach must maintain a vigilant eye for efforts to use the coach to further a vested interest.

The unforgivable sin of coaching is failing to maintain confidentiality. As noted earlier, trustworthiness is the currency of coaching—once confidentiality has been violated, wittingly or not, the executive may be damaged and the coach will lose credibility. Ethics and experience guide effective coaches through the inevitable temptations to talk more than they should. One of the most common attempts to breach confidentiality occurs when a more senior executive or an HR person asks the coach for an evaluation of the executive's potential or capabilities. The naive coach, not versed in the politics of organizational life, will be caught off guard. When one company's VP-HR asked me to provide an estimate of a coachee's executive potential for use in succession planning, I offered to willingly provide the estimate *after* and *if* the coachee gave his consent; the VP-HR backed off immediately.

Executive coaches, like it or not, have a kind of power in the organization not unlike that of other consultants. That power is different, however, because of the personal sensitivity of much of the information that conveys the power and because of the special relationship that typically evolves between the executive and the coach.

Bellman's (1990) discussion of the consultant's use and abuse of power applies equally as well to executive coaches as to other types of consultants. He gives numerous examples that include violating confidentiality, aligning oneself with the chief executive officer when that person is not the client, or undermining someone whom the consultant sees as ineffective (p. 164). Bellman lists four major classes of power abuse:

- Knowing best—playing God.
- Manipulation—pursuing hidden ends or not revealing the means used to pursue ends.
- Pretending—to know or understand more than they do, exaggerating accomplishments.
- Deception—presenting themselves as different from what they are, such as making false claims on a résumé.

A common question that arises is whether to use internal or external coaches. Each has its advantages and disadvantages—Hall, Otazo, and Hollenbeck (1999) present both the pros and the cons. Neither internal nor external coach, however, is exempt from dealing with issues involving the abuse and use of power. The solution to avoiding these dangers is an understanding of the issues that are likely to arise, a realistic view of the way organizations work, and an ethical foundation to work within. Ethics is not the exclusive property of any one group of professionals, although my bias is toward the type of ethical standards developed and endorsed by psychologists. Flaherty's *Coaching: Evoking Excellence In Others* (1999) is an excellent example of a broad-based book that gives serious consideration to the responsibilities of the coach.

Another pitfall of executive coaching revolves around coaches who want to do psychotherapy rather than focus on performance, and executives who are sometimes all too willing to participate. Most executives are far too sophisticated to go there unless they want to, but organizations with growing executive coaching expenses have a vested interest in keeping the focus on performance; coach selection, as noted, can be the best place to screen out coaches whose interest is therapy.

Executive coaching does have its dangers and downsides. Careful selection and monitoring of coaches, however, combined with attention to the factors that contribute to coaching effectiveness, should go a long way toward avoiding the dangers.

Factors That Affect the Effectiveness of Executive Coaching

Although people change all the time, specific, targeted change is seldom easy. Change may be fragile at best, and many factors contribute positively or negatively to whether executive coaching is effective or ineffective, a success or a failure. Even with the best coach in the world, executive performance may not improve, and even where the coaching exercise may get high marks at the time, there is no guarantee that the executive will maintain any gains made.

Simple as it sounds, the first requirement of a successful coaching assignment is that the executive wants to change. One problem with "everybody gets a coach" programs is that at any particular point in time not everybody will want to change. Models of how people change have as a primary success element that the person *wants* to change. (Dalton & Hollenbeck, 2001, specifically address the process of executive change; Prochaska, Norcross, & DiClemente, 1995, present a more general change model of how people change, why they do and why they don't.) Those whose stock in trade is helping adults to change soon develop a healthy respect for the view that no one can change other people, they change themselves.

Feedback—360-degree feedback, a surprise performance appraisal that is harsher than expected, a missed promotion or a promotion achieved when it was not expected, any of these can be important motivators for executive change. The dynamism of the credible coach is partly at least reflected in the coach's ability to engage the executive in the change effort. Unless the executive can be engaged in the process, the coaching assignment is unlikely to succeed.

The boss is a key factor in successful coaching, whatever form that boss takes. At the chief executive officer level, the boss may be the Board of Directors. Whoever the boss is, the boss will play an important role in providing feedback, helping with setting goals for development, providing resources, opening doors for learning, and providing an environment where new behavior is accepted, rewarded, and encouraged.

The greater the organizational support that can be garnered for executive change in the coaching process, the more likely the change will take place. When Microsoft provides high-potential executives with a coach, it also provides a network of support for the targeted changes; the network includes the boss, the corporate HR person who oversees the high-potential pool, the business unit HR director, and, of course, the coach. Even though no one of these besides the coach is privy to what happens behind closed doors, the executive working with the coach gets a lot of support for changing and is not left to (nor allowed to) fend for himself.

Executive success does not take place in a vacuum. Neither does executive change. Executive coaching is subject to the same constraints that affect other leadership development programs—unless the organization supports the developed leader, the developmental changes, even if they take place, are unlikely to last. Organizations with climates that support change have systems (such as compensation and performance appraisal) that respond to changes and are themselves adaptive, and likely to take advantage of the potential of executive coaching. Rigid, highly politicized, dysfunctional organizations are unlikely to be fertile ground for executive coaching.

What Is the Future of Executive Coaching?

This chapter argues that executive coaching has grown so rapidly because it meets the need for a leadership development tool that responds to the changes in the business environment. As Kotter said, "The whole game changes, and a lot of people are trying to keep up, learn how, not fall off." Executive coaching, flexible and performance focused as it is, offers to help. At its best, when done well by competent practitioners in supportive organizations, executive coaching can be a catalyst that speeds up the executive development process and contributes to better executive performance.

Is executive coaching a fad, or does it have a future? It looks as though the factors that are pulling executive coaches into the leadership development process are unlikely to subside. Organizations everywhere are asking, "How can we accelerate the development of leaders, how can we make better use of what we have, how can we prevent failure?" As one chief executive officer told me, his corporate plans *require* that executives succeed—with ambitious plans and in a war for talent, there are few ready replacements. As the world of business globalizes, executive coaches have a potentially very useful contribution to make in helping executives learn the skills of that world. Working in teams (whether virtual or face-to-face) is one of those skills.

Executive coaching has a great deal to offer in such a world. The array of available coaches will probably differentiate itself in terms of competence and the focus that coaches take. Organizations will differentiate also in their use of coaching—they will be more selective in how they choose coaches and more demanding in the results they expect. Personal coaching seems to be a genie out of the bottle in a world awash in personal choices. Not all of those choices are likely to be supported by organizations; it seems unlikely that organizations will provide a personal coach for every executive. But executive coaches who provide significant value added to busy executives in high-performing organizations will, like the executives themselves, find their services at a premium.

References

Bellman, G. M. (1990). "The darker side of consultant's power." In *The consultant's calling: Bringing who you are to what you do,* p. 164. San Francisco: Jossey-Bass.

Biederman, P. W. (2000, Tuesday, August 8). "Someone to help resolve all your 'issues.'" *Los Angeles Times,* ID #0000074004. Available online.

Block, P. (1999). *Flawless consulting: A guide to getting your expertise used* (2nd ed.). San Francisco: Jossey-Bass.

Dalton, M. A., & Hollenbeck, G. P. (2001). "A model for behavior change." In C. Timmreck, D. Bracken, & A. Church (Eds.), *Handbook of multisource feedback,* pp. 352–367. San Francisco: Jossey-Bass.

Dottlich, D. L., & Cairo, P. C. (1999). *Action coaching: How to leverage individual performance for company success.* San Francisco: Jossey-Bass.

Edelstein, B. C., & Armstrong, D. J. (1993). "A model for executive development." *Human Resource Planning, 16*(4), 46–51.

Evered, R. D., & Selman, J. C. (1989, Winter). "Coaching and the art of management." *Organizational Dynamics,* pp. 16–32.

Flaherty, J. (1999). *Coaching: Evoking excellence in others.* Boston: Butterworth-Heinemann.

Groder, M. G. (1991, Winter/Spring). "A grand vizier: Every chief executive needs one." *Consulting Psychology Bulletin, 43*(1), 4. (Originally published in *Boardroom Reports,* 1982.)

Hall, D. T., Otazo, K. L., & Hollenbeck, G. P. (1999, Winter). "Behind closed doors: What really happens in executive coaching." *Organizational Dynamics,* pp. 39–53.

Hollenbeck, G. P. (1996). "An essay on issues in executive coaching." In *Current practices in 360 feedback and coaching for executive evaluation and development.* Boston: Executive Development Roundtable, Boston University.

Kaplan, R. E. (1998). "Getting at character: The simplicity on the other side of complexity." In R. Jeanneret & R. Silzer (Eds.), *Individual psychological assessment,* pp. 178–227. San Francisco: Jossey-Bass.

Kotter, J. P. (1990). *A force for change.* New York: Free Press.

McCauley, C. M., & Hughes-James, M. (1994). *An evaluation of outcomes of a leadership development program.* Greensboro, NC: Center for Creative Leadership.

Morris, B. (2000, February 21). "So you're a player. Do you need a coach?" *Fortune,* pp. 144–154.

Peters, T. J., & Austin, N. K. (1985). *A passion for excellence: The leadership difference.* New York: Warner Books.

Peterson, D. B. (1993, April 30). "Measuring change: A psychometric approach to evaluating individual training outcomes." Paper presented at the Society for Industrial and Organizational Psychology annual conference, San Francisco.

Peterson, D. B. (1996). "Executive coaching at work: The art of one-on-one change." *Consulting Psychology Journal: Practice and Research, 48*(2), 78–86.

Peterson, D. H., & Hicks, M. D. (1996). *Leaders as coaches: Strategies for coaching and developing others.* Minneapolis, MN: Personnel Decisions International.

Prochaska, J. O., Norcross, J. C., & DiClemente, C. C. (1995). *Changing for good.* New York: Avon Books.

Thompson, J. H. (1991). "Working in the executive suite." *Consulting Psychology Bulletin, 43*(1), 5–9.

Useem, J. (2000, January 10). "Welcome to the new company town." *Fortune,* pp. 62–70.

Witherspoon, R., & White, R. P. (1997). *Four essential ways that coaching can help executives.* Greensboro, NC: Center for Creative Leadership.

Zander, R. S., & Zander, B. (2000). *The art of possibility: Transforming professional and personal life.* Boston: Harvard Business School Press.

CHAPTER 7

Developing Executives

Val H. Markos

At the helm of virtually every successful organization is an effective leader. Those organizations concerned about continued success, as almost all are, recognize that having effective leadership is necessary for that success. This recognition is the driving force for companies to develop current leadership and to identify and develop future leaders. It is often said that one of the most important roles of an organization's leader is to ensure succession of leadership. But how is such succession ensured? How do executives actually develop? How does an organization systematically develop talent to ensure effective leadership for today and for the future? This chapter will look at how organizations approach this task of developing leaders and at how an organization integrates practices and programs to maximize such development.

This chapter discusses four areas critical to executive development systems. An early issue that an HR practitioner must address in establishing development efforts is determining the level of organizational commitment and identifying the sponsor or champion. Next, the identification of executive talent and the evaluation or diagnosis of an executive's development needs should be determined. Although virtually all managers in an organization can develop, not all can or will develop into an executive and not all executives will develop to be a successful chief executive officer. Third, the activities that are commonly used to enhance executives' development need to be identified. The final area is the continuing education and development of current executives and the methods to help them continually grow and maintain effectiveness.

This chapter focuses on the practice of leadership development. It will not discuss in depth on theories or definitions of leadership. Many of the conclusions drawn in this chapter come from the experience of the author. Where there is research published on the specific topic, it is cited. However, much of what is documented in this chapter comes from the author's decade of experience in the area of leadership development.

Sponsorship

A critical aspect of an effective system of executive development is sponsorship and commitment. The commitment of the organization is needed because these efforts are not without their costs in time, dollars, and resources. Executive development efforts require a long-term perspective and balance between maximizing today's business and investing in tomorrow's business. When a position opens that is critical to the success of the organization, should the organization staff it with a seasoned veteran or with an executive who has not performed in the role and will have a learning curve but whose experience in the position will pay great dividends to the organization in the long term? Obviously the answer is not the same for each specific situation. It is necessary to balance commitments to develop future leadership and to run today's business—and it is far too easy to lose that balance. The HR practitioner who is asked to manage an executive development system can have a great system on paper and create innovative plans but can have very little impact without organizational sponsorship and commitment.

For example, when an executive is unwilling to release a high-potential manager to take a new position or to attend a critical developmental experience, it is difficult to proceed without top sponsorship. Unless the chief executive officer of the organization is involved and committed, development progress across the organization will be limited. Some developmental assistance may be provided to the individual, but the chief executive officer must be committed in order to maximize the development opportunities.

To show that commitment, one chief executive officer formed a development council that met quarterly to discuss and review succession, development, and diversity progress. He chaired the council and established a monthly report that listed the number of upper management positions filled from an identified pool of high-potential individuals. The report included the number of high-potential individuals released from each leader's unit to another unit in the corporation and the number received into each leader's unit. It also listed the number of positions filled by diversity candidates. (He was very interested in having his executive ranks reflect the diversity that existed in the markets served by the corporation.) He then gave each member of his leadership team specific objectives for the year in each of the categories measured. He did not take away their decision authority or freedom to select or develop talent, he simply received a commitment from each of them to develop and move critical leaders in the business. He also gave each member on his team credit or grief for the efforts reflected by the report. At the quarterly meetings, the report was discussed and progress was highlighted.

So how does an HR practitioner gain that commitment from the top? The HR practitioner cannot unilaterally create or dictate commitment. But the practitioner can help the chief executive officer see the need for development efforts by raising thought-provoking questions, providing useful data, and creating tracking reports that lead to certain conclusions. For example, does the leadership of the past ensure future success? Do we have the talent to fill the critical positions we have now or will have in the near future? Do we struggle to find the right talent each time an executive position comes open? Or do we have in place the talent to take us to a new level of competitiveness that is demanded by the market?

Just as critical as helping others to see the need is helping to fashion a practical and powerful approach for addressing the need. The head of the organization must own the process by continually being involved in the shaping of it. There is no substitute for such commitment and involvement. With that sponsorship the process can begin with the identification of those managers who have the potential to have the greatest impact on the organization's future.

Leadership Talent Identification

All employees, from the chief executive officer to the mail room clerk, should continually develop their ability to perform in their current job and to their build skills for future responsibility. However, not all employees or managers can be given the same opportunities or need the same development. Not all managers have the potential to be the chief executive officer. How does an organization identify those with high potential and how does an organization accelerate the development of those identified? It is very common for organizations to identify pools of high-potential managers for such accelerated development. These "hi-pos" are watched, tracked, offered stretch assignments, and provided with educational and development opportunities. Such opportunities require commitment, investment, and risk on the part of both the individual and the organization. So how are the decisions made on who is high potential and what development needs will be addressed?

This identification process has to rely initially and principally on the relationship between individuals and their supervising manager. It is their performance on the job and their interactions with the managing supervisor that are the first measures of their potential and ability. The identification process typically relies on supervising managers throughout the organization to identify individuals with the potential to develop beyond their current position. The criteria used to identify managers with executive leadership potential usually include the potential to rise multiple levels in the organization, to move across functions, or to move up within a relatively short period of time.

The identification process often includes a tiered or roll-up step in which a supervising manager's nomination of a high-potential manager is reviewed or approved by the next level of managing supervisor, thus "rolling" the nomination up the organization. This provides for a management review and evaluation beyond that of the immediate supervising manager. All managers should be working with their employees to ensure that they develop to their greatest potential. However, for high-potential employees the specific development opportunities and challenges may go well beyond those the supervising manager is capable of providing. Consequently, a roll-up process is usually more selective than a process that simply requires a supervising manager's nomination.

Rolling up the nominations also has the advantage of having the input of more managers, thereby providing a more thorough evaluation of candidates. This process is most effective when there are specific criteria to evaluate managers and executives, when evaluating managers are informed and well-trained, and when there is a rigorous review of the evaluations by an objective person or group. This objective third party is usually an HR practitioner who manages or works with the high-potential pool. The rigorous review process may include a review of the supporting nomination and interviews with individuals who know and work with the nominated manager. The objective is to gain enough information to corroborate the identification of a high-potential manager.

In some instances, formal assessment is also incorporated into the process. This assessment can range from paper-and-pencil testing to assessment center activities with behavioral observations. The latter is useful for both the rich information it generates and the developmental feedback it provides, which can easily be incorporated into a development plan. However, the expense of an assessment center is substantial, and the administration of individual and group exercises can be logistically challenging.

In any identification process it is important to establish clear criteria for selection that are based on the critical leadership skills that the process is trying to develop. For example, if the need in the organization is to develop general managers who can manage across multiple functions and manage business units, then the criteria should include the ability to work in or direct multiple functions. The criterion for identification into a high-potential process could be seen as the "ability to move up two levels of management and across multiple functions."

The criteria for targeted development should also include a commitment by the individual to participate in such career opportunities. It is all too common to find a manager or an executive with great potential to move beyond a discipline or up in the organization but whose values, personal aspirations, or personal life situation point in a different direction. That is why it is critical to involve the individual in any identification process for such opportunities. This does not necessarily mean self-nomination but it certainly means self-confirmation of a nomination.

Leadership Development Planning

Even when the identification process with specific criteria results in a very selective group of high-potential managers or rising executives, there is a great variation in their needs, strengths, and backgrounds. Although expediency drives an organization to create a single program that all executives must pass through, the most efficient and effective use of resources dictates that the development of such talent be tailored to the specific needs of the individual. Executives are generally very much in favor of participating in development activities, but they quickly disengage if the experience is not personally meaningful. Consequently, there is a need for an accurate, tailored, and current plan for the development of each executive.

Development planning and the preparation of a development plan should not be reserved solely for high-potential managers and executives. Every employee should have a development plan and should be engaged in development activities. However, for individuals with the highest potential, there should be particular attention given to the scope and depth of such a plan. As executives advance in the organization, there is a tendency on their part to avoid such exercises and pay less attention to a formal development plan. Often they believe that the only purpose of development is to bring them to their current position, not to help them continue to grow in effectiveness. This resistance presents a challenge for the HR practitioner.

Development planning follows a basic model as depicted in Figure 7.1. The model includes four basic steps: the identification of need (what to develop), the plan on how to obtain the development (how to develop it), the actual development, and the evaluation of the development (was it developed). The diagram depicts the model as a cycle because once completed, it can begin again, focusing on different needs or a different level of development in a given area.

In creating the development plan, an evaluation or assessment of individual needs should be conducted. The assessment has two critical components. First is a leadership competency model that serves as a common framework for articulating individual strengths and development needs. Many companies have developed and use models of executive competencies. A review of many of these

Figure 7.1. Model of Executive Development Cycle.

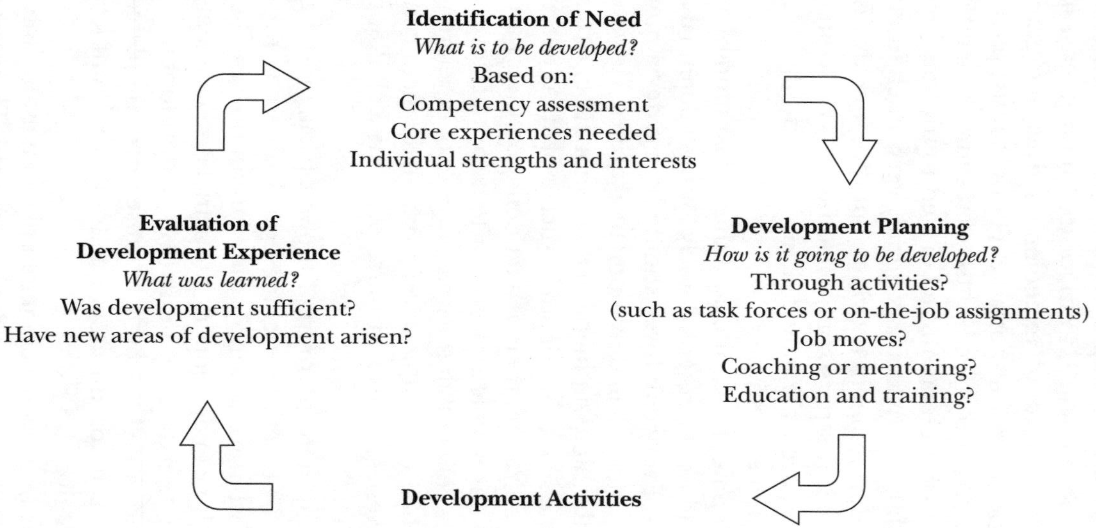

Identification of Need
What is to be developed?
Based on:
Competency assessment
Core experiences needed
Individual strengths and interests

Development Planning
How is it going to be developed?
Through activities?
(such as task forces or on-the-job assignments)
Job moves?
Coaching or mentoring?
Education and training?

Development Activities

**Evaluation of
Development Experience**
What was learned?
Was development sufficient?
Have new areas of development arisen?

models shows a substantial overlap in the competencies across organizations. There is little evidence that further research is needed to arrive at a model that provides the needed direction for most executive development efforts. What is needed is simply the support and acceptance by the organization that a given competency framework reflects the needs of the organization. Among the benefits of such a common framework for evaluation and planning is the ability of an organization to collectively review the plans, identify broad organizational needs, and design and implement special initiatives that ensure organizational competency in a particular area.

The second component of development assessment and planning is a group of core or targeted experiences that can help an individual develop, demonstrate, and practice such competencies. These core experiences include the varied and challenging building blocks of an executive's career. They can include such experiences as line and operations responsibility, staff and strategy positions, profit-and-loss responsibility, large team leadership, and customer interaction opportunities. These development experiences not only provide the development of skills and perspectives but also allow for multiple and varied observations of the executive's skills and abilities. Such a range of experiences further assists in identifying the development needs of the executive.

While most assessment and planning processes have these two common components, companies and organizations vary widely on how the process is managed. Approaches to assessment and planning range from an individual and a managing supervisor rating an individual and initially discussing a development plan to very elaborate assessment centers with behavioral observations, simulations, psychological testing, and trained assessors. Obviously such approaches differ greatly in costs with commensurate differences in the richness and thoroughness of the information. The level of sophistication in the process must fit the need of the organization and be consistent with the support and commitment level inside the organization.

The assessment and planning effort results in an evaluation of the individual, an identification of the competencies and skills to be strengthened or leveraged, and some recommendations on developmental opportunities and experiences. These recommendations may include education, special assignments, coaching, and involvement in community efforts. Often included are specific classes offered by the company or by universities aimed at specific topics such as strategic planning or managing critical resources. If coaching is needed, the specific area of focus (for example, interpersonal skills, strategy development, communications, or working with peers) is described. The plan should also include the next targeted experiences for which the executive should be considered. This plan then becomes the basis of the executive's development and a guide for individual growth. The managing supervisor uses it in planning for and assigning opportunities for the manager. The organization uses it in staffing decisions to take advantage of management vacancies for both performance and development purposes.

Development Activities

As I mentioned earlier, individual growth and development come primarily from experience and therefore the focus of executive development is mostly on experiences—and work experiences to be more precise. Further, different experiences will provide different lessons and perspectives, and will strengthen different skills. Morgan McCall's *Lessons of Experience,* now over a decade old, remains an excellent source of information on executive development, as is other related research at the Center for Creative Leadership (McCall, Lombardo, & Morrison, 1988).

Job Rotation and Orchestrated Staffing

Such research identified or confirmed some major experiences that are most commonly seen as developmental. For example, a move from a staff position to a line position or from a line to a staff position involves a significant change in the perspective and skills needed to perform successfully. This is especially true when the line position is one that has responsibility for hundreds or thousands of people serving the customer. I have listened to many executives discuss the challenges they personally have faced in such moves. The executive who grew up in a staff role is challenged by the fast pace and constant pressures of a line position and the demands of managing so many people. One executive who had moved from a staff role to managing a services organization requiring 24-hour service to thousands of business customers commented how she was routinely awakened during the night with issues for the first six months of the assignment. As she grew and learned the skills of large team management and delegation, the midnight questions came less frequently. Executives moving from the line to staff often have even more difficulty adjusting to staff positions with their greater ambiguity, longer project cycle times, and their need to influence without having direct authority. These adjustments can cause great frustration and the executives often complain that they are not accomplishing anything. Such job moves help to develop the skills and perspectives needed to lead and to provide an understanding of various organizational functions for the executive.

McCall cites several such development opportunities, including a significant increase in scope of responsibility or an opportunity to start up an operation from scratch or to turn around an operation that is in trouble. Of course, at the executive level these usually represent major job changes and significant effort on the part of the organization and the individual to balance the needs for development and performance. Without a commitment to development, for example, an opportunity to lead or turn around a troubled organization will likely go to a turnaround artist—someone who has done it before and has proven ability to perform in that type of situation—rather than to someone who needs a development assignment.

To the extent that developmental assignments include placing managers in new and challenging positions, there are a few critical points to keep in mind when managing a process of staffing positions for developing executive talent. These points represent real challenges in staffing such positions. It is critical that the assignments used to develop executive talent are positions that allow for success or failure. They can't be training positions—"make-work" jobs where results and decisions are not expected. Without real responsibility, no one is likely to show substantial development, so the individual's capabilities to develop cannot be assessed. This means that some individuals will succeed and others may not do well in such positions. All too often we see the executive placed by a mentor or senior advocate into a role that provides exposure to the leaders of the business but no opportunity to fail. Almost as often we see the same executive, when later placed in a significant role with such an opportunity to make a difference, struggle because of the lack of experience in positions with real risk and responsibility.

The greater the stretch in the assignment, the greater the development opportunity as well as the greater the risk of failure. The decision on placement must balance the amount of stretch with the amount of risk involved. It is important that the length of the assignment be sufficient for the individual to learn. I have often seen executives in stretch assignments say they are ready to move in six to eight months having "learned all they are going to learn"—when in fact they have received very little feedback on the impact or effectiveness of their actions in that time frame. Often the learning really comes with seeing the results of their decisions and the implementation of their plans such as a new marketing program or a reengineered service order process. Frequently, such results do not come immediately, meaningful feedback is difficult to receive, and learning may require months or even years. In many organizations, a year and a half to two years is considered a minimum interval for major job rotations. For most assignments that time frame is probably accurate, though there are a host of other factors that may indicate less or more time in a position.

Not all development through experience has to involve a job move. Assignments and on-the-job opportunities on a smaller scale can be used to provide such development. Serving on corporate or nonprofit boards, internal and external councils, or advisory boards are just a few examples of development experiences that are frequently used to strengthen relationship-building skills or influencing skills and develop a broader or different perspective. Such opportunities can provide excellent "practice fields" for executives to develop or change leadership styles. Of course, if the opportunities are not frequent, the expectations for change must also be appropriately lowered. Meeting quarterly on an outside board doesn't have the same intensity as working day in and day out for a solid year in a developmental assignment.

So how is such staffing systematically accomplished in a large organization where many high-potential executives seek development opportunities? There are really two approaches that are common and are often used together. One is replacement planning and the other is centrally managed staffing. The first takes a proactive approach to the identification of development opportunities and allows more decision latitude by individual leaders in the field. The second approach controls executive staffing from a central staff that ensures a balance between developing tomorrow's leaders and maintaining performance today. This approach allows selections only from a slate of candidates prepared by the central staff.

Replacement planning ensures that important positions are reviewed and a plan is established for the replacement of the incumbents. Such plans may include immediate replacements as well as longer-term potential replacements—people who may not be ready now to replace the incumbent but may have the potential to do so in the future. Such plans are often established by the incumbent or the supervising manager of the position and suffer from the tendency to consider only talent in close proximity to the position. To avoid such a tendency the process may force the inclusion in the plan of candidates from other business units. Providing information on other potential candidates to the preparer of the replacement plan helps the preparer become familiar with such talent. This process of socializing their profiles is critical to leveraging development opportunities and to moving talent across a large organization.

Centrally managed executive staffing approaches the issue by requiring that staffing decisions for important positions (typically defined as top 1 percent or 2 percent of positions) be processed through a central clearinghouse to ensure they are staffed to maximize corporate objectives. Generally, this means a slate of candidates is created centrally and the hiring manager is given latitude to select from the slate. To be effective, this approach requires an evaluation of the development potential of the position to be filled, a complete database of talent in the organization, and a well-communicated commitment in the organization to consider development in staffing decisions. The database must include an evaluation of the skills, development needs, and interests of candidates as well as other information (such as mobility) that will allow for initial screening. This approach is often challenged by strong leaders who proactively identify talent in their own organizations to fill vacancies or anticipated vacancies. To succeed, the HR practitioner must help these leaders understand the value of moving talent in and out of their organization for the benefit of both the company and the individual executives involved.

Actually, the most effective process combines a little of both approaches. A consistent process of sharing development information on executives with leaders who will be making staffing decisions greatly facilitates the placement of these executives. This information, coupled with clear expectations that the leader become acquainted with the executives, increases the likelihood of actually placing them when an opening arises. Whether that happens through a replacement planning exercise, a process of socializing profiles, or even an orchestrated meeting between the developing executive and the hiring leader is not important. What is important is that the hiring leader should have some familiarity with the executives and their skills prior to the executives' being placed on a candidate slate.

All too often, a proactive leader will have filled a vacancy on his team prior to seeing any candidate slate from a central staff. And while an organization that is committed to development may choose to force a selection choice on a leader, such a move decreases the probability that any development will actually occur. Removing the hiring leader completely from a staffing decision is not the way to ensure the development of talent or a commitment to performance objectives.

Coaching for Development

The primary focus of executive development is on work experiences and job assignments, but other contemporary resources are frequently used to enhance learning based on experience. One of the strongest trends in executive development in the last decade has been the use of executive coaches in assisting development. A decade ago, most coaches worked with executives who were seen as having one or more fatal flaws. Before they were removed from their positions, they were given an opportunity to work with a coach. Having a coach working with you in those days was not a good sign for an executive's future in the organization and few executives would ever mention their work with a coach.

Today the situation has changed dramatically. Rarely is a "last chance" executive assigned a coach, although he may have worked with one earlier if there were previous signs of derailment. Now many executives are assigned coaches and the distinction of having a coach is a sign that the company sees further potential in the executive! Today the chief executive officer frequently has a coach and talks about it. Many of the highest-potential executives are paired with a coach, and coaches often work with groups of executives to improve individual and team performance.

George Hollenbeck covers the topic of coaching well in Chapter 6. But a few comments here are warranted about coaching as a tool for executive development. *Coaching* describes any relationship in which one person is consciously and openly assisting another person to improve skills or to perform more effectively. With this definition a coaching relationship can be established between any two individuals at any level in the organization, between peers, between a manager and a development professional in the organization, or between an executive and an external professional.

In developing executives it is very beneficial to have leaders who can effectively coach high-potential talent. Where excellent coaches exist in the organization they should be working with high-potential managers who can benefit from their experience. Often such coaches are openly recognized and rewarded for their skills. This further reinforces their commitment and energy to such a valuable task even as they see those they coach advance beyond them in the organization.

Typically in developing executives, external coaches are employed. In this case, as in all coaching relationships, establishing specific goals and timetables maximizes the experience. Specific goals and times should imply a finite life to the relationship. While a coached executive may opt to renew the contract or extend the relationship, the contract should be explicit and expectations established regarding the time frame of the engagement. Periodic reviews to assess the effectiveness of the relationship and redirect its focus or terminate it should also be a part of the up-front agreement.

A key element of a successful coaching relationship is the confidence the executive has in the coach. The selection of coaches and matching of coaches with executives must be done with credibility and trust in mind. The choice of an ideal coach depends on the specific situation. However, an effective coach usually has a great understanding of organizational behavior and individual development, and also has had experience in a business or organization, preferably in a line role. The coach must also be comfortable giving negative feedback and holding up a mirror to the person being coached to ensure that the executive is attentive to the feedback.

Multisource Feedback for Development

One of the most valuable roles a coach plays is to provide the executive with feedback and often this feedback is from multiple sources. The term *360-degree feedback* has been coined to describe the process of providing feedback from all angles; from the supervisor, peers, customers, suppliers, and subordinates. This form of feedback has been very popular over the last decade and for good reason. If it is provided in an effective manner and coupled with some direction and assistance in identifying ways to improve, such feedback can be a very powerful tool in capturing the attention of managers, in initiating efforts to change and improve behavior, and in monitoring and measuring development. This approach is most effective for the development of interpersonal skills and behaviors that are easily observable by those surrounding the manager.

Multisource feedback has become a key part of most executive development efforts. It is typically collected in a formal written fashion with an established set of questions that allow for collection of normative data. However, technology now allows leaders to tailor their quest for feedback to the specific areas of behavior that they are addressing in their development. Research conducted by Marshall Goldsmith (1996) has shown this to be extremely powerful and effective in capturing the attention of the developing executives. Goldsmith's research demonstrates that if an executive follows a few basic steps after receiving such feedback and involves those who gave the feedback, then improvement by the executive on the dimension being addressed can be virtually ensured.

The desire of many organizations for even further progress or improvement in behavior has caused a shift in the approach to multisource feedback. Most multisource feedback efforts have been introduced into organizations through development programs. The intent of such programs is to allow managers to own feedback they receive (that is, nobody else in the organization has access to it). The lack of dramatic improvement in behavior from many involved in such programs has caused some companies to approach multisource feedback differently. Some have used such feedback in an evaluative sense with more consequences in terms of financial incentives tied to improvement. Although this can increase the impact, it can also introduce dynamics that are not consistent with the intent of the initiative.

There are several key elements to the successful use of multisource feedback. The first is a clear understanding by all involved of the purpose of the feedback. This intervention has been so popular that it often seems like a tool in search of an application. It is important to determine whether the purpose is for development or evaluation. Should it be used to reinforce or initiate an organizational culture change or a shift in managerial style within the organization? As in any intervention, the tool is not the purpose. The tool should support the purpose.

All participating individuals must understand the purpose for gathering the feedback, how the feedback will be used, and any policies regarding anonymity and confidentiality. Protecting the confidentiality of the data is critical for any further feedback efforts. Who sees the individual results? Everyone should be clear about this before gathering the feedback. Inevitably, someone in the organization will ask to see someone else's results. It may be for a very positive and honorable reason. Nonetheless, the answer to the question of who sees the feedback should be formulated before the question is asked. If the feedback is purely for development purposes, most agree that only the recipient of the feedback should see it. Others argue that supervising managers cannot coach without knowing what to coach, and so they should be privy to the feedback. Still others claim the feedback should be open to supervising managers and leadership to ensure incentive and motivation to improve. These are all viable ways to approach multisource feedback. The critical element is that everyone understands how it will be used and who will see it.

Many organizations have addressed the issue of confidentiality, coaching, and incentives by first protecting the confidentiality of the specific feedback. However, they require recipients to create a development plan specifically to address areas of development. The recipients are also required to share the plan with their supervising managers. Other organizations make it clear that the feedback is company property and as such is shared with leaders just as performance measures are used as a type of report card. The most effective approach for an organization recognizes and addresses the purpose of the initiative and the environment of the organization.

Another key element for success with multisource feedback effort is the richness of the data in terms of behavioral and actionable feedback. The more actionable the feedback, the more likely action can be expected as a result of the feedback. This means careful upfront preparation and thought should be given in the development of feedback items. If at all possible, the opportunity to provide written comments regarding strengths and needs should be encouraged. Such comments can add greatly to the richness of the data and the power of the process. Often such comments pinpoint behavior, reinforcing positive acts and identifying development needs that might be missed using only a finite number of items. Written comments are not without their costs, however, since the processing of such verbatim comments from a paper-and-pencil instrument can be the most expensive part of the feedback process. The use of the Internet or an intranet to collect the feedback can reduce the expense of verbatim comments as well as the total cost of administration of multisource feedback.

Mentoring

In addition to coaching, a similar and quite popular approach— and one that is often confused with it—is mentoring. Whereas coaching is generally aimed at assisting the participant in developing skills of leadership, mentoring is aimed more at navigating through the organization, and understanding the norms and unwritten rules. A mentor often provides tips and suggestions on skills and approaches to leadership. The most effective mentorships happen when an unselfish, willing executive assists someone lower in the organization. Such relationships are formed when both parties have a commitment to both the relationship and the mentoring goals, even when the goals are not explicitly stated. Often companies try to program mentoring connections by matching executives with high-potential managers based on the participants' needs and interests. In these cases, most relationships do not turn into true mentorships but they can still add significant value to the organization and the individuals involved.

The likelihood that mentoring will be effective can be enhanced by careful selection and matching of partners consistent with the objectives of the program. Selecting mentors and participants based on their development needs, commitment to development and the mentoring process, and their credibility within the organization are factors that contribute to the success of the effort. Matching partners that have some common interests and background, as well as complementary views within the organization, will help produce a true mentorship. Even without the relationship developing into a true mentorship, however, such an opportunity provides great insight and perspective for the participant from someone who has navigated through the political channels of the organization and who has faced the big picture. Likewise, the mentor or senior partner in the relationship can gain a perspective from another level of the organization and can become familiar with talent that exists within the organization.

Another systematic approach to mentoring is to simply educate executives on the concept and then request or require them to form their own relationships with high-potential managers of their choosing. This approach increases the likelihood that the relationships formed will in effect be true mentorships. However, if left completely up to the mentors the partnerships formed tend to be with participants closely surrounding the mentor. That is, when left to identify their own participants, executives tend to select managers who are known to them, who are in their same organization, and who have a very similar background to their own. These individuals are not necessarily the managers most in need of a mentoring experience and may not be the ones who most benefit from the experience.

Education and Training

Many managers asked to define executive or management development will immediately turn to education and training. Education is often one component of executive development and might include

- Company-sponsored and internally delivered programs for high-potential managers
- Non-degree executive education offerings from major universities and business schools
- Executive MBA programs
- Other business education programs

Education and training play a substantial role in the development of future and current executives. The role described here is that of executive education, not the supervisory skills training that is aimed at providing newly identified first-level managers with the skills required for their new position.

Research by George Hollenbeck (Dalton & Hollenbeck, 1996) on the impact and contribution of publicly offered executive education (such as Harvard's Advanced Management Program) found two primary benefits. The first is that it broadens a manager's perspective. Such an experience introduces new concepts and ways of approaching issues. It may be broadening from a functional to a general management perspective, from a domestic to a global perspective, or even from a focus of individual and organizational competition to one of collaboration and partnership. Such experiences can be great trigger points for growth of the individual.

The second documented benefit from an executive education experience is the expanded peer group and network the participant develops during the experience. This peer group offers an opportunity for further learning and is a great source of information and ideas. Association and interaction with such a network also provides the participant with a sense of confidence. Relationships developed during such encounters are often maintained and developed over time to benefit the individuals and organizations represented. I know of one executive from the United States who attended such a program and met a participant from China and a relationship was formed. Almost a decade later, the U.S. executive's company was starting up a small venture in China, and this executive sought out his friend—who was now the mayor of the very city where the venture was formed. These experiences and relationships can be extremely beneficial to the participants as well as the sponsoring companies.

Ongoing Development of Executives

Once executives have arrived at the pinnacle of an organization, how do they continue to grow and develop? How does an HR practitioner assist in that process? How does an HR practitioner leverage individual development activities for organizational growth and development?

Recently a chief executive officer of a major corporation was asked, a year after his appointment, "What has been the biggest surprise during your time in the top position?" His response came quickly. The biggest surprise was the incredible demand for learning since the first day on the job. This chief executive officer had been in the industry 25 years prior to his current position and had been in positions reporting directly to the previous chief executive officer for several years. Yet he saw continued development and learning as an enormous part of this job. Continued development at the top is critical if leaders are to effectively address the issues of a dynamic and global marketplace. Yet many HR practitioners find it difficult to engage or influence the senior executives in such development. Why? To answer that question let me describe these executives.

Executives and leaders of major corporations today are usually extremely bright and highly successful individuals who have focus, determination, and opinion. They have been reinforced for their approach and behavior financially as well as socially throughout their careers with continual recognition and numerous promotions. They are extremely busy individuals; the corporate and civic demands on their time could easily fill all 24 hours of their day if they allowed it to happen (and sometimes they do). Time is extremely valuable to an executive. They also have hosts of managers, consultants, advisers, and others competing for an audience with them to share an almost infinite number of ideas, concepts, and business cases. These executives are successful, forceful, busy, and somewhat "crusted" by the multiple factions vying for their attention. It is easy to see why executives can be a tough audience when it comes to an HR practitioner's attempts to change their behavior or even to assist in their development.

How does an HR practitioner influence the executives' ongoing development? There are several keys to the success of a practitioner's efforts but the first and foremost is to gain credibility with the executives. Developmental experiences are likely to push the executives out of their own comfort zone. To embrace an opportunity in an uncomfortable territory, the executives have to have some confidence in the person taking them there, that is, making the development recommendation. Once they have that confidence, they are more willing to step out, to listen, to try, and to take advantage of opportunities the HR practitioner suggests.

So how does an HR practitioner gain credibility with the executive team? It comes down to the topic I introduced at the start of this chapter—sponsorship. If the HR practitioner can act as a partner with the chief executive officer, the efforts and activities come with instant credibility to the rest of the team. I once committed to the chief executive officer that I would not offer education or development initiatives without his sponsorship. In turn, I asked for his involvement in guiding our efforts—not day-to-day guidance but a high-level direction of our educational classes and development activities. The first initiative we launched with that commitment was a class for the chief executive officer and his team on leadership. We then rolled out the class to the other leaders of the company who were all invited by the chief executive officer. It was now his initiative. Sponsorship is critical, especially in educational and development efforts that are aimed at aligning leadership or influencing culture. There is no substitute.

Another critical component of credibility for the HR practitioner is to understand the business and the issues facing the executives and the company. Development efforts must address the needs of those involved. To address the needs, the HR practitioner must know the needs and be able to articulate the needs and the recommended intervention in terms that the target audience understands. Further, credibility is aided if there is some apparent or face validity to the recommendations. This is why the wise practitioner will spend plenty of time gathering information about the issues and asking many questions prior to rendering opinions, designing programs, or recommending interventions.

Often, timing is critical to effectively influence development at the executive level. Timing can mean the difference between an effective development intervention (individual or group) and one that doesn't get off the ground. Making the right recommendation at the right time requires staying close to the business and the executives as well as recognizing opportunities to assist the executives. On an individual level, the development recommendation is much more likely to be accepted if the executive sees the need for that development. So asking a question like "What is keeping you awake at night" triggers possible efforts on the practitioner's part to meet those needs.

Ideally, the practitioner can be close enough to the action to recognize leading indicators—advanced signs of challenges facing the organization—rather than seeing the challenges only after the organization or the executive is really suffering from them. I remember one day I was pilot testing an executive intervention on customer focus and a market-driven approach for the organization. In such a class I usually invite a small group of executives who are thought leaders in the organization and who are very open in providing their feedback. On this occasion one of the participants, an executive with line customer operations responsibilities, told me she would miss 45 minutes on the second morning of the class because of a scheduled conference call requiring her participation. On the morning of the call, she excused herself and returned 45 minutes later. Upon returning to the class she interrupted the discussion and announced that the call had involved an issue from the marketplace, the very issue addressed in class prior to her departure. She told the class she was glad to see our education efforts addressing the very issues she is wrestling with in the business. Timing is critical to credibility and effectiveness.

Finally, when it comes to maintaining credibility, there is no substitute for delivering quality programs and services. If participants see a program as helpful, if they find the experience valuable, and if they can see a difference because of the recommendations, they will come back for more. But if they don't, it will be difficult to get their commitment or engagement next time around.

Education as a Tool to Continue Growth of Executives

Efforts to educate and train executives can have different purposes. Some efforts are aimed at individual development or at the improvement of individuals in a particular area. Others are aimed more at aligning the organization or reinforcing a cultural shift in the organization. These different objectives drive different approaches to education design and delivery.

Most of the traditional educational programs at universities and business schools have been aimed at individual development. For example, a general management program at a business school is aimed at providing the participants with an understanding of multiple functions (such as marketing, finance, and operations) that are crucial to an expanded role with broad responsibilities. The experience may be delivered to groups for efficiency of delivery or for increased learning as the participants learn from one another. Nonetheless, the primary goal of the experience is individual development and not the alignment or strengthening of a team for future effectiveness.

Educational experiences whose primary purpose is the development or reinforcement of a cultural shift or alignment of the group are designed differently from the experience for individual development. For example, an organizational development experience will probably have teams attend together or over a very short period of time. This will increase the likelihood that lessons will be transferred to the workplace and reinforced in the work environment. Further, it is likely that members of the group will probably have assignments from the experience that extends the experience for the group back to the workplace. Business schools and other providers of executive education are addressing the need of companies to use education as an organization development intervention. Business schools frequently customize educational programs specifically for companies and deliver the education to a specific business unit or by inviting teams from one company to attend together. The existing knowledge on organization development provides great assistance in the design and delivery of such experiences. The HR practitioner must understand the basic differences in the objectives of such educational experiences and the different success factors associated with each.

For executive education to be effective, it must start with top-quality faculty. Each faculty member must have credibility as an authority on the subject matter. Often, internal trainers are not subject matter experts but versatile trainers who can quickly gain an understanding of a topic by being trained themselves by experts. Such a train-the-trainer approach is common in management development efforts (such as in teaching supervisory skills, time management, performance management). However, this approach will not be effective in executive education. The faculty must be knowledgeable in the subject matter as well as its application to the industry and the company. The faculty's ability to respond to challenging and skeptical questions from the audience is extremely important to the effectiveness of the experiences. The questions will almost certainly come since executives are generally extremely bright and usually enjoy an intellectual challenge. They also like to challenge others intellectually. If the message is to be accepted by the executives, the faculty must be able to have a relevant and challenging conversation on the topic with them.

The phrase *world-class faculty* is often used to describe the level of expertise and credibility desired. This implies seeking faculty from universities and consulting firms from around the world. Substantial time and effort is required to seek out such faculty and follow up on references to determine the level of capability. Nonetheless, having a world-class faculty is an important aspect of executive education.

If *world-class* describes the level of expertise desired in the faculty, in publicly offered programs another important key to maximize the learning is world-class *participants*. An executive who attends an educational program on global business issues expects to learn both from the faculty and from the other participants in the class. So in a course on global business issues, it is critical that participants represent global businesses. If the purpose of the experience is to help an executive understand competitive marketing, the executive will learn much more in a class where the participants are from companies with strong marketing reputations. Regardless of the subject of the course, the learning is increased if the participants assist in the teaching by sharing relevant perspectives.

I remember when I recommended a program at a well-known institution to a general manager who had great skills and abilities but who could have benefited from the leadership lessons offered by the program. After he attended he told me that he learned very little. He complained that virtually all the other participants in the class were less experienced and from companies smaller than the organization he ran. He believed that none of the participants had a broad enough perspective on the subject because of their lack of experience at his level. He learned little from the program, not because the topic or faculty was wrong, but that he could not get past the point that the other participants were not at his level. I was disappointed that he gained so little—I believe there were lessons there to learn, but he couldn't see them. Not all executives are as difficult as that one, but such a mismatch can make the experience less effective. Attention to the participants in an educational program is important to its effectiveness.

Education Aimed at Developing Organizations

Executive education aimed at aligning the organization or reinforcing a cultural shift in the organization uses variations of the principles of world-class faculty and participants. With regard to participants, it is important to "get the right people in the room"— that is, to invite as participants those executives whose roles and actions relating to the topic are most influential in the organization, and those who can learn from one another. It is important that education include participants whose continued collective learning can benefit them and the organization. Often executives from across the organization meet and form relationships only through their exposure at forums and programs like those I have discussed. Again, this may seem a very basic lesson—but more often than not, a great educational effort will simply miss the targeted audience or will not have much impact because those most influential in the organization are not engaged.

As for faculty, the qualities discussed earlier are also critical here—especially the ability to respond to challenges and intellectually joust with the participants. It is often helpful to partner an external, world-class faculty member with an internal leader for both the external view and the internal application. This approach brings the message closer to home and is a great developmental experience for the leader who is teaching or leading the discussion. It is also further evidence of sponsorship and credibility for the initiative. A powerful closing session to a financial values course one company offered was to have the chief financial officer review the business cases developed by the class participants and discuss the merits of the cases with the class.

Using executives as faculty is an excellent way to assist in the development of those executives. It not only provides the opportunity for them to deliver "teachable points of view," as Noel Tichy describes them (Tichy, 1997), it also provides the executives with an opportunity to listen to managers from across the company. It positions the executive to get feedback, information, and views from managers outside the executive's usual circle of interactions. Such a forum often raises the issues that are bubbling up in the organization. I have seen leaders who have regularly served as discussants or as faculty grow in their thoughts and approaches to issues because of the consistent and challenging questions raised in such classes.

So how does one design an educational intervention aimed at the executive body? It certainly must start with the identification and articulation of the purpose of the education. The purpose is virtually always related to a change in behavior, perspective, or culture of the organization. The purpose must be articulated clearly in order to communicate to both participants and faculty. Executive education, in many respects, is more about sending and reinforcing messages to the audience than about training; it is more about changing perspective than about building skills, and more about motivating the audience to change than about delivering information. With these ideas in mind, the design of an educational intervention is rarely effective in achieving its purpose without using elements of drama, symbolism, or significant uniqueness in the delivery to reinforce the lessons. Simply delivering information through a traditional classroom approach doesn't have the necessary impact. That is why experiential learning methods have become so prevalent in executive education. The experiential learning approach provides an experience in which the learner can test and apply the lessons of the course or can arrive at the conclusions desired by the design through experience, not just from hearing the concepts. Two approaches to experiential learning methods are simulations and action learning. I have worked with both approaches and both can be powerful.

Simulations

This approach simply tries to create a simulated environment in which the participants can wrestle with the actions and decisions of the leaders in that environment. With the introduction of some concepts in the course, participants can then apply them in the simulation. The simulations can range from the purely behavioral (such as role-playing) to sophisticated computer modeling of a situation in which interaction with the computer guides the simulation. In either case, the key to learning is for the participant to experience the situation and, most important, receive feedback on the actions taken or behavior demonstrated. Feedback is critical to the design since the learning primarily comes from an understanding of the impact or effectiveness of the decisions made by the participant in the simulation. The simulation allows for such feedback in a controlled setting and in substantially reduced time cycles. In the business world, it often takes weeks, months, or even years for an executive to determine whether decisions are effective and have the intended impact. Even the most perceptive and development-minded executive learns slowly from these experiences simply because of the length of the decision-feedback cycle. By using a computer simulation, an executive team can simulate four quarters or four years of business situations and receive feedback on their actions and decisions in an afternoon.

The fact that executives can get feedback rapidly using a simulation can make this method very effective in helping executives learn. It is important during the experience that time is taken to debrief what is happening, what decisions were made, what the impact was, and what the connection is between the decision and the impact. The design of the experience should include ample time for the discussion of results of the simulation to ensure that the participants make the connection between their decisions and the results.

Another critical success factor is that participants must be able to connect the actions required in the simulation to the issues they are facing in their organization. The simulation doesn't have to mirror their organization issues perfectly, but they should be able to see the relationship between the action required in the simulations and their role in the organization. The simulation then allows them to experiment in a safe environment with actions and decisions that would be somewhat risky in the real world. With the advances in information technology, it is now possible to make simulations and models accessible to executives at their desks to reinforce the learnings or to allow for further experimentation beyond the classroom.

Action Learning

Another approach to executive education is action learning (Dotlich & Noel, 1998; Tichy, 1997) and some of the same critical factors apply. Action learning takes many forms but essentially it is the application of the learned concepts to real issues. This approach does not separate the learning from the work or actions of the executive. Typically, the design requires a little education in the traditional classroom approach and then an extended period of time (days, weeks, or months) in which the participants, in groups or individually, work on projects where they can apply those concepts. The projects are either selected by the program sponsor (such as the chief executive officer) or identified by the participants using specific criteria. For example, the criterion might be that a project must be aimed at growing revenue, increasing productivity, or more fully utilizing existing assets. Following the period of time spent on the projects, the participants typically reunite to report their progress to the sponsor and to discuss projects and learnings in the larger group.

This approach has become very popular, partially because the sponsor of the effort can show real work being accomplished along with some education. From time to time, what started as a six-week or three-month project flourishes into a new business or market and the participants are assigned to lead the effort beyond the action learning phase. Given the description of this win-win approach, it is easy to see why it is so appealing. It is not education in a vacuum or education separated from the real work. It is, however, a difficult task to accomplish the learning goals with this approach without great effort and resources. My experience is that without strong facilitation, the participants jump into action on the projects but don't necessarily apply or learn concepts. It becomes just action as opposed to *action learning*. This action can be quite valuable in its contribution to the company's progress. But if the design does not facilitate reflection and review of the action, learning always takes a backseat to doing.

Nonetheless, even without such facilitation, learning to work with their assigned team and forming relationships with teammates are certainly positive and expected outcomes. If the projects are identified by the designer and not left to the decision of the participants, the projects themselves can provide the participants with substantial learning regarding the nature of the work involved. Such projects can range from developing a marketing plan for entering a new country or market to redesigning an order fulfillment process for improved efficiency or customer satisfaction. The projects should have a champion who expects results and holds the participants accountable for those results.

In many cases, the projects come from disciplines or geographic areas of the company where the participants have not worked before and where they have no authority to redirect efforts. In these cases, the expected outcome may simply be a recommendation on a given issue. If this is the case, the sponsor should be ready and willing to implement the recommendation if it is reasonable. The final report session may be designed to precipitate a decision by the sponsor, preferably to accept the recommendation and move into the implementation stage. This forces accountability and reinforces the importance of the project.

Again, with facilitation and good debriefing, real lessons can be gained for individuals and teams. Some designs even call for the teams, once they have been assigned to their projects, to identify what further information or education would be helpful. Such partnership between training and the client is a significant challenge for the HR practitioner to source and prepare in real time. Nonetheless, it can be very powerful and effective.

Use of Drama and Symbolism in Education

Beyond the experiential learning designs, executive education aimed at changing or reinforcing a change in the organization is greatly enhanced by the use of drama and symbolism to create a memorable experience. The drama might be created by providing feedback on the competitive (or lack of competitive) performance of the organization or by including customers, partners, and even competitors in the learning process in order to provide unfiltered feedback and perspectives to the participants. The use of metaphors to introduce or reinforce lessons can also create drama. I once used the metaphor of a symphony and its conductor to discuss some aspects of organizations and leadership. To strengthen the power of this metaphor we invited a symphony orchestra to play for our executives and had the executives sit among the members of the symphony and observe and discuss the organizational behavior of the orchestra. We invited a few of our executives to stand with the symphony leader and conduct the orchestra with him. We then involved the members of the orchestra in our discussion. Earlier in the day we had discussed several aspects of leadership and the orchestra conductor was prepared to address those aspects in his remarks during the symphony experience. Such use of a metaphor coupled with the experiential approach both gained the attention of the audience and left an enduring impression as they returned to their roles in the company.

In one session I had participants read a play in preparation for a Socratic discussion on values and leadership. Rather than simply discuss the play we enlisted the drama department of a local college to perform several acts of the play for our participants. We arranged the classroom with seats in a large circle so the participants sat around and close to the actors. At a point in the play in which a difficult values decision was being acted out, the actors invited the class members to participate in the play. After the play we continued a Socratic discussion on the decisions made. For many of the participants the invitation to participate was a powerful reminder of the leader's responsibility to maintain integrity and consider the welfare of the people he is leading.

In another program I asked frustrated customers to attend an executive class on customer service and to express their frustrations and describe their specific service problems to executives. We designed a module of the class to focus on the customers' experience and to identify the policies and practices that helped or hindered the service to the customer. It was painful for the participants to listen to the frustrations of the customers. Invariably, the executives would commit to changing the process to address the customer complaints. Frequently, the executives would make calls back to their organization before the module was complete to make changes in the approach and to solve the specific customer's problem. Such a dramatic, symbolic, and unique experience can greatly reinforce the message or objectives of the education—and anything that makes the experience more meaningful also makes the lessons from the experience more memorable.

Information Technology's Role in Executive Education

As the age of information continues and technology touches all aspects of our lives, it is valuable to discuss the role of information technology in executive education. Much of training in today's organizations is being pushed to the desktop with online learning and desktop training efforts. In the executive realm the move to online learning isn't happening nearly as rapidly. It will head that way, but at the beginning of this 21st century, very little education at the executive level is web-based. The role of information technology in executive education remains as a help in logistics and registration, but not in the enhancing of the education. I have seen progress in successfully using the web and online services to provide information or understanding in a just-in-time manner.

BellSouth is using it to provide updates to executives on technology. From a web site the company has created, the executive can obtain information and training ranging from a description of all the company's products through a glossary of technical terms to online courses regarding the latest technology. This is a valuable use of technology in executive development—to deliver just-in-time training and information.

This avenue for the delivery of information, while helpful, is not the greatest role the Internet will play for executive development. A critical piece of executive education is learning from and growing with a team or group of colleagues, and if the primary way such a group can learn requires being in the same place at the same time, then there are obvious limits to the growth of the group and the individuals. If the relationships and the sharing of information and perspective is free from the need to be in the same physical place at the same time, or even to be in the conversation at the same time (as on a conference call), such growth can be exponentially increased. Web-based communication allows for just such an opportunity.

Institutions and organizations are just now beginning to understand the use of this tool to connect students with faculty, students with students, and companies with clients. While we are in the early stages of using this tool for executive development, the Internet has the potential to greatly enhance the education of the executives primarily by connecting them together to learn and reinforce lessons learned. It may not replace the classroom or live group discussion for some time yet, but it will certainly enhance and extend the learning from such approaches.

Summary

This chapter has addressed several aspects of executive development: the need for top sponsorship, the identification of executive talent, and the many activities that contribute to the development of that talent. It also described the continuing development of executives and executive teams through executive education. A final thought in summarizing this chapter is that the impact of all these aspects is leveraged greatly by the coordination of their activities. If we can integrate the identification of and development planning for executive-level talent with the staffing process at the executive level, we greatly magnify the impact of the processes. If we can coordinate the education opportunities with the development plans of the executive talent, we optimize the development investment for the greatest gain. If our mentoring efforts and coaching programs are coordinated with our high-potential identification and planning, we again maximize the effectiveness of the efforts. Developing executives is a complicated and multifaceted process and the coordination of the many activities involved can dramatically increase the impact of each of the activities in the organization.

References

Dotlich, D. L., & Noel, J. L. (1998). *Action learning: How the world's top companies are re-creating their leaders and themselves.* San Francisco: Jossey-Bass.

Dalton, M. A., & Hollenbeck, G. P. (1996). *How to design an effective system for developing managers and executives.* Greensboro, NC: Center for Creative Leadership.

Goldsmith, M. (1996). Ask, learn, follow up, and grow. In M. Goldsmith, F. Hesselbein, & R. Beckhard (Eds.), *The leader of the future: New visions, strategies, and practices for the next era,* pp. 227–237. San Francisco: Jossey-Bass.

McCall, M. W., Jr., Lombardo, M. M., & Morrison, A. M. (1988). *The lessons of experience: How successful executives develop on the job.* Lexington, MA: Lexington Books.

Tichy, N. M. (1997). *The leadership engine: How winning companies build leaders at every level.* New York: Harper Business.

CHAPTER 8

Rewarding Executives

Marianna Makri, Luis Gomez-Mejia

Executive compensation has proven controversial because of the widely held belief that executives are grossly overpaid. Some view the continuing explosion in the pay of top executives—at the expense of shareholders and workers—as obscene, arrogant, and self-serving. For example, Kennedy-Wilson—an international real estate firm—paid its chairman and chief executive, William McMorrow, $3.7 million in 1999, a year when the company's net income was only $5.6 million! (Moore, 2000). Others, however, counter that executives are rightfully compensated for the increase in growth and innovativeness of American businesses over the last decade. They contend that with businesses booming, some of the results may need to be credited to the abilities of their leaders, beyond just pure luck.

A Mercer study (Lublin, 2000), based on the latest proxy statements from 350 major U.S. companies, indicated an upward trend in top executive salary as well as bonuses. Specifically, in 2000 the highest executive's median salary and bonus climbed to $1,688,088. Looking at the trend in total pay during the past decade, executives in the year 1999 got paid, on average, 442 percent more than their colleagues did in 1990 (Reingold & Grover, 1999). During the same period, the wages of non-exempt employees increased an average of just 34 percent (Gomez-Mejia, Balkin, & Cardy, 2001). The disparity in pay between those at the top of the corporate ladder and those at the bottom is increasing. For instance, while in

1965 top executives were paid 44 times a blue-collar worker's pay, that figure had jumped to 209 times by 1997 (Abrams, 1999).

The underlying objective of the compensation design is to encourage executives to pursue strategic decisions that provide the firm with a competitive advantage. The reward system plays a major role in how executive decisions are made because executives are very responsive to what they perceive will lead to a personal payoff. They are especially responsive to the incentive schemes designed for them, and will formulate policies for the entire organization if they believe they will help them to achieve the objectives needed to trigger incentive payments. Consequently, goals and objectives built into the executive compensation plan are likely to have a multiplier effect on the entire workforce. Simply put, because the top executive is the main strategist for the firm, his compensation package may have a significant effect on business decisions affecting the future of the entire organization.

In particular, executives are in a position to employ organizational resources to pursue objectives that might not be in the best interest of stockholders (Tosi, Werner, Katz, & Gomez-Mejia, 1999). Policy choices concerning growth, cutbacks, expansion, product diversification, investments in capital equipment, and R&D are the responsibility of top management. As a result, a pay package designed to reinforce the wrong strategic choices (for example, rewarding short-term results at the expense of long-term performance) can be highly detrimental to the firm's future success. Therefore, the use of incentives that reward executives for outcomes important to shareholders is fundamental. The purpose of this chapter is to provide an overview of key dimensions of compensation design, its major determinants, and its consequences for executives and the firm.

Executive Pay Dimensions

The pay mix of the compensation package affects the decision-making process of the chief executive officer. Pay mix can be analyzed in terms of fixed components (salary and benefits) and variable components (bonuses and long-term income). Table 8.1 presents the key elements of executive pay.

Table 8.1. Dimensions and Effects of Executive Pay Mix.

Fixed Components		Variable Components	
Salary	*Benefits*	*Bonus*	*Long-term income*
• Between 40 percent and 80 percent of total pay.	• Usually not linked to the achievement of specific goals.	• Short-term incentives linked to annual goals.	• Stock option plans encourage long-term strategic focus. However, their motivational value is highly dependent on the market.
• Less likely to influence strategic decisions because it is taken for granted.	• Include health care, life insurance, financial planning, health club membership, use of company cars or private jets, vacation packages, and so on.	• Since they are contingent on meeting certain expectations, the criteria used to trigger them must be carefully considered.	• As with bonuses, the dimensions on which stock options are granted can affect long-term firm performance.
• Encourages short-term strategic focus.	• Are difficult to justify.	• Some companies use guaranteed bonuses to attract and retain talented executives.	• The time frame for payoffs is critical, and restrictions need to be imposed on when options can be exercised.

Fixed Components of Executive Pay

The fixed dimension, also referred to as base pay, usually ranges between 40 percent and 80 percent of total executive compensation. The way in which fixed pay is determined is controversial, and determining what percentage of total pay the fixed components should consist of is more an art than a science. Firms face a choice of paying managers the same amount on a fixed basis or providing a portion of the manager's income on a variable basis. Fixed pay is less likely than variable pay to interfere with executive decision making since it is generally taken for granted. Heavy reliance on base salary can become dysfunctional, because if a large proportion of the executive's salary is taken for granted the executive will not be motivated to perform better. Also, because fixed pay is received annually, it encourages the executive to focus on the firm's performance for the fiscal year and to pay relatively little attention to long-term strategic issues.

Benefits are provided to the executive as a condition of employment, but they are usually not coupled with the achievement of strategic objectives. Benefits may include items such as health club membership, use of private jets, and vacation packages. For a growing number of chief executives a new batch of benefits promises a lifetime of care. These are "permanent perks," good for the life of the executive, and sometimes that of his spouse as well. Among these lifetime perks are a company car and driver, access to aircraft, and financial planning (Schellhardt & Lublin, 1999). Because these benefits are difficult to justify, they have been a target of criticism by those who feel executives earn more than they deserve. However, although the direct link between benefits and firm performance is weak, it could be argued that these perks can indirectly affect the executive's productivity. For example, providing a company jet or a car and driver for the executive could eliminate or minimize some distractions such as waiting in busy airports for delayed flights.

Variable Components of Executive Pay

Bonuses are short-term incentives linked to specific annual strategic goals. Because bonuses are contingent on meeting certain expectations, they carry more risk to the executive than the fixed components, but at the same time they can be more motivating. Executives are highly motivated individuals in terms of their work ethic, so in the context of executive pay the term *motivation* refers not to the level of effort exerted by the executive but to whether that effort is in keeping with the best interests of the shareholders. Although the primary interest of shareholders is an increase in the stock price of the firm, the executive could be interested in increasing the size of the firm through an acquisition—after all working for a larger company would justify an increase in her pay.

A major concern in executive compensation is that managers may take advantage of their position to pursue personal objectives at the expense of shareholders when shareholders are *widely dispersed*. This potential misalignment of interests can be controlled through the compensation design, using the bonus component of the pay scheme to align the goals of the company and its shareholders with the personal goals of the executive. Both quantitative and qualitative goals can be used as contingencies for bonus awards. Quantitative goals include earnings per share, dividends paid, revenues, return on equity, and net profit. Qualitative goals might include obtaining a government contract or investing in science and technology. Executive bonuses vary widely by industry, and in some industries, such as pharmaceuticals, bonus plans can reach 100 percent of base salary (Gomez-Mejia & Balkin, 1992). Although executive bonuses are extremely popular, they should be used with caution. Executives are likely to maximize whatever criteria are used to trigger the bonuses, sometimes at the expense of meeting other crucial goals such as customer relations and investments in R&D. As the bonus component approaches two-thirds of the executive's fixed salary, its effect on the executive's behavior can be powerful (Gomez-Mejia & Balkin, 1992).

Today it's not enough for executives to receive an enormous salary, a bonus, and a grant of stock options. Many of them are also accumulating "special" bonuses. In their proxy statements, companies explain these bonuses by citing a special achievement by the executive. Sometimes the described achievements sound like part of the job that the chief executive is already being rewarded for through all that other pay. For example, Thomas Unterman, executive vice president and chief financial officer of Times Mirror Co., received a $1 million award in 1998 for the "successful completion" of three divestitures (Schellhardt, 1999b). CEO Douglas Pinner of Tokheim Corp., a gasoline-pump maker, received a $150,000 bonus "for directing and accomplishing" an acquisition. In all, nearly 9 percent of companies in 1999 gave special awards to top executives, up from just 2 percent in 1995, according to William M. Mercer Inc., which analyzed the proxy statements of 350 major U.S. companies (Schellhardt, 1999b). In the past decade chief executive officers have not only received great increases in salary but also significant enhancements in contingent pay. This upward trend is not likely to change any time soon.

Some directors say they are using special awards to retain executives and avoid losing them to rivals. The Playtex Products chief executive officer, Michael Gallagher, got a special $1 million bonus in 1999 when the company's stock hit a threshold of $15 a share, then stayed at or above that price for 30 days. Under a "special price-based incentive" program, he could receive three additional $1 million awards if the stock price hit $20, $25, and $30 before June 30, 2000. The proxy statement for Playtex, an apparel maker based in Westport, Connecticut, indicates that the special award reflects the company's need to attract, retain, and motivate a chief executive officer of Gallagher's caliber.

Frustrated by the tight talent market, more companies now promise extended bonus payouts that aren't tied to performance. Hotly pursued executives are winning multiyear guaranteed payouts—often in addition to signing bonuses. Hewlett-Packard, for example, gave a $3 million signing bonus to its new chief executive officer, Carly Fiorina, to lure her away from Lucent Technologies in 1998. She also received a $365,000 guaranteed bonus for 1999 and was assured an additional $1.25 million bonus for 2000. The Internet consulting firm Lante Corp. enticed its president, Rudy Puryear, from Andersen Consulting in June 1999 with a three-year guaranteed bonus: $125,000 for the remainder of 1999, $250,000 in 2000, and $125,000 in 2001. That's on top of his $500,000 base salary, considered high for an Internet start-up. The whole point of a bonus is that it is supposed to rise and fall depending on firm performance. A guaranteed bonus is really contrary to that purpose. Many pay consultants say this practice attracts executives by minimizing the risks they face in leaving stable employment (Jurgens, 2000).

Long-term incentives are very complex. The wide variety of available plans can be divided into two groups: stock-based programs that make the executive part owner of the firm and plans that combine cash with equity-based compensation. The dimensions on which stock options are granted can have tremendous effects on a firm's long-term plans. If growth in market share is used as a criterion for providing stocks to the executive, the incumbent may be tempted to pursue an aggressive merger and acquisition program even if this is not in the best interest of shareholders. If stock options are granted based on profitability ratios, the executive may be tempted to reduce investments in R&D. Alternatively, if stock options are granted based on the number of patents granted to the firm, the quality of those patents may be overlooked.

A Mercer survey in 2000 suggests an increasing trend to grant stock options. Specifically, during 1999, 143 top executives cashed in stock options with a median gain of $2,857,676, exceeding the prior record of $2,770,185 set in 1998 (Lublin, 2000). One drawback of using stock options as motivational tools is that executives can anticipate personal financial gains regardless of their firm's performance as long as the stock market stays strong. The upward trend in granting options, however, does not parallel comparative increases in firm performance. The median total shareholder return of 350 major companies in 1999 was -3.9 percent even though their executives' total compensation jumped 10.8 percent to a median of $2,782,482. Companies often display a serious disconnection between pay packages and stock performance. Although Coca-Cola shares dropped 13 percent in 1999, forcing CEO Douglas Ivester into early retirement, he still received a generous exit package and consulting deal. And the value of his accumulated stock options rose $50 million, bringing his total compensation package to almost $70 million. Bank of America shares dropped nearly 17 percent, but CEO Hugh McColl appropriated $49 million in salary, bonuses, and restricted stock awards. Tyco International shares rose an anemic 3.4 percent, but CEO Dennis Kozlowski nonetheless pulled in $30.6 million in pay and bonus and exercised options for a $140 million gain. One consultant noted that options are the one part of the pay package where there's no discipline. *Business Week* (Foust, 2000) also noted a sudden rise in restricted stock grants, which generally don't link pay to performance, as well as in stock options. The reason for the restricted share surge is that stock options aren't attractive to executives at many "old economy" companies because their shares are suffering in a market infatuated with high-technology firms. Restricted shares or stock grants, on the other hand, are essentially gifts of stock, and unless they are linked to performance targets, executives get them simply by sticking around.

Even though the link between stock options and firm performance is not always positive, stock option plans serve to tie the executive's fate with that of the firm over the long run. Options can motivate executives to resist a takeover, and to encourage short-term risk taking by linking pay to longer-term results. Simply put, the motivational value of stock options lies in their shifting the executive's attention to the long-term fate of the firm. In some cases, restricted share grants are necessary to keep talented executives on board, especially in highly competitive industries. "When you have people in key positions and the company is making a lot of money, you can't lose them—you just can't," says B. Kenneth West, a Motorola director and senior corporate-governance consultant for TIAA-CREF, the world's largest pension fund. "It's a real conundrum. It puts compensation committees and boards in an uncomfortable position" (Lublin, 2000).

The most important drawback of stock options is that they reward absolute performance, with big financial rewards going to anyone who can get the stock to inch above the exercise price. Option plans do not take into account relative performance in either the overall market or in a company's industry group. Given recent years' bull markets, everyone has been able to make money out of options. However, giveaways of stock may not last. Excessive executive pay is a hot-button issue for disgruntled workers, shareholder activists, and corporate governance experts, who contend that the broad use of stock options reduces corporate earnings. The increasing use of options and restricted shares poses new risks to companies and shareholders. As more stock is issued to executives, other shareholders increasingly find their ownership diluted or weakened. In fact, under pressure from shareholder rights activists, restricted stock grants have fallen out of favor lately (Zuckerman, 2000). That's because—unlike options, which can become worthless if the price of the underlying stock falls—restricted stock grants can always be converted into cash once they mature. The only justification for giving grants that entitle executives to stock at some future date is to keep them from jumping to rivals. If the executives defect before their grants become due, they can't collect.

In summary, when designing long-term income plans, the time frame for payoffs must be carefully considered. If no restrictions are imposed on when stock options can be exercised, the executive may unload the stock when the stock price is higher. In high-technology firms, 3 years is an appropriate time horizon for dispensing rewards. In service industries, 10 to 15 years is more appropriate. The reason for this difference is that firms in high-technology industries experience greater variability in stock price than firms in service industries. In high-technology industries the rate of growth is faster and the probability for success lower due to constant product innovation demands. Therefore, it is suitable to allow executives of high-technology firms to "cash in" their stock options more frequently and benefit from an increase in stock price. Another important issue is whether executive tenure should be included as a criterion for exercising stock options. If longer tenure is desired, then tenure should be explicitly built into the formulas for exercising options. In high-technology firms, however, a shorter tenure may be desirable if the firm wishes to promote innovativeness. Limited executive tenure in these firms can result in fresh ideas being brought into the company and greater strategic experimentation by giving executives an opportunity to try new things. An additional important pay policy choice is whether the plan is contributory. Sharing part of the costs increases personal risk and aligns the executive's interests with the interests of the company. Finally, if continuous reinforcement is desired, stock purchase plans can be used to allow the executive to purchase stock at any time.

To conclude, the executive pay mix communicates what the organization values, what it desires, and what it rewards. When designing an executive compensation package it is essential that the rewards being proposed encourage the appropriate type of behavior. Annual salary and bonus serve to motivate executives in the short term while stock option plans serve to align their actions with the long-term performance of the firm. Firm performance at any given time is not a hard number measurement but only an estimate derived by using accounting conventions. Even if the firm is periodically audited by an independent accounting firm, executives enjoy great discretion in choosing the methodology to use in assessing the financial well-being of the company. To the extent that this same information is used for executive compensation purposes, there is an incentive for executives to develop a narrow focus to accomplish whatever will trigger the reward at the expense of other important dimensions of performance and even at the expense of stockholders. For example, if executives are being rewarded for bottom-line results at the end of the year—such as Return on Equity—they are more likely to select accounting choices that increase short-term reported earnings. This is where stock option plans come into play, to reward executives for enhancing firm performance measured by market value.

Variables That Explain Executive Pay

Firm Performance and Firm Size
Although firm performance is the most researched executive compensation criterion, its link to pay is weak at best. Objective measures of performance (such as ROE, ROA, market share, assets, market-to-book ratio) have been shown to be weak predictors of chief executive officer pay. Specifically, Tosi et al. (1999) found that accounting measures of firm performance explain only 5 percent of the variance in total chief executive officer pay. An extensive stream of research in performance appraisal in disciplines of industrial/organizational psychology and human resource management suggests that objective performance criteria are deficient because they contain many irrelevant factors, and that boards of directors should turn to measures of performance that include both objective and subjective assessments of the executive's performance. For example, in high-technology firms, basing executive pay on the number of patents granted to the firm per year would motivate executives to patent innovations at every step of the innovation process to reach their performance goals, and to neglect the quality of those patents since their compensation is not based on this criterion. Including a more subjective criterion for

assessing the executive's performance, such as the effectiveness of the research and development process, would lead to a better alignment of the executive's actions and to greater benefits for the firm in the long run.

Firm size, on the other hand, has been found to be an important predictor of the magnitude of the executive pay package. Empirical research to date points toward a weak relationship between firm performance and chief executive officer pay and a high correlation between company size and chief executive officer pay. In fact, firm size has been found to explain more than 50 percent of the variance in chief executive officer pay (Tosi et al., 1999). Although greater firm size (as represented by market share) tends to insulate firms from the downside effects of business cycles and may also create economies of scale and scope, it also has a dark side. For example, larger size can be accomplished through acquisitions, a strategy that has been shown to result in a decrease in stock price. In fact, acquisitions don't create value for acquiring firms. Acquiring firms' shareholders often get less than they pay for while those of target companies get stock gains of 20 percent to 30 percent (Inkpen, Sundaram, & Rockwood, 2000). Therefore, the appropriateness of using firm size as a criterion to set executive pay depends on strategic and contextual factors.

Labor Market

To attract and retain qualified executives a firm needs to maintain some parity with the market's going compensation rate. Very limited empirical research has been conducted on how the labor market rate affects the design of the executive compensation package—perhaps because it is difficult to define the market, or because executive pay packages are highly individualized and depend on the idiosyncrasies of the situation and the negotiation skills of both parties. Given the wide range of pay rates for executives even within the same industry, it's usually easy to gather and interpret market data to justify or legitimize a high compensation package for a particular executive. Thus determining the market rate is a difficult task. In addition, the people who set the executive's pay (that is, the members of the compensation committee) are usually friends of the executive, so there is an inherent conflict of interest that makes the judgment process subjective.

Peer Compensation

Social comparison theory argues that the compensation of selected peers may play a role in setting executive pay. Board members may use themselves as a reference point and base their executive pay recommendations on their own compensation. To underpay or overpay the incumbent against this standard produces cognitive dissonance, which executives from other firms who are members of the board's compensation committee will try to redress or bring into balance. From this perspective, firm performance plays a minor role in setting the executive's pay. In addition, executives themselves may have compensation expectations based on their comparisons with their own social reference points and might influence the board to discount the role of firm performance in measuring their worth. Compensation consultants tend to raise the bar for executive pay by examining pay packages and planned raises in a company's peer group. Typically, they'll recommend an executive be compensated in the 50th to 75th percentile of their peer group. "No compensation consultant is going to recommend that an executive take a paycut. They'll lose their job. It's part of the reason that chief executive officer pay is a never-ending spiral that always goes up" (Strauss, 2000, p. 1B).

Ownership Structure and Institutional Investors

Ownership concentration is associated with greater monitoring of the executive: Stockholders who own small amounts of stock will exercise less monitoring because they have less at stake in the firm. On the other hand, stockholders who own a significant fraction of a firm's stock (usually defined as 5 percent or more; Tosi & Gomez-Mejia, 1989) exhibit more intense monitoring of executives, and this is reflected in a tighter linkage between pay and firm performance, R&D investments, and level of diversification. In addition, greater ownership concentration is linked to fewer mergers and acquisitions that may be used to justify higher pay, less manipulation of firm performance data, less reliance on firm size as a basis to set executive pay, as well as less power and influence of the top executive on the board of directors. In management-controlled firms (that is, when management owns more than 5 percent of equity in the firm), top executives have the best of both worlds: their base salary is more strongly related to size, a relatively stable factor, and their bonuses are related to firm performance. On the other hand, in owner-controlled firms, firm performance is closely linked to top executive pay, but firm size is not. In this case, executives are in a riskier position because they are primarily rewarded for performance.

Institutional investors also have power over a firm's management through their large aggregate ownership, and they have recently emerged as an important group of shareholders. In fact, they have a direct effect on both the level and mix of top executive compensation; the presence of institutional stockholders is associated with a lower level of top executive compensation and a higher proportion of long-term incentives in the total compensation package. However, this relationship holds only for investors who can resist pressure—those who do not depend on firms they invest in for their own business and, therefore, are less likely to be affected by executive pressure.

The source of financing can also influence executive pay. Firms financed by venture capitalists tend to design the executive compensation package with a short-term orientation because their backers are more interested in short-term results. Pension funds, on the other hand, do not have similar pressures for immediate returns because of the longer time horizons of pensioners and the funds' habit of often holding stock for up to a decade. For that reason, pension funds have a long-term orientation when it comes to designing the executive compensation package.

Individual Characteristics

Human capital theory focuses on individual characteristics as predictors of executive pay. This perspective holds that executives accumulate "human capital" over time based on their learning. The total amount of learning at any given point determines how valuable the executive is to the firm and, in turn, how much the firm is willing to pay for the executive's services. Executives are generally highly educated and possess many years of work experience requiring much personal sacrifice. Therefore, their higher pay may be seen as a return on this human capital investment. Research suggests that human capital (as measured by years of education and firm and job tenure) and job responsibility level explain 69 percent of the variance in base pay level and 24 percent of the variance in bonus as a proportion of base pay (Gerhart & Milkovich, 1990). Therefore, human capital may help explain the relationship between firm size and executive pay; as firms get bigger, the executive's job becomes more demanding, so the executive would be compensated accordingly for the additional human capital required. As summarized by Agarwal (1981, p. 39) in a classic empirical paper on this issue: "The amount of human capital a worker possesses influences his productivity, which in turn influences his earnings. The same general reasoning should hold for executive workers as well. Other things being equal, an executive with a greater amount of human capital would be better able to perform his job and thus be paid more."

Role, Position, and Managerial Discretion

The weakness in the pay-performance connection may be tied to the executive's position or organizational role. Pay differentials between top executives and lower or middle managers can be deliberately designed to motivate lower and middle management performance: The top executive's position is presented as a prize to stimulate others to achieve it. This proposition is based on tournament theory (Lazear & Rosen, 1981), which postulates that the chief executive officer in a firm is seen by other people in the organization as the winner of a lottery. The enormous compensation he receives has little to do with personal performance; rather, it is used to energize the behavior of other managers.

Another way to explain the weak relationship between executive pay and firm performance is by considering the role of the executive as an arbitrator and a strategist. Executives are often expected to manage multiple coalitions within the firm and cater to the needs of those groups through personal charisma, bargaining, and consensus building. Therefore, executive pay could be based on how the executive's behaviors help meet the needs of those groups inside and outside the firm.

The opportunity for managerial discretion also influences executive pay; the greater the level of managerial discretion, the higher the level of pay. The greater the level of discretion, the greater the potential impact of the executive on the firm and, therefore, the greater the compensation level (Hambrick & Finkelstein, 1987). This can also be explained in the context of information processing.

In the case of high-discretion industries, multiple courses of action are possible; therefore, the level of information processing and the complexity of problems increase. In addition, as firms become more international, executives face more complexity and information processing. Consequently, the degree of internationalization is a predictor of executive pay. Adding to this, a firm's diversification strategy and level of R&D activity contribute to the information processing demands on the executive. Specifically, R&D activity is positively related to both long-term pay and total pay, and the degree of diversification is positively related to all three forms of executive pay (base salary, long-term compensation, and total compensation). Product diversity also increases the information processing demands on the executive, pushing the pay higher.

Capital intensity (that is, the amount of money invested in plant and equipment) is another important factor that affects managerial discretion and, subsequently, executive pay level. Capital intensity tends to make an organization less flexible and less accommodating to changes in strategy. When capital intensity is high, investment opportunities are limited, and managerial discretion is low; therefore, executive compensation is low. On the other hand, when capital intensity is low, executives have more discretion and their jobs are more complex, demanding, and risky, calling for higher levels of compensation.

Industry Structure and Market Conditions

Industry risk, complexity, and turbulence interact with compensation risk and influence the effectiveness of the executive compensation design. Research (Miller, Wiseman, & Gomez-Mejia, 2001) has shown that in highly complex and turbulent industries as well as in industries that are very stable, executive pay should be loosely linked with firm performance. When complexity is moderate, however, the link should be stronger. Another important factor that has implications for executive compensation is industry concentration. A highly concentrated industry would be one for which sales come from a few large companies. On the other hand, in industries that are less concentrated, the number of competing firms is greater. Less concentrated industries might require more capable executives to address the greater range of options and opportunities they face; therefore, they should be paid more than executives in more concentrated industries. Market growth also affects executive compensation because high-growth industries provide executives with more managerial discretion than low-growth industries, which in turn leads to higher pay.

Boards of Directors and Remuneration Committees

The job of the board is to assess executive performance and develop an appropriate compensation package. A firm's board is the primary internal corporate governance mechanism and represents shareholders. Personal interactions between executives and board members encourage the development of close relationships that go beyond the purely economic value created by the interaction. These relationships may influence both the longevity of the compensation contract (by allowing the executive to stay on beyond his useful contribution to the organization) and the price of the contract (by paying the executive a premium for his loyalty). Furthermore, trust between executive and board relaxes the need for clear performance criteria and increases the expectation that the evaluation of performance will be fair and reflect the changing conditions surrounding the contract (Zajac & Westphal, 1995).

Executive tenure has two effects on the pay-performance relationship. First, the more that owners or board members learn about the abilities of the executive, the less need there is to link executive pay to firm performance. This learning explanation suggests that, over time, owners or board members may trust the executive even in the absence of formal controls. Second, as executives become more entrenched, they can use their personal influence with the board to weaken the relationship between pay and performance. This suggests that, over time and in the absence of controls, the executive can take advantage of owners and board members. Therefore, longer executive tenure suggests that a close relationship exists between the executive and the board, which in turn helps to explain the lack of a consistent relationship between pay and performance.

Executive pay decisions are often delegated to a subgroup of the main board called the remuneration or compensation committee. In the absence of compensation committees, executives may have the opportunity to give themselves pay raises that are not congruent with shareholder interests. The members of a firm's compensation committee should be independent directors who are not managers in the firm. Even though compensation committees potentially have a positive role in the exercise of control, they are subject to influence by the top executive. In addition, chief executive officers may offer independent directors attractive contracts and consulting agreements with the firm. Finally, there is evidence that executive pay is significantly higher in companies that adopt remuneration committees (Daily, Johnson, Ellstrand, & Dalton, 1998). This observation can be explained by a social comparison model, which suggests that because executives set each other's pay on compensation committees, it is in their own best interest to set a high pay level for others as a means of raising their own pay level. A chief executive officer looking for personal enrichment could just select a compensation committee whose members earn more than she does. Because chief executive officer pay is related to the pay level of the board of directors, the power of chief executive officers to influence their boards helps to explain the weak pay-performance linkage.

Risk and Decision Making

Risk plays an important role in the design of an executive compensation package. Three types of risk are relevant here. First, *employment risk* represents the possibility that the executive will be terminated either due to unsatisfactory performance or insolvency of the business. Second, *compensation risk* represents the potential variability in the executive's future compensation represented by the proportion of variable pay in the total compensation package. Third, *risk in executive decision making* reflects the uncertainty inherent in decisions that are made in turbulent and dynamic competitive environments. All three types of risk can affect the risk tendencies of executives in their strategic decisions on behalf of the firm. This conclusion is based on research in decision making, which indicates that the risk preferences of individuals vary with other individual factors such as current wealth, likelihood of goal attainment, and the prospect for future change to personal wealth (Currim & Sarin, 1989; Kahneman & Tversky, 1979).

Although shareholders would prefer that the executive select investment options for the firm that carry higher potential returns (and thus higher risks), executives typically exhibit more risk-averse preferences in their strategic choices to minimize the probability of personal financial loss. Put differently, executives would prefer a low-risk/low-return strategy, shareholders would prefer a high-risk/high-return strategy (Hill & Snell, 1988). Executives exhibit risk-averse or risk-seeking behavior when choosing among strategic options based on their compensation contingencies.

Prospect theory (Kahneman & Tversky, 1979) helps explain why executives exhibit a consistent bias in their selections for or against risk. Specifically, it argues that the risk propensities of individuals change with the firm's performance context. According to prospect theory, executives who anticipate high firm performance would become risk averse. On the other hand, executives of firms with below-average profitability would prefer riskier alternatives to improve firm performance. So, when executive pay is strongly linked to firm performance, managers are risk seeking when facing poor firm performance, and risk averse otherwise. The implication here is that the incentive properties of the executive compensation package should match the expected performance horizon of the firm. A declining firm may prefer to promote risk taking by the chief executive officer in terms of investments in R&D by providing incentives that are linked to a financial turnaround. Simply put, the nature of the executive compensation package—and, consequently, the financial risk that is shifted onto executives—can have a major behavioral impact. The board of directors needs to anticipate how the incentive features in the executive compensation package will influence the executive's behavior. It is important to note, however, that the impact of the compensation mix emphasizing high or low risk sharing depends on the individual's propensity to take risks. Because risk orientation is idiosyncratic, an executive's response to risk, although influenced by the compensation contract, also depends on his personal decision-making approach.

As discussed earlier, the compensation package can be outlined along two dimensions: variable pay (such as bonuses and stock options) and fixed pay (salary and perks). They each represent different aspects of executive wealth, carry different risks or threats to wealth, and exert varying influences on executive risk taking. Fixed pay represents a moderate threat to wealth as uncertainty in fixed pay can lead to an erosion of buying power (that is, fixed pay is tied directly to the executive's customary standard of living). Bonuses represent the least threat to wealth because they are not counted as part of wealth until they are actually awarded (that is, they are an unreliable source of income). In cases where bonuses are regularly awarded, they become more like an entitlement and thus more like fixed pay. However, contingent pay such as stock options is subject to more uncertainty than fixed pay because the amount and timing of the former are not known in advance. Although stock options can be valued in the present, this value represents only an estimate of their ultimate value as the value actually realized from those options when they are eventually exercised is dependent on firm performance at that time. Because variable pay carries more uncertainty than fixed pay, increases in the proportion of variable pay to total pay transfers more risk to the executive by placing more of his own wealth at risk. As a result, the executive may become risk averse. The amount of compensation risk incurred by the executive is expected to have a direct effect on managerial decisions such as capital investments, R&D expenditures, diversification, and mergers and acquisitions.

What Is the Ideal Level of Risk?

The amount of risk transferred to the executive through compensation design can have both positive and negative effects on risk-taking behavior. On one hand, stronger links between executive pay and firm performance presumably reduce risk aversion by executives if the executive perceives a positive relationship between risk and returns. In contrast, a tight link between pay and performance can lead executives to become risk averse if they perceive a negative relationship between risk and performance, thereby avoiding risky strategic options. One resolution is to moderately link pay to firm performance, which can facilitate the "right" strategic decisions. But after a certain point, more risk shifting to the executive might encourage overly cautious and conservative decision making (Wiseman & Gomez-Mejia, 1998).

Motivational Effects of Executive Pay

Firm performance can be significantly affected by the degree to which executive compensation strategies reinforce or match corporate strategies. However, it is unclear whether compensation decisions guide the selection of strategy or follow strategy. In any case, aligning executive pay with the firm's short- and long-term strategic goals is of paramount importance because executives are the ones responsible for investing the firm's capital and also for making investments pertaining to R&D.

Compensation experts recently have focused on other intermediate factors affecting executive pay such as the degree of international diversification and the level of R&D investment. Whether executives affect firm performance directly or indirectly through their investment decisions and acquisition and diversification strategies, the manner in which they are rewarded is a salient and enduring concern. Executives may become overly conservative and adopt a shorter time horizon, by investing less in R&D, if their compensation package has a substantial downside risk or if the return on that R&D investment falls below expectations. In addition, the growth strategy adopted by the firm may be influenced by how executives are rewarded. If their pay is closely linked to firm size, they may be inclined to diversify or pursue mergers and acquisitions. Also, executives may avoid entering product markets characterized by volatile stock prices if a substantial portion of their pay is linked to equity market performance measures.

Finally, if the executive compensation package provides for a substantial lump sum payment (golden parachute) in case of a takeover, the executive may lack the motivation to fight the takeover or to perform exceptionally well. A *golden parachute* is a contractual obligation to provide top executives with a large lump sum payment if they are involuntarily replaced, and is intended to be a bridge to the executive's next opportunity. At the managerial level a typical severance package includes two to three weeks of salary for every year of service; at the executive level, it includes three to five years of earnings. Recent evidence of generous parachutes granted to departing top executives suggests that failure often pays. Even if a company moves against an underperforming chief executive officer, it must pay out as much to get the officer to leave as it would have paid if the chief executive officer had been successful. Examples include the ousting of Procter & Gamble CEO Durk I. Jager, who pocketed a $9.5 million bonus for 17 months' worth of not-so-great work (P&G's stock dropped by 50 percent during that period, costing shareholders more than $70 billion in wealth). In addition, Halliburton's board awarded CEO Richard B. Cheney an exit package worth $13.6 million, and Mattel granted ex-CEO Jill E. Barad a $50 million exit package, excluding stock options, following three quarters of losses (Foust, 2000). Often, these departing chief executive officers do not even have to pay taxes on the money. According to Executive Compensation Advisory Services, in 1999, 52 percent of companies had agreed to pay any taxes resulting from "excessive" parachute payments (Reingold & Grover, 1999). Simply put, most chief executive officers nowadays can bank a hefty farewell kiss from former employers, despite failing performance.

Another reason why executive pay is so important is because of its cascading effect on the compensation structure of the entire organization. Differences in pay between managerial levels revolve around 33 percent so that higher pay at the top is associated with higher pay at lower management levels (Gomez-Mejia, Tosi, & Hinkin, 1987). In addition, an executive whose pay package is tied to financial measures of performance is likely to develop an incentive system for lower-level managers that rewards similar types of indicators.

Contagion Effect Across International Markets

Trends in the past few years suggest that executive pay policies are imitated across U.S. borders, in response to the increasing globalization of markets. Performance-based bonuses are on the rise at the average European company, and in the majority of countries, more managers are receiving bonuses that form a bigger portion of their overall compensation package, according to a study conducted by a group of European compensation specialists in 1999 (Richter, 1999). In Europe, many companies are considering adding a stock option component to their compensation design, in part to keep competitive parity with U.S. firms. Even in Japan, where egalitarian pay structures have long been considered the norm, an increasing number of companies are trying out options. A 1999 Mercer study (Schellhardt, 1999a) found that the base salary of U.S. chief executive officers averaged 40 percent higher than that of their British counterparts, and their bonuses averaged 210 percent of base salary, compared with just 50 percent for the British chief executive officers. The biggest difference, however, was in the level of unrealized stock-option gains. The American chief executive officers, on average, were sitting on an astounding $80 million in paper gains, their British counterparts had $2 million each in such unrealized gains.

In the Netherlands, 72 percent of top executives received bonuses valued at 25 percent of their base salary for 1999 (Rocks, 1999). A year earlier, 56 percent of received bonuses were valued at 20 percent of their base pay. In some countries, the shift toward variable pay came at the expense of increases in base pay. Despite the recent economic turnaround in France, French companies "are still not increasing base salaries across the board. They prefer to make payments more individual by increasing variable pay" (Rocks, 1999). Overall, Switzerland's top managers were Europe's top earners, leading the list with an average base pay of 229,000 euros ($239,000). Denmark and western Germany follow with 227,000 euros and 192,000 euros, respectively (Rocks, 1999).

In Central Europe, most executive pay packages are simple enough: salary plus performance-linked bonus, with the bonus rarely exceeding the salary (Rocks, 1999). Consider Svatoslav Novak, the chief executive of Czech-based SPT Telecom. His bonus is based on profitability, consumer satisfaction, and network growth, all of which can be quantified with surveys and statistics. But one thing is often missing: a link with the company's stock market performance. The concept of building shareholder value into the compensation equation—as is often done in the United States via stock options—is only just starting to catch on abroad. Consider the impact at a company like Ceske Radiokomunikace. Shares nearly tripled over the last 12 months, with market capitalization rising by 26.7 billion korunas ($894.3 million). The company's chief executive officer, Miroslav Curin, says he earned less than 100,000 korunas a month last year; his bonus wasn't linked to the share price. His total compensation: less than $80,000 a year. "Options should be one of the instruments used to motivate managers to focus on shareholder value," Curin says, "but they haven't really taken off here yet." Some companies are testing different approaches, especially in the two other large Central European countries: Hungary and Poland. Thus, in Central Europe, companies are trying to figure out how to introduce options.

Executive-compensation growth in Canada is accelerating but still lags well behind U.S. pay scales, according to an international study by Towers Perrin (Greenberg, 1998). Towers Perrin found in its 1998 Worldwide Total Rewards survey of 23 countries that the average total compensation for a chief executive in Canada was $498,118 a year, well below U.S. chief executive officers' average pay of $1.07 million. Executive wages are clearly moving up in Canada to try to catch up with the United States. The problem is that the United States keeps pulling ahead.

Concluding Remarks

It is evident that the nature of the executive compensation design affects a range of executive decisions, and that selecting incongruous criteria to reward executives could lead to negative consequences for firms. Let's not forget Albert Dunlap, chief executive officer of Scott Paper, who—after working for less than two years—walked away in 1996 with nearly $100 million in salary, bonuses, stock gains, and other perks. Some have argued that he earned that money by pumping short-term results at the expense of long-term performance by reducing R&D investments by 50 percent and introducing 107 so-called new products to the market through simple changes in packaging (Byner & Weber, 1996, p. 44).

Practitioners face a wide variety of options when designing executive pay packages, and many judgment calls need to be made because prescriptive statements are of little value. At most companies, the standard for executive compensation planning is a pay package that can attract, motivate, and retain employees combined with pay-for-performance guidelines designed to enhance shareholder value. However, the effectiveness of the reward system depends on the fit between the pay strategies in use and the nature of the firm. Under conditions of very high or very low environmental uncertainty, Miller, Wiseman, and Gomez-Mejia (2001) found that the link between chief executive officer pay and firm performance is almost zero; under conditions of medium uncertainty this link is fairly large. This suggests that the performance criteria on which executives would be evaluated should be based on the firm's idiosyncratic circumstances. For example, the incentive system for firms competing in high-technology markets should induce executives to make resource allocation decisions that would assist the firm in sustaining its innovation capability (Balkin, Markman, & Gomez-Mejia, forthcoming). Because innovation requires making long-term investments in R&D projects that may have a negative impact on more immediate financial statements (Hoskisson, Hitt, & Hill, 1993), high-technology firms should link executive pay to evidence of innovation efforts. At the same time, because complexity makes the relationship between executives' actions and firm performance very uncertain in high-technology markets, executive compensation packages may be loosely coupled with accounting performance outcomes. In short, the design of the executive compensation package should reflect the firm's unique characteristics and the particular conditions facing it.

In summary, there are some key issues to keep in mind when rewarding executives:

- Executives will tend to maximize whatever is being rewarded. In this sense they are not any different from most employees. However, the stakes are very high in that executives make fundamental decisions that affect the entire organization.
- In designing executive compensation programs, it is important to examine the behavioral implications of the criteria and the pay mix being used to reward the executive. For instance, reliance on quantitative criteria may lead to manipulation of those criteria, something that can be extraordinarily difficult to detect. Likewise, transferring too much risk to the executive may lead to lost opportunities for shareholders as the executive responds by becoming overly cautious.
- Developing an effective executive compensation program is more of an art than a science. The board needs to consider a variety of factors, many of which require clinical judgment. No two firms are alike, so the board needs to consider the firm's strategy, its market niche, performance trends, scale of operations, its particular labor market for executives, and the desires of large shareholders.

- The way executives are rewarded provides a vivid example for all employees of what the organization considers important. This is likely to affect the climate of the entire organization. For instance, providing lavish perks and lucrative stock options exclusively for the top executive may demoralize lower-level managers—particularly when these rewards are seen as undeserved, as is often the case when they are offered during periods of declining performance.

References

Abrams, R. (1999, February 5). "Wear clean underwear: Business wisdom from Mom." *Business Week,* online edition.

Agarwal, N. C. (1981). "Determinants of executive compensation." *Industrial Relations, 20*(1), 36–46.

Balkin, D. B., Markman, G. D., & Gomez-Mejia, L. R. (forthcoming). "Is CEO pay in high technology firms related to innovation? Some empirical evidence." *Academy of Management Journal, 43*(6), 1118–1129.

Byner, J. A., & Weber, J. (1996, January 15). "The shredder." *Business Week,* pp. 44–49.

Currim, I., & Sarin, R. K. (1989). "Prospect versus utility." *Management Science, 35,* 22–41.

Daily, C. M., Johnson, J. L., Ellstrand, A. E., & Dalton D. R. (1998). "Compensation committee composition as a determinant of CEO compensation." *Academy of Management Journal, 41*(2), 209–220.

Foust, D. (2000, September 11). "CEO pay: Nothing succeeds like failure." *Business Week,* online edition.

Gerhart, B., & Milkovich, G. T. (1990). "Organizational differences in managerial compensation and financial performance." *Academy of Management Journal, 33*(4), 663–691.

Gomez-Mejia, L. R., & Balkin, D. B. (1992). *Compensation, organizational strategy and firm performance.* Cincinnati, OH: South-Western.

Gomez-Mejia, L. R., Balkin, D. B., & Cardy, R. (2001). *Managing human resources.* Upper Saddle River, NJ: Prentice Hall.

Gomez-Mejia, L. R., Tosi, H., & Hinkin, T. (1987). "Managerial control, performance, and executive compensation." *Academy of Management Journal, 30*(1), 51–70.

Greenberg, L. M. (1998, December 23). "Canadian professionals' compensation trails that of their U.S. counterparts," *Wall Street Journal,* online edition.

Hambrick, D. C., & Finkelstein, S. (1987). "Managerial discretion: A bridge between polar views of organizational outcomes." In L. L.

Cummings & B. M. Staw (Eds.), *Research in organizational behavior* (Vol. 9), pp. 369–406. Greenwich, CT: JAI Press.

Hill, C. W., & Snell, S. (1988). "External control systems and relative R&D investments in large multi-product firms." *Strategic Management Journal, 9,* 577–590.

Hoskisson, R. E., Hitt, M. A., & Hill, C. W. (1993). "Managerial incentives and investment in R&D in large multiproduct firms." *Organization Science, 4,* 325–341.

Inkpen, A., Sundaram, A., & Rockwood, K. (2000). "Cross-border acquisitions of U.S. technology assets." *California Management Review, 42*(3), 50–71.

Jurgens, R. (2000, April 6). "Look out below: Does a big pay gap between the top executive and the next tier feed turnover?" *Wall Street Journal,* online edition.

Kahneman, D., & Tversky, A. (1979). "Prospect theory: An analysis of decisions under risk." *Econometrica, 47,* 262–291.

Lazear, E. D., & Rosen, S. (1981). "Rank order tournaments as optimum labor contracts." *Journal of Political Economy, 89,* 841–864.

Lublin, J. S. (2000, April 13). "Executive pay: Dot-com bonanza spills over. Old economy firms adopt new compensation strategies." *Wall Street Journal,* online edition.

Miller, J., Wiseman, R., & Gomez-Mejia, L. R. (2001). "The influence of business risk on executive pay," Unpublished manuscript, University of Wisconsin, Milwaukee.

Moore, L. B. (2000, May 31). "Kennedy-Wilson's cheap stock may not counter CEO's rich pay," *Wall Street Journal,* online edition.

Reingold, J., & Grover, R. (1999, April 19). "Special report: Executive pay." *Business Week,* online edition.

Richter, K. (1999, June 30). "Performance-based bonuses become more popular in Europe." *Wall Street Journal,* online edition.

Rocks, D. (1999, January 25). "Central Europe's top 10 executives: Fresh incentives: For top jobs, the East-West pay disparity virtually vanishes." *Wall Street Journal,* online edition.

Schellhardt, T. D. (1999a, April 8). "A marriage of unequals: When executives at one merger partner make a lot more than their counterparts, it can make for some rocky times." *Wall Street Journal,* online edition.

Schellhardt, T. D. (1999b, April 29). "Pay: To a pile of CEO perks, add the 'special' bonus." *Wall Street Journal,* online edition.

Schellhardt, T. D., & Lublin, J. S. (1999, July 6). "Career matters: All the rage among CEOs: Lifetime perks." *Wall Street Journal,* online edition.

Strauss, G. (2000, April 5). "The Billionaires Club: New economy rockets CEO pay into the stratosphere." *USA Today*, pp. 1B–3B.

Tosi, H. L., & Gomez-Mejia, L. R. (1989). "The decoupling of CEO pay and performance: An agency theory perspective." *Administrative Science Quarterly, 34*(2), 169–218.

Tosi, H. L., Werner, S., Katz, J., & Gomez-Mejia, L. R. (1999). "How much does performance matter: A meta-analysis of CEO compensation studies." *Journal of Management, 26*(2), 301–339.

Wiseman, R. M., & Gomez-Mejia, L. R. (1998). "A behavioral agency model of managerial risk taking." *Academy of Management Review, 23*(1), 133–153.

Zajac, E. J., & Westphal, J. D. (1995). "Accounting for the explanations of CEO compensation: Substance and symbolism." *Administrative Science Quarterly, 40*, 283–308.

Zuckerman, S. (2000, March 21). "BofA paid CEO $76 million last year. Some analysts call it major overpayment." *San Francisco Chronicle*, p. C1.

PART THREE

Understanding Executive Perspectives

CHAPTER 9

Finding the Key to the Executive Suite

Challenges for Women and People of Color

Karen S. Lyness

Although women and people of color have made progress in attaining managerial positions, they are still not well represented at executive levels. Morrison and von Glinow (1990) suggested that female managers and managers of color encounter a "glass ceiling," defined as "a barrier so subtle that it is transparent, yet so strong that it prevents women and minorities from moving up in the management hierarchy" (p. 200). Current thinking is that instances of overt discrimination are becoming increasingly rare. Rather than disappearing altogether, however, discrimination against women and people of color has become more subtle and may be reflected, for example, in cultural norms or work practices that inadvertently disadvantage these groups (for example, see Meyerson & Fletcher, 2000). For instance, in organizations where contributions are measured by "face time" rather than actual accomplishments, women who spend less time at work due to their family responsibilities are at a disadvantage. Although men who spend less time at work would be similarly penalized, the majority of domestic responsibilities are still carried out by women (Shelton & John, 1996), suggesting that mostly women are disadvantaged by this practice. Also, selection of executives may be based on subjective factors such as informal networks and the comfort level of other executives, which may result in subtle selection bias favoring those who demographically resemble current executives (that is, white males).

Much of the published research literature about executives has focused on white males—the traditional incumbents in these jobs. Less is known about the careers of nontraditional executives, including women and people of color, perhaps because until recently few had made it to senior management. The goal of this chapter is to review what we know about nontraditional executives, including their current representation in managerial and executive jobs, the organizational barriers and challenges they face, and factors contributing to their career advancement. The chapter concludes with some action steps and recommendations for organizations that want to increase diversity at senior management levels.

Current Representation at the Executive Level

Table 9.1 presents an overview of the current representation of women and people of color in managerial and executive positions. In 1999 women held about 45 percent of the executive, administrative, and managerial jobs, which is similar to their representation in the labor force (U.S. Department of Labor, 2000). However, women were better represented at management levels in the public sector, where they held about 51 percent of the management positions, than in the private sector, where they held less than 33 percent of the management positions (U.S. Equal Employment Opportunity Commission, 1998).

Within Fortune 500 companies the majority of senior managers are men, with women holding only about 12 percent of the corporate officer positions, 6.8 percent of the line corporate officer positions, and 3.3 percent of the top-paying corporate officer positions (Catalyst, 1999a). Less is known about current gender composition of executives beyond the Fortune 500, although women were reported to hold only 3–5 percent of senior management positions in the largest 1,500 U.S. companies in 1992 (Glass Ceiling Commission, 1995). Even within the Internet industry, which has claimed to be free of traditional prejudices, only 8 percent of chief executive officers of 150 public Internet companies are women, and women hold 15 percent or less of several other key officer positions in these companies (Silverman, 2000).

Table 9.1. Representation of Nontraditional Managers and Executives.

			Percentage		
Demographic Group	U.S. Labor Force[a]	Executives, Administrators, and Managers[a]	Public Sector Officials and Administrators[a]	Private Sector Managers and Officials[b]	Fortune 500 Corporate Officers[c]
Women	46.5	45.1	51.1	32.7	11.9
Women of color					1.3
African Americans	11.3	7.6	14.0	5.9	
Hispanic Americans	10.3	5.6	4.9	3.9	
Asian Americans & Pacific Islanders				2.8	
Native Americans & Alaskan Indians				0.4	

Source: (a) U.S. Department of Labor, 2000; (b) U.S. Equal Employment Opportunity Commission, 1998; (c) Catalyst, 1999a.

People of color are less well represented than women among the managerial ranks. African Americans held about 8 percent and Hispanic Americans held about 6 percent of the executive, administrative, and managerial jobs in 1999, which is somewhat less than their proportions in the labor force (U.S. Department of Labor, 2000). African Americans held 14 percent of public sector management positions and about 6 percent of private sector management positions, and Hispanic Americans held less than 5 percent of the management jobs in either sector. Asian Americans held about 3 percent and Native Americans held less than 1 percent of the private-sector management positions (U.S. Equal Employment Opportunity Commission, 1998).

In 1999 the Catalyst census presented separate statistics for women of color, who were found to hold only 1.3 percent of the corporate officer positions in Fortune 500 companies (Catalyst, 1999a). African American women occupied the majority of these positions (67), followed by Asian Americans/Pacific Islanders (21) and Hispanic Americans (17).

There is also evidence of occupational segregation, such that women and people of color tend to work in support functions, including human resources, communications, public relations, diversity management, and customer relations (Glass Ceiling Commission, 1995), which often have less potential for advancement and lower compensation than line positions or jobs in core business functions. There are also differences in the types of jobs held by different minority groups. For example, Asian American women were found to be less likely to manage other people and more likely to work in engineering or research and development jobs than African American or Hispanic American women (Catalyst, 1999b).

Why a Glass Ceiling?

A number of explanations have been offered for the glass ceiling (for example, Collins, 1997; Cox, 1994; Morrison & von Glinow, 1990; Nieva & Gutek, 1981; Powell, 1999). The major categories include the following:

- *Person-centered explanations* attribute lack of advancement of women and people of color to gender or racial and ethnic differences in necessary educational qualifications, experience, skills, behaviors, or traits. For example, it has been suggested that not many women have made it to senior management due to gender differences in leadership abilities, political savvy, or willingness to work long hours. Other reasons for lack of advancement include self-selection and personal choices, such as a preference for staff positions like human resources or community relations, or taking time off to raise a family.

- *Explanations based on structural factors* (for example, Kanter, 1977a) attribute lack of advancement by women and people of color to discrimination and segregation in the labor market, resulting in their confinement to less desirable jobs than those held by white males. For example, women and minorities tend to be tracked into staff positions with limited authority and advancement potential rather than into core business functions that lead to executive positions (Collins, 1997; Ragins & Sundstrom, 1989).

- *Explanations based on stereotypes* (for example, Heilman, 1983, 1995; Ruble, Cohen, & Ruble, 1984) attribute lack of advancement by women and people of color to biases of organizational decision makers who make assumptions about individuals based on beliefs about gender or racial groups, resulting in discrimination against nontraditional candidates (that is, women or minorities) for executive positions. For example, women may be less likely to be chosen for executive positions that are typically held by men due to beliefs that women in general are less likely than men to have the attributes needed to succeed (Heilman, 1983).

Opinions differ about whether the progress to date, as reflected by movement of women and people of color into lower and middle management, should lead to optimism that over time they will be well represented at executive levels as well. According to the *pipeline argument,* because women and people of color have now moved into management, they are in the pipeline for further advancement and over time can be expected to advance to senior management. It has been argued, for example, that in order to reach the highest level corporate positions, managers need many years of organizational experience as well as degrees from well-regarded educational institutions; representation of women and people of color will not increase at executive levels until these individuals have accumulated the necessary experience and credentials (Ward, Orazem, & Schmidt, 1992). Optimism about the pipeline argument is due in part to beliefs about the underlying causes of the glass ceiling for women and minorities. If all nontraditional candidates need is more experience and a chance to develop their skills, then time should help to rectify these shortcomings. If, on the other hand, there are well-entrenched organizational barriers to their advancement, it is harder to be so optimistic (Gutek, 1993). It is important that we have an accurate understanding about why the glass ceiling persists for nontraditional managers because our definition of the problem can determine our approach to solving it (Nieva & Gutek, 1981).

Women's Career Issues

In this section I review barriers to advancement for women, the challenges they face as nontraditional executives, and factors shown to facilitate their career success.

Barriers to Advancement for Women

Comparable Qualifications Do Not Ensure Comparable Career Success
There is less evidence to support person-centered explanations about the glass ceiling for women than explanations based on structural factors or stereotypes (Morrison & von Glinow, 1990; Powell, 1999). For example, longitudinal studies tracking comparably qualified female and male MBA-program graduates have found that the women had made less progress in career advancement and compensation than had their male counterparts (for example, see Cox & Harquail, 1991; Olson, Frieze, & Good, 1987; Schneer & Reitman, 1994). Also, male managers have been found to gain more in compensation than have female managers by changing companies (Brett & Stroh, 1997). In addition, research has indicated that female managers in Fortune 500 companies who had "all the right stuff," including education, work experience, and willingness to relocate, lagged behind their male counterparts in compensation (Stroh, Brett, & Reilly, 1992). There is evidence that even after controlling for age, education, tenure, salary grade, and

type of job, women were rated by their supervisors as having less promotion potential than their male counterparts (Landau, 1995). Other research found that structural factors influence women's evaluations such that women received lower performance ratings than men when their work groups had a small proportion of women, even after the researchers controlled for any male-female differences in abilities, education, and tenure (Sackett, DuBois, & Noe, 1991).

Taken together these studies suggest that comparable qualifications do not necessarily ensure comparable career success for women and men. In fact, women's advancement may be hindered by organizational barriers such as those shown in Table 9.2 and discussed in subsequent sections.

Difficulties Obtaining Mentoring

Evidence is mixed about gender differences in access to mentoring relationships (see Ragins, 1999), but research has shown that women often face barriers to obtaining mentors, such as the lack of women at senior levels and potential mentors being unwilling to enter relationships with them. On the other hand, women reported a greater need for mentoring than men (Ragins & Cotton, 1991), suggesting that lack of access to effective mentoring could be a significant barrier to their advancement. Other research on graduates of nine MBA programs found that women were less likely than men to have white male mentors, and that having white male (but not female or minority) mentors was associated with greater earnings (Dreher & Cox, 1996).

Not Being Given Stretch Assignments

Development of critical skills needed for advancement often occurs through *stretch assignments*—exposure to challenging job assignments and novel situations that require managers to use previously untested skills and approaches. Yet female managers may be less likely than male managers to be given certain types of stretch assignments, including jobs involving risk or exposure to new parts of the business (Ruderman, Ohlott, & McCauley, 1990; Van Velsor & Hughes, 1990), opportunities for overseas assignments (Adler, 1984; Lyness & Thompson, 2000), and line assignments (Olson et al., 1987). An unanswered question for some of these studies, however,

Table 9.2. Examples of Organizational Barriers for Nontraditional Managers and Executives.

	Women	People of Color
Barriers to Advancement for Managers	• Difficulties obtaining mentoring • Not being given stretch assignments • Selection bias due to sex stereotyping • Tracking into dead-end jobs • Being held to a higher standard • Difficulty balancing work and non-work responsibilities	• Lack of informal networking • Lack of role models from their own racial/ethnic group • Racial stereotypes and prejudice • Not being given stretch assignments or visibility • Difficulties obtaining mentoring • Being held to a higher standard • White managers' lack of comfort with people of color • Difficulties obtaining sponsors
Additional Challenges for Executives	• Not fitting the (male-dominated) organizational culture • Less personal support • Stress of being tokens • Social isolation • Being stereotyped as women rather than executives • Performance pressure due to their heightened visibility • Femininity-competence double bind	• Tracking into jobs related to their cultural backgrounds • Stress of being tokens • Loss of group identity • Social isolation • Being viewed as representatives of their racial or ethnic groups rather than executives • Not fitting the organizational culture

is exactly why women were less likely to get these critical opportunities. It is possible, for example, that women may be less interested in certain types of assignments or relocations that may help to advance their careers.

Selection Bias Due to Sex Stereotyping

Both women's lack of advancement and failure to receive stretch assignments may also be due in part to gender bias in staffing or promotion decisions due to sex stereotyping and preconceptions of organizational decision makers. Sex stereotypes are defined as widely shared beliefs about the attributes of women (for example, nurturance) and the attributes of men (for example, achievement orientation) (Heilman, 1983; Ruble et al., 1984). Skills and attributes thought to be needed for management jobs are more similar to characteristics traditionally associated with men rather than with women (Heilman, Block, Martell, & Simon, 1989; Schein, 1973, 1975). Also, jobs become gender-typed according to whether they are typically held by men or women (Krefting, Berger, & Wallace, 1978). According to Heilman's lack of fit model (1983), men are more likely to be chosen than women for male gender-typed jobs because men are thought to be more likely to perform successfully since they have the needed skills and personality characteristics. Because many critical developmental assignments (for example, line jobs) are typically held by men, these assignments may be male gender-typed, resulting in subtle gender bias against women when decisions are made about filling these positions. Also, organizations are sometimes more cautious about taking risks on women than men in promotions to jobs with unfamiliar responsibilities (Ruderman, Ohlott, & Kram, 1996). By missing out on important developmental assignments, female managers may find it more difficult than male managers do to acquire and demonstrate that they have the skills needed to advance to senior management.

Tracking into Dead-End Jobs

According to contextual explanations such as Kanter's structural theory (1977a), staffing decisions tend to be biased in favor of the dominant group (that is, men) because they tend to select others who are similar to themselves. This may lead to organizational tracking processes that perpetuate gender differences in careers by tracking entry-level men into high-power career paths, while tracking women into dead-end jobs in departments with limited opportunity for promotion (Ragins & Sundstrom, 1989).

Being Held to a Higher Standard

In addition to potential bias in staffing decisions, there is evidence that women may be held to a higher standard for promotions (Cannings & Montmarquette, 1991; Gerhart & Milkovich, 1989). Also, if women are successful in male gender-typed jobs, their performance may be discounted by attributing it to luck or effort rather than more stable internal characteristics such as ability (Greenhaus & Parasuraman, 1993). Thus, even if women are successful in jobs not typically held by women, their performance may not have as much organizational payoff or may be less likely to lead to advancement than similar performance by their male counterparts.

Difficulty Balancing Work and Non-Work Responsibilities

Although societal norms are changing, many women still devote more time to family and other non-work responsibilities than do their male counterparts. Non-work responsibilities can take time away from the long hours that are required for advancement. Also, organizations often have cultures that reflect male values (Acker, 1990; Kanter, 1977a). Employees who are viewed as committed only to their jobs tend to be rewarded with promotions, but employees who divide their commitments between their jobs and family are plateaued at lower levels (Acker, 1990). Support for the theory that organizational cultures reflect male values was provided by longitudinal research showing that managers who had taken family leaves of absence received fewer subsequent promotions and smaller salary increases than did managers who had not taken leaves, even with controls for performance ratings (Judiesch & Lyness, 1999). Although this study found similar penalties for male and female managers who took leaves of absence, almost 90 percent of the leaves were taken by women, suggesting that the leave penalties applied primarily to women's careers.

Additional Challenges for Executives

Female executives face many of the same organizational barriers as female managers (see Table 9.2.), plus other challenges that may be due in part to the small number of executive women in most organizations. For example, women at higher management levels reported greater obstacles, such as not fitting the (male-dominated) organizational culture and less personal support, than did women at lower management levels, but these differences by level were not found for men (Lyness & Thompson, 1997). Even in organizations with a good track record of promoting women, women at higher levels in the management hierarchy might receive fewer promotions than men at comparable levels (Hartmann, 1987; Lyness & Judiesch, 1999). In addition, a study of comparable female and male executives found that the women reported less satisfaction with future career opportunities at their organization than did the men (Lyness & Thompson, 1997). Other challenges for female executives include stress associated with their token status and the femininity-competence double bind.

Stress of Being Tokens

According to tokenism theory (Kanter, 1977a, 1977b) the skewed sex ratios at senior levels can affect interactions between the dominant group (men) and the token group (women). For example, men may exaggerate differences between themselves and the token women, leading to negative consequences for the women including social isolation, being stereotyped as women rather than executives, and performance pressure due to their heightened visibility.

Support for this theory was provided by a survey of women at the vice presidential level or above, who reported "male stereotyping and preconceptions of women" as the greatest barrier to their advancement (Catalyst, 1996, p. 37). Also, women at the highest corporate levels reported being excluded from informal networks with male peers (Davies-Netzley, 1998; Moore, 1988). In addition, female executives reported that they had experienced greater barriers to advancement than did their male counterparts, including lack of fit with the (male-dominated) culture, exclusion from informal networks, and difficulty with work-life balance (Levey, Johnson, & Civian, 1999; Lyness & Thompson, 2000). The personal consequences of token status were illustrated by a British study where women reported stress due to lack of same-gender role models, gender stereotyping, and men appearing to be uncomfortable working with them (Davidson & Cooper, 1986).

Femininity-Competence Double Bind

One of the most difficult dilemmas faced by competent women in executive positions that are typically held by men has been termed the "femininity-competence double bind." This insidious phenomenon results from the assumption that behaviors required to succeed as an executive, such as assertiveness, leadership, and decisiveness, are inconsistent with traditional concepts of femininity, such as nurturance, passivity, and warmth (Jamieson, 1995). On the other hand, women who are successful female managers tend to be described with attributes associated with men and the managerial role (Heilman et al., 1989). Although being described in less feminine terms may not sound like a problem for women, other laboratory research has shown that women who were competent at male gender-typed positions may be disliked (Heilman, Battle, & Barocas-Alcott, 1998). Whereas perceived competence was generally predictive of an individual's ability to influence others, this did not apply to competent women, for whom likableness was a better predictor of ability to influence others (Carli & Eagly, 1999). Other research has found evidence of a small bias in evaluations favoring male leaders over female leaders, and female leaders who used an autocratic or directive leadership style (that is, a stereotypically male style), received more negative evaluations than other women, particularly from male raters (Eagly, Makhijani, & Klonsky, 1992). This research may help to explain why 96 percent of female executives reported that an important career advancement strategy for women was to "develop [a] style that men are comfortable with" (Ragins, Townsend, & Mattis, 1998, p. 29). Real-world negative consequences of the femininity-competence double bind were illustrated by the 1989 Supreme Court case of Ann Hopkins, who (as the only woman out of 88 candidates) was denied partnership at Price Waterhouse due to being stereotyped as too masculine, despite her undeniable productivity and bottom-line contributions to the firm (American Psychological Association, 1991; Jamieson, 1995). Thus, it appears that in order to succeed, women must avoid being perceived as too feminine, because feminine characteristics are thought to be inconsistent with the characteristics of a competent executive, or too masculine, which may lead to criticism for failing to live up to the traditional feminine ideal and negative perceptions about their interpersonal skills.

Factors That Facilitate Advancement

Although much has been written about barriers to women's advancement, less is known about what helps them succeed. Perhaps because women must overcome the barriers that were reviewed in the preceding section, some factors are more important for their advancement than for men's, but other factors appear to be equally important for both women and men. In this section and Table 9.3 I summarize what we have learned from studies of successful female executives; organizational initiatives are reviewed in a later section.

An interview study with executive women in Fortune 1000 companies (Gallagher, 2000) concluded that these women succeeded because of their

- Understanding of themselves and their goals
- Understanding of their companies and the unwritten rules about how to succeed
- Ability to emulate successful role models

Gallagher's study suggested that the critical factors that determine whether women will advance are their competence, outcomes, relationships, and endurance. In addition, based on her research and experience as an executive coach, Gallagher cautioned women that perfectionism can be career-limiting, and she stressed the need to take calculated risks such as being willing to make decisions in difficult or ambiguous situations and taking on challenging line assignments.

Developmental Job Assignments and Broadening Experiences

Developmental job assignments are critical for managers' skill development (for example, Howard & Bray, 1988; McCall, Lombardo & Morrison, 1988; McCauley, Ruderman, Ohlott, & Morrow, 1994), and developmental job assignments have also been identified by successful female executives as an important factor in their advancement (for example, Mainiero, 1994; Morrison, White, & Van Velsor, 1987; Ragins et al., 1998). In fact, recent research found that success for both female and male executives was related to developmental assignments and breadth of experience, such as having

Table 9.3. Examples of Career Facilitators for Nontraditional Managers and Executives.

Women	People of Color
• Understanding themselves and their goals • Understanding their companies and the unwritten rules about how to succeed • Ability to emulate successful role models • Ability to take calculated risks • Developmental job assignments and broadening experience • Good track record • Relationships and networking • Powerful sponsors • Opportunities to prove their competence to organizational decision makers • Mentoring • Personal characteristics, such as competence, strength, perseverance, internal standards and judgment, and passion for their work	• Access to high-visibility assignments • Performing over and above expectations • Communicating well • Powerful sponsors • Mentoring • Network groups • Education and training • Opportunities to prove their competence to organizational decision makers • Developmental job assignments and broadening experiences • Personal characteristics, such as competence, strength, perseverance, internal standards and judgment, and passion for their work

held both line and staff assignments and worked in multiple functional areas (Lyness & Thompson, 2000).

Good Track Record

One of the most frequently identified facilitators of advancement for women is having a good track record of successful accomplishments (for example, Mainiero, 1994; Ragins et al., 1998). In fact, having a good track record was given higher ratings by female executives than by male executives as a facilitator of their advancement (Lyness & Thompson, 2000). It is possible that having a good track record is more important for female executives because gender stereotypes may be overcome when unambiguous and job-relevant information is available for staffing decisions (for example, see Heilman, Martell, & Simon, 1988; Tosi & Einbender, 1985).

Relationships and Networking

Another career facilitator that is frequently identified in studies of successful women is developing relationships and networking (for example, see Mainiero, 1994; Ragins et al., 1998). Comparative studies have also found developing relationships to be reported as a more important facilitator by female executives than by their male counterparts (Davies-Netzley, 1998; Lyness & Thompson, 2000). Developing relationships may be particularly important for women at executive levels as a way of overcoming social isolation if there are few other women at their level in the management hierarchy. Also, developing relationships may help competent female executives be perceived as likable and may help to offset the femininity-competence double bind. In addition, women frequently report that other people contribute to their development and learning about corporate culture (Bierema, 1996; Van Velsor & Hughes, 1990).

Powerful Sponsors

Research has shown that promotions tend to go to men with the largest networks, but promotions go to women who have strong ties to strategic sponsors, suggesting that women are not fully trusted and therefore need stronger sponsorship than men do in order to get promoted (Burt, 1992; Ibarra, 1997).

Opportunities to Prove Their Competence
to Organizational Decision Makers

Studies have found that women were more likely to be promoted to senior management when they worked in the hiring department (Powell & Butterfield, 1994) or had corporate headquarters experience (Hurley & Sonnenfeld, 1998), both of which might be due to organizational decision makers' being personally acquainted with the female candidates and aware of their track records. The need for female managers to prove their competence to organizational decision makers may also have been reflected by research showing that relative to men, women were more likely to be promoted than hired into management positions (Lyness & Judiesch, 1999). This research, along with Brett and Stroh's (1997) finding that male managers benefit more than female managers do by changing companies, suggests that female managers should be advised not to underestimate the value of staying at a company where they are known and can capitalize on their internal track records, networks, and sponsors.

Mentoring

Numerous studies have found that mentoring relationships facilitated career success (for example, Dreher & Cox, 1996), and a survey of female executives found that the majority viewed mentoring as a key strategy for advancement (Ragins et al., 1998). As was mentioned earlier, having white male mentors was associated with greater earnings (Dreher & Cox, 1996). On the other hand, women may benefit from female mentors who can serve as role models and offer firsthand advice about overcoming the organizational barriers that women face (Ragins, 1997), and executive women have also found it beneficial to have multiple mentors or sponsors rather than relying on a single individual (Mainiero, 1994).

Career Issues for People of Color

In this section I review barriers to advancement for people of color, the challenges they face as nontraditional executives, and factors shown to facilitate their career success.

Barriers to Advancement

Managers of color report many of the same barriers to career advancement that were found for women (see Table 9.2). For example, a survey of professional and managerial women of color (Catalyst, 1999b) reported that their major barriers included

- Not having influential mentors or sponsors
- Lack of informal networking with colleagues
- Lack of role models from their own racial or ethnic group
- Lack of high-visibility assignments

A survey of human resource professionals identified these same barriers as well as stereotyping or preconceptions based on race or ethnicity as the major barriers to advancement for people of color (Society for Human Resource Management, 1999). Some of the major organizational barriers to the advancement of managers of color are shown in Table 9.2. They are also reviewed here.

Racial Stereotypes and Prejudice

Prejudice and stereotypes about racial or ethnic minority groups have been identified as perhaps the most important barrier to advancement for members of these groups (Thomas & Gabarro, 1999). However, racism and prejudice in today's organizations are often subtle and hidden rather than the overt bigotry and hostility of earlier decades (Bell & Nkomo, 1994). For instance, a study found that "prejudice and treating differences as weaknesses" were the top barriers to advancement for nontraditional managers, and that prejudice can also contribute to other barriers: "By permeating policies and practices in very subtle ways, prejudice continues to deprive nontraditional managers of advocates, resources, and power" (Morrison, 1992, p. 39). Prejudice can lead to numerous negative consequences for people of color, including difficulties developing trusting relationships with members of the majority group, uncertainty about whether to believe negative feedback or attribute it to discrimination, self-fulfilling prophecies related to lower performance expectations for people of color, and racial harassment, such as hearing coworkers tell jokes about their racial or ethnic group (for example, Cox, 1994). There is also evidence that women of color may face barriers associated with their gender, such as lack of acceptance in authority roles, in addition to the barriers encountered by men of color (Bell & Nkomo, 1994).

Stereotype content has been found to differ across various racial and ethnic groups. However, all of these identity groups tend to be described with characteristics not typically associated with successful managers, which may result in bias against them when staffing decisions are made. For example, Asian Americans were perceived to be technically oriented but not good at supervising others or communicating, Latinos were perceived to be unassertive, and African Americans were perceived to be incompetent (Morrison, 1992). As with stereotypes of women, the danger lies in associating these attributes with individuals who are members of these groups, forcing the individual to have to disprove the stereotype rather than starting on neutral ground. Also, managers of color have the additional burden of needing to monitor their own behavior to avoid being stereotyped. For example, African American managers who display strong emotions may be labeled "aggressive" but similar behaviors of white managers may be discounted or viewed less negatively (Ruderman & Hughes-James, 1998).

Not Being Given Stretch Assignments or Visibility

African American managers reported that they had received fewer developmental assignments associated with advancement, including opportunities to start up a new business, to turn a business around, or to work on special projects or task forces, than had comparable white managers (Douglas, Ruderman, & Davidson, 1999). Cianni and Romberger's (1995) research, which was one of the few studies that compared the experiences of different racial and ethnic groups within the same Fortune 500 organization, found that Caucasians reported more assignments that increased their contact with higher-level managers and more special project assignments than did Latinos, and Caucasians reported more encouragement to assume new responsibilities than did African Americans. These findings suggested that managers may have been more reluctant to take risks or provide visibility for people of color, and as a result, may have provided fewer opportunities for these individuals to develop the skills and relationships needed to advance. The supervisors' behavior may also have reflected an organizational culture that did not respect cultural differences as illustrated by the finding that Latinos who spoke with an accent were not chosen to make presentations to senior managers, and thus were denied career-enhancing visibility (Cianni & Romberger, 1995).

Difficulties Obtaining Mentoring

A longitudinal study of MBA graduates found that even after controlling for factors such as age, job performance, work experience, and company size, African Americans reported less access to mentors as well as lower satisfaction with their careers and advancement than did white MBAs although the two groups did not appear to differ in the hierarchical levels they had attained (Cox & Nkomo, 1991). As was discussed earlier, Dreher and Cox (1996) found that only MBAs with white male (but not minority or female) mentors were found to earn more than those without mentors. Their data showed, however, that African American and Hispanic American MBA graduates were less likely than white MBAs to have white male mentors, but no difference in access to white male mentors was found between Asian American and white MBAs (Dreher & Cox, 1996).

Being Held to a Higher Standard

Research examining supervisors' performance attributions for matched samples of African American and Caucasian managers found that the performance of African Americans was less likely to be attributed to ability or effort and more likely to be attributed to help from others than was comparable performance of Caucasian managers (Greenhaus & Parasuraman, 1993). Other research in a Fortune 500 company found that whites received higher ratings of promotion potential from their supervisors than did African Americans or Asian Americans, even after controlling for age, tenure, salary grade, and type of job (Landau, 1995).

White Managers' Lack of Comfort with People of Color

Thomas and Gabarro (1999) reported results of a fascinating and insightful three-company case study comparing careers of 20 executives of color (most of whom were African American and male) to those of 13 white executives and 13 plateaued managers of color. Thomas and Gabarro concluded that several barriers to minority advancement were related to white managers' unfamiliarity and lack of comfort with people of color. For example, the managers of color had to repeatedly prove their lack of inferiority to organizational decision makers. Also, their white managers' lack of comfort resulted in lack of bonding with white supervisors, and exclusion from informal networks and social activities. In addition, it was difficult for these managers to obtain white sponsors because of potential sponsors' concerns that sponsoring managers of color was riskier than sponsoring comparable white managers who would not be scrutinized so closely by other managers. Female executives of color also reported that a key barrier was having to develop relationships with top executives who were uncomfortable with racial differences (Gallagher, 2000).

As a result of the barriers they face, it may take longer for people of color to get promoted. For example, Thomas and Gabarro (1999) found that even though their credentials were comparable when they were hired, the executives of color took more years to reach middle management than did the white executives. This was not due to the minority managers' lack of competence, but rather to the extra time that was needed for the minority executives to overcome the organizational barriers and challenges they faced. Specifically, these managers needed extra time to prove their competence over and over in new assignments and with new bosses, in order to establish credibility, overcome the negative stereotypes, reach the higher promotion standards expected of their racial or ethnic groups, and give others time to recognize their potential.

Additional Challenges for Executives

Perhaps due to their limited representation in senior management, studies about executives of color are relatively sparse and often either look only at African Americans or combine all minority racial and ethnic groups. As a result, not much is known about issues unique to other groups, such as Latinos, Asian Americans, and Native Americans, or about unique issues for women of color. A recent cross-industry survey of 280 executives and managers of color found that the majority reported discriminatory experiences, including "double standards in delegation of assignments" and "harsh or unfair treatment of minorities by Whites" (Korn/Ferry International & Columbia Business School, 1998, p. 33). Also, this study noted that African Americans reported more discriminatory experiences and Asian Americans reported fewer discriminatory experiences than did other groups. Some of the additional challenges for executives of color are listed in Table 9.2. They are also reviewed here.

Tracking into Jobs Related to Their Cultural Backgrounds

A study of well-educated African American executives in white-owned companies found that although many were originally hired into line positions, the majority of these executives had been tracked into "racialized" jobs, such as affirmative action or urban affairs, that were far removed from the corporate mainstream (Collins, 1997). Whereas these jobs were initially viewed as having high organizational status and providing a route for talented African Americans to advance rapidly, in fact the African American executives who had worked mainly in these types of jobs advanced less than did their African American counterparts in mainstream jobs. Also, because the racialized jobs resulted in underdevelopment of critical skills and less access to organizational networks, over time the executives in these jobs became less competitive for further advancement or movement into mainstream departments with greater authority (Collins, 1997).

Stress of Being Tokens

Another study of African Americans in elite positions, including executives, politicians, academics, and other leaders, found evidence of "token stress" (for example, loss of black identity, having to demonstrate more competence than peers, and a sense of isolation), which increased as the proportion of African Americans in an individual's work setting decreased (Jackson, Thoits, & Taylor, 1995). Nontraditional executives may also be viewed as representatives of their racial or ethnic groups and asked to serve as role models or speak about their experiences to organizational groups or the media (for example, Ruderman & Hughes-James, 1998). Thus it appears that in work settings where the majority of senior managers are white, executives of color may be singled out in various ways and may face some of the same challenges as women do in male-dominated management hierarchies.

Not Fitting the Organizational Culture

Just as female executives face the challenge of maintaining their femininity while holding leadership roles in companies with male-dominated cultures, executives of color face similar challenges due to differences between their own racial or ethnic cultures and their companies' cultures, which are often European American in origin (Bell & Nkomo, 1994; Cox, 1994). Nontraditional executives may have difficulty figuring out how to fit in, and there may be stress and tension associated with leadership roles that require acting in ways that don't feel natural or are associated with a loss of cultural identity (Cox, 1994). Interviews with African American managers revealed, for example, that some had been cautioned that in order to be perceived as leaders, they should conform to corporate expectations regarding hairstyles, dress, and emotional expressiveness (Ruderman & Hughes-James, 1998).

Factors That Facilitate Advancement

Most factors that have been identified as facilitators of advancement for people of color are similar to those in the earlier section about facilitators of advancement for women (see Table 9.3). For example, a survey of professional and managerial women of color (Catalyst, 1999b) found that the factors reported to be most important for success included

- Access to high visibility assignments
- Performing over and above expectations
- Communicating well
- Having an influential mentor or sponsor

Many of the factors mentioned most often as facilitators undoubtedly facilitate the career advancement of white males as well as people of color. On the other hand, some studies suggest that, as with women, certain facilitators (for example, influential sponsors, mentors who can help them understand the corporate culture, and a proven track record of accomplishments) are particularly important for managers and executives of color because of the barriers and challenges they face.

Mentoring

A frequently mentioned factor associated with advancement for people of color is mentoring relationships, and a study of MBAs found that white male mentors provided greater advantage in terms of compensation growth than did female or minority mentors, regardless of the protégé's race or gender (Dreher & Cox, 1996). Similarly, a study of federal government workers found that protégés of color were more successful when they had male mentors than when they had female mentors (Daley, 1996). Perhaps because white males hold most of the senior positions, they serve as gatekeepers to critical career networks, and people of color must gain access to these networks in order to get promoted (Daley, 1996).

However, benefits have also been reported for racially homogeneous mentoring relationships. Thomas (1990) found that African American protégés reported receiving more psychosocial support from African American mentors than white mentors. Other research found that among African American MBA graduates, those who participated in minority network groups at their organizations expressed a higher degree of optimism about their careers than did those who did not participate in minority network groups; further analysis indicated that this difference was due to enhanced mentoring opportunities provided for African American employees by the minority network groups (Friedman, Kane, & Cornfield, 1998).

Education and Training

Research with federal government employees found that education and training were particularly important for people of color. Specifically, level of education was a better predictor of hierarchical level attained by managers of color than by white managers, and denial of training opportunities had more of a negative impact on advancement of people of color than of whites (Daley, 1996). Another study that examined the effect of race on promotion decisions to top management positions in a federal government department also found a positive relationship between level of education and promotions (Powell & Butterfield, 1997). In addition, Gallagher's (2000) study of female executives found that more executives of color than white executives had earned advanced degrees, including the Ph.D., J.D., or MBA, and the female executives of color said that earning advanced degrees was a way of proving themselves by overachieving in order to overcome the barriers they faced.

Opportunities to Prove Their Competence

Research has found that women of color were more likely to be promoted into senior management positions when they were employed in the departments with the job openings (Powell & Butterfield, 1997). As with similar findings related to the advancement of women in general, it is possible that working in the hiring department led to promotion because the decision makers were personally acquainted with the women of color and were aware of their skills and accomplishments. Also, a study about racial differences in performance attributions found that these racial differences in attributions to ability (for example, that the performance of African American managers was less likely to be attributed to their ability or effort and more likely to be attributed to help from others) were smaller when supervisors had worked with African American subordinates for more than a year. The researchers observed that this suggests that the additional time may have given these managers opportunities to demonstrate their competence and counteract negative stereotypes or biases that their supervisors may have had about African Americans (Greenhaus & Parasuraman, 1993).

Developmental Job Assignments and Broadening Experiences

The in-depth Thomas and Gabarro case study (1999) underscored the importance of developmental job assignments as a facilitator of career advancement for people of color. Those who had attained executive positions differed from their plateaued colleagues because of their deep grounding in their work during their early careers. Specifically the executives tended to have had a focused pattern of early assignments within the same department that allowed them to be at the cutting edge of technical work that they liked, while the plateaued managers' early assignments were more fragmented with frequent moves that sometimes took them out of the mainstream in exchange for small promotions or title changes. As they rose through middle and upper management ranks, the minority executives' career paths differed from those of the plateaued minority managers because the executives had more critical skill-building developmental assignments and broadening experiences such as changes in function, line-to-staff responsibilities, or location.

Personal Characteristics

Thomas and Gabarro (1999) concluded that the executives of color had succeeded because of their competence, credibility, and confidence. Also, an in-depth qualitative study of the career development of 18 prominent, highly achieving African American and white women concluded that these women's success was due to their strength and perseverance in overcoming the challenges of racism and sexism, their reliance on internal standards and judgment, passion for their work, and strong relationships with other people (Richie et al., 1997). In addition, based on her interviews with executive women of color, most of whom were African American, Gallagher (2000) concluded that they had succeeded due to their competence, outcomes, relationships, and endurance, (that is, the same success factors that she had identified for white women). However, Gallagher also noted that additional characteristics were required for the female executives of color to succeed, such as the ability to develop relationships with white managers who were uncomfortable with racial differences, and the motivation to overachieve in order to prove themselves.

Common Career Issues

This review suggests that women and people of color face many similar barriers to advancement that might help to explain their underrepresentation at executive levels (see Table 9.2). For example, there is evidence that both groups have to contend with organizational barriers such as difficulty in obtaining developmental assignments, being tracked into staff jobs that don't facilitate advancement, difficulty in obtaining influential mentors or sponsors, and being excluded from informal networks where critical information and career opportunities are shared.

Some similar organizational barriers were found for nontraditional managers in executive positions as for nontraditional managers in the pipeline for these positions. However, because the relative proportion of white males tends to increase with each move up the hierarchy, women and people of color in executive-level jobs may encounter additional stress associated with their token status. As these individuals advance to executive positions, there is increasing pressure to change to fit corporate behavioral expectations, as well as negative consequences of token status such as social isolation and performance pressure due to being seen as a highly visible representative of a demographic group rather than as an individual.

Although there are many similar barriers for women and people of color, there are unique issues for each group as well. Particularly at the executive level, women who perform well in jobs that are typically held by men may be seen as unfeminine, and may be disliked for violating societal gender role prescriptions. Also, the challenges of balancing work with family or non-work responsibilities tend to be exacerbated with the pressures and time demands of executive jobs. These work-family balance issues are more difficult for female executives than for the current generation of male executives, who are more likely to have a nonworking spouse to handle most of the family and non-work responsibilities (for example, Lyness & Thompson, 1997).

In addition, the typical experiences and stereotype content differ across various racial and ethnic groups, with African Americans and Latinos reporting more discriminatory experiences and Asian Americans reporting fewer such experiences. Also, African Americans and Latinos are stereotyped as incompetent while Asian Americans are stereotyped as highly competent but not very likable (Glick & Fiske, 1999), suggesting that individuals in these groups may face different types of organizational challenges and barriers.

Studies of women and people of color who have attained executive jobs have also identified factors that are thought to have facilitated their advancement and career success (see Table 9.3). Not surprisingly, these studies tend to underscore the importance of factors such as competence, relationships with mentors and sponsors, and developmental assignments that foster skill development and broad experience, which are probably as important for white males as for women and people of color. However, comparative studies have suggested that certain factors may be more important for advancement of nontraditional executives than for their white male counterparts because of the barriers the nontraditional managers face. For example, having a good track record and developing relationships were reported to be more important for female executives than for male executives (Lyness & Thompson, 2000). It is possible that a good track record helps women to overcome stereotypes that they lack requisite management skills while relationships help offset social isolation due to their token status. Similarly, Thomas and Gabarro (1999) concluded that opportunities to prove their competence enabled executives of color to overcome stereotypes and gain support of powerful mentors and sponsors.

Several personal characteristics have also been identified that might enable women and people of color to overcome barriers to advancement. For example, those who had succeeded were found to have the strength and perseverance to overcome prejudice, as well as passion for their work, self-confidence, and internal standards. There is also some evidence that the current generation of nontraditional executives may have been willing to work within the system to adapt their personal styles to fit their corporate cultures, and some have gone to great lengths to avoid being stereotyped. For example, the term "macho maternity" was coined to describe professional women who work as close as possible to their delivery dates and then return to work as soon as possible after childbirth (Brooks, 1997) to avoid the perception that they place family needs before work. Also, some female executives of color have reported that they had to overachieve to avoid being perceived as inferior (Gallagher, 2000).

Action Steps for Organizations

Given the numerous organizational barriers and challenges facing women and people of color, it is unlikely that their representation will dramatically increase at executive levels without some type of organizational intervention. Many authors have provided advice to organizations about how to increase diversity in their executive ranks. (See, for example, Catalyst, 1998, 1999b; Glass

Ceiling Commission, 1995; Morrison, 1992; Ruderman & Hughes-James, 1998; Thomas & Gabarro, 1999.) Based on the career issues identified in this review, common themes in the literature, and my own experience, some key action steps and recommendations for organizations are summarized in Exhibit 9.1 and reviewed here.

Link Initiatives to Business Objectives with Bottom-Line Payoff

Like many other types of organizational change initiatives, diversity management programs are more likely to succeed when they have top-level management support and hold managers accountable for specific outcomes. One of the best ways to make this happen is to develop initiatives that are clearly linked to business objectives with significant bottom-line impact, such as improving the company's ability to recruit and retain talented employees or to respond to needs of diverse customers. For example, Ernst & Young LLP created an Office of Retention to improve its retention rate among women. Based on survey responses identifying the critical issues, it created a program called Women's Access to increase opportunities for mentoring and networking with organizational

---

Exhibit 9.1. Action Steps to Increase the Advancement of Women and People of Color.

1. Link initiatives to business objectives with bottom-line payoff.
2. Make sure top management is personally committed and holds managers accountable.
3. Identify the organizational barriers.
4. Take action to tear down or reduce key organizational barriers, such as lack of role models, social isolation, difficulties getting mentoring, and lack of accommodation of non-work responsibilities.
5. Remember that jobs are key—ensure that women and people of color have access to visible, mainstream jobs throughout the management hierarchy.
6. Enhance retention of nontraditional executives and managers by attending to their needs.

---

leaders and one called Flexible Work Arrangements to improve life-work balance; the initiatives were well received by employees and have saved the firm over $21 million (Cole, 1999). Also, Avon Products, which has a female chief executive officer and is among the four Fortune 500 companies with the highest percentage of female corporate officers (Catalyst, 1999a), initiated its ambitious diversity programs in the 1980s to move more women and people of color into senior management in order to better understand and meet the needs of its female and culturally diverse customers.

Top Management Must Be Personally Committed and Must Hold Managers Accountable

Because the organizational barriers for nontraditional managers are often systemic and subtle, meaningful change is likely to require many years of sustained leadership and effort. For instance, one of the reasons that Avon Products is thought to have been so successful in its early diversity initiatives is the commitment and leadership of the chief executive officer at the time, Jim Preston.

Key success factors for diversity initiatives include having a well-articulated vision that makes it clear why increasing diversity is a business imperative, and effectively communicating this vision throughout the organization, which usually involves diversity training for employees. This vision must be backed up by the willingness to commit the necessary resources, tracking measurable success indicators, and holding managers accountable for their performance. For example, at companies such as AT&T and Digital Equipment Corporation, managers' success in advancing women and people of color is a factor in their performance appraisals (Deutsch, 1996). Diversity initiatives must also be well integrated with other human resource activities.

Identify the Organizational Barriers

Given the role of subtle organizational factors in limiting the progress of many nontraditional managers, it is important for employers to identify the specific barriers and issues in their organizations before embarking on any initiatives to increase the representation of women and people of color at executive levels.

As the federal Glass Ceiling Commission pointed out, *"no two companies are alike,"* and "successful programs begin by identifying the internal barriers specific to the corporate culture and the working environment of minorities and women" (Glass Ceiling Commission, 1995, p. 39).

Organization-specific research is important to ensure that accurate information is available to guide diversity efforts and, in some cases, to educate top management—who may not fully understand the organizational barriers for nontraditional managers. Research has found, for example, that chief executive officers cited factors such as lack of line experience and not enough time in the pipeline as the top barriers, while executive women reported that male stereotyping and exclusion from informal networks were the most important barriers for women (Ragins et al., 1998).

As with other organizational change initiatives, failure to accurately identify the problems may lead to misdirected attempts to solve them. For example, some companies have responded to the underrepresentation of women at executive levels by sending women to leadership development programs, based on the apparent assumption that lack of advancement is due to women's deficits in leadership skills (a person-centered explanation). If, on the other hand, the problem is actually due to barriers related to a male-dominated culture or selection bias against women, even the best leadership development program is likely to have little effect on women's advancement. More important, if women are blamed for their own lack of advancement, organizational responsibility is removed and the systemic barriers remain unexamined and unchanged (Gutek, 1993).

Diagnosis of the underlying issues and barriers can best be accomplished with a combination of quantitative and qualitative data. Organizational databases can provide hard facts about current gender and racial or ethnic representation across functions and hierarchical levels, as well as longitudinal trends regarding access to developmental assignments, advancement, turnover, performance ratings, and rewards. Current data can be used to identify areas where improvements are needed and develop key indices for tracking the impact of diversity initiatives. Employee focus groups, surveys, and exit interviews can be used to illuminate the reasons behind the data, such as perceived organizational barriers to advancement for nontraditional managers; similar information should also be collected from white males for comparison. In addition, analysis of the career paths and developmental experiences of successful executives can provide useful benchmarks to ensure that women and managers of color in the pipeline are getting access to the kinds of opportunities that have enabled others to advance.

Take Action to Tear Down Key Organizational Barriers

Diversity initiatives should be developed to address key organizational barriers for women and people of color, such as those summarized in Table 9.2. In addition to providing developmental assignments, organizations need to help nontraditional managers and executives overcome barriers such as lack of role models, exclusion from informal networks, difficulties obtaining mentoring, and the challenges of balancing work and non-work responsibilities. For example, a number of companies have achieved positive results from establishing employee network groups made up of women or members of specific racial or ethnic groups. In addition to providing opportunities for members to benefit from information exchange and mentoring, these groups can provide insights for senior managers or human resource officers about the organizational barriers and suggestions for improvements.

The value of organizational diagnosis for directing diversity initiatives was illustrated by IBM's recent efforts to extend its successful domestic diversity programs to address global issues for female managers and executives. Prior to its 1997 and 1998 Global Women Leaders Conferences, IBM administered surveys to identify perceived barriers for female managers and executives, and found that the top barriers were as follows (White, 1999):

- The "male-dominated culture" of the organization
- Difficulties balancing work and personal responsibilities
- Lack of networking and mentors
- Difficulty getting access to key positions
- A "culture that doesn't take risks with women"

Although the same barriers were found for all geographic regions, specific initiatives were designed and carried out within each region, such as work-life surveys, mentoring and networking programs, and increased focus on women in leadership roles. Based on another study of issues for women of color (also described in White, 1999), IBM implemented programs to provide enhanced networking and career development for women of color. In addition to careful diagnosis of problems, the IBM initiatives also benefited from reliance on the expertise and insights of the women themselves about how best to address the issues.

According to Thomas and Ely (1996), the most common organizational approaches to diversity are either to encourage women and people of color to assimilate into the dominant (white male) culture or to recognize differences by placing them in jobs that are related to their backgrounds, such as responsibility for diversity or for interfacing with customers from their own cultural backgrounds. The latter approach is built on the assumption that the primary contribution that nontraditional managers can offer to the organization is an understanding of their own demographic groups, but ignores the fact that nontraditional managers might make a greater contribution by bringing new perspectives and approaches to doing the work itself. Thomas and Ely argue instead for what they call the "learning and effectiveness paradigm," which retains some of the positive features of earlier paradigms, such as an emphasis on fairness and recognizing value in cultural differences, while placing greater emphasis on openness to change and learning from the diverse perspectives of the employees.

On the other hand, Meyerson and Fletcher (2000) advocate an organizational change strategy built around "small wins," or experimentation and incremental changes directed at replacing organizational practices that produce inequity with practices that work better for all employees. For example, they had worked with an organization where time was poorly managed with frequent meeting overruns, last-minute schedule changes, and late-night meetings, all of which were particularly difficult for female managers who typically had more family responsibilities than their male counterparts. The organization implemented a more disciplined use of time, which benefited everyone and also led to improved work quality. Thus, both the Thomas and Ely and the

Meyerson and Fletcher approaches differ from earlier approaches focused only on increasing demographic diversity because the newer approaches attempt to bring about more fundamental (and potentially valuable) changes to the way in which work is done. They also illustrate the value of inclusive programs where everyone benefits.

Remember That Jobs Are Key

One of the strongest themes running through the review of career issues for women and people of color is that getting the right job assignments is critical for advancement. Therefore, it is essential to ensure that women and people of color have access to visible, mainstream jobs throughout the management hierarchy. Developmental assignments provide opportunities for nontraditional managers to develop skills needed for promotion to bigger jobs, the chance to demonstrate competence to senior managers, and opportunities to develop relationships with key managers and potential sponsors throughout the organization. High-quality organizational career management and assessment systems, including succession planning, challenging assignments, career workshops, coaching, and feedback, can also help to offset some of the disadvantages associated with lack of mentoring and informal networking (for additional information, see Dreher & Dougherty, 1997; Ruderman & Hughes-James, 1998). In addition to developing the individuals, placing women and people of color in visible, mainstream jobs throughout the management hierarchy sends an important signal to other talented women and people of color that this organization is a good place to work.

Giving women and people of color access to mainstream jobs that can enhance their development and chances for advancement requires ensuring that staffing decisions are based on merit and not influenced by biases or stereotypes. Stereotyping and biases can be reduced by the following steps:

- Clarifying selection criteria and ensuring that all candidates are evaluated on the same dimensions
- Communicating the selection criteria to guide career development

- Basing selection decisions on objective performance data or other job-related factors
- Implementing a standardized selection process with good documentation and clear managerial accountability for decisions

The value of procedural safeguards was illustrated, for example, by research that found no evidence of gender bias in executive promotion decisions in a government setting with standardized procedures, careful documentation, and accountability for decisions (Powell & Butterfield, 1994). Many companies also require that candidate slates for management positions at all levels include women and people of color to increase the selection of nontraditional candidates. Given the evidence that women are more likely to attain management positions through internal promotion than external hiring, it is important to ensure that external candidate slates include nontraditional candidates as well.

There are other challenges to organizational diversity management programs, such as concerns about reverse discrimination and resistance from those who favor the status quo. Although some of the barriers facing nontraditional managers and executives are due to their token status, simply increasing the number of the minority group does not always improve their situation and may result in backlash or harassment (Martin & Collinson, 1999). In addition, there is research evidence that women who are portrayed as "affirmative action hires" tend to be perceived as less competent than others (Heilman, Block, & Stathatos, 1997), suggesting that there may be a stigma of incompetence associated with women or people of color who are thought to have been hired or promoted to increase diversity in the management ranks rather than because of their qualifications. This underscores the need to make it clear that the staffing decisions are based on merit and qualifications rather than other factors.

It is also important that nontraditional candidates be given access to stretch assignments where they are exposed to new areas of the business or are given the chance to develop and demonstrate previously untested skills. This requires taking risks on nontraditional managers to the same extent as with white males. Also, it is important not to limit consideration to candidates who resemble the previous job incumbent demographically, as for example, when men are considered to be better candidates for line positions because these positions have usually been held by men. In addition, it is important to offer assignments requiring relocation to women and people of color with family responsibilities or working spouses rather than making an assumption that they would not be willing to relocate. Finally, organizational decision makers should guard against tendencies to trade off managers' potential career advancement in favor of short-term organizational benefits, as, for example, when competent women or people of color are kept in support roles where their talents are directed toward working behind the scenes to make others look good rather than being moved into visible leadership roles.

Enhance Retention of Nontraditional Executives by Attending to Their Needs

In today's tight labor market, retention of talent has become an increasingly critical issue for organizations, and turnover among women and people of color is a significant expense for many companies (Robinson & Dechant, 1997). There is evidence, for example, that managerial women may have higher turnover rates due to more limited advancement opportunities (Stroh, Brett, & Reilly, 1996) and greater family responsibilities (Schwartz, 1989) as compared to managerial men. Also, there is evidence that some women are leaving corporations to start their own businesses, and that desire for challenge, concern about managing families and work, and frustration about blocked career advancement are the most commonly mentioned reasons for the transition from corporate to entrepreneurial settings (Buttner & Moore, 1997).

On the other hand, some recent research offers ideas about how to improve retention of nontraditional managers. For example, a survey found that women of color who intended to stay at their organizations were more likely to have managers who (Catalyst, 1999b)

- Provided opportunities for visibility
- Explained organizational policies
- Mapped out clear developmental goals

Women of color who intended to stay at their organizations were also more likely to report that their organizations had supportive diversity practices, senior management committed to hiring a diverse workforce, and diversity training for managers (Catalyst, 1999b).

There is evidence that female managers who perceived limited opportunities for career advancement expressed greater intention to resign than did male managers with similar opportunities (Stroh et al., 1996). On the other hand, a longitudinal study of factors predicting voluntary turnover found that female managers who had received recent promotions were less likely to resign than male managers who had received promotions (Lyness & Judiesch, forthcoming). This study also found the negative effect of promotions on both female and male managers' turnover persisted for less than a year, suggesting that other types of retention tools (for example, stock options) with longer-term payouts should be considered as well.

Many companies have implemented family-friendly benefits, such as flexible hours and emergency day care services, to help employees manage non-work responsibilities that can interfere with work. Employees at organizations that offer family-friendly benefits have been found to express more commitment to their companies and lower intentions to leave (Grover & Crooker, 1995; Thompson, Beauvais, & Lyness, 1999). However, the positive effects of family-friendly benefits can be undermined by an unsupportive organizational culture or supervisors who penalize employees for taking advantage of these programs or policies (Thompson et al., 1999), suggesting that companies need to ensure that attention is given to these factors as well.

Conclusions

As this review has shown, there is considerable evidence about the barriers to advancement for women and people of color, suggesting that the playing field is not yet level. Examples of these barriers include being stereotyped based on demographic group membership, difficulty obtaining developmental assignments or mainstream positions, and lack of mentorship and sponsorship. Nontraditional managers may also be held to a higher standard or scrutinized more closely, and as a result their advancement may take longer. Upon reaching the executive ranks, they may face additional challenges such as social isolation and not being fully accepted by others.

In writing this review I have been struck by how much more we seem to know about barriers for women and people of color than about how best to overcome the barriers. At the individual level, there is some evidence that having the right educational credentials, access to challenging developmental assignments, a proven track record of accomplishments, and relationships with powerful organizational sponsors may help women and people of color to overcome some of the barriers they face. At the organizational level, success in advancing women and people of color to the executive level requires integration of diversity initiatives with business objectives, top management commitment, managerial accountability, initiatives targeted at identified barriers, and ongoing measurement of progress against specific objectives. On the other hand, the challenges of increasing the representation of women and people of color at executive levels have been underscored by recent publicity about how even a well-managed company such as General Electric has almost no diversity among its top executives—in fact, there were no women and only one African American among the executives running the 20 businesses that provided 90 percent of GE's earnings in 1999 (Walsh, 2000).

The careers of today's executives are often characterized by many more interorganizational moves than were typical of executives in previous decades. Although changing companies has often been recommended as a good way for ambitious managers to advance their careers, recent research found that changing companies provided greater career benefits for white males than for women or people of color (Dreher & Cox, 2000). Because many organizations now fill key management positions through external hiring rather than traditional promote-from-within strategies, this study has troubling implications for the careers of nontraditional managers if they continue to be disadvantaged in the external labor market as compared to their white male counterparts. Despite the organizational barriers to advancement, nontraditional managers should not underestimate the value of staying at an organization where they have already demonstrated their competence and established important relationships. In addition, organizations seeking to increase the proportion of women and people of color in their executive ranks need to ensure that nontraditional managers and executives are given full consideration regardless of whether positions are filled internally or externally.

Many of the current generation of nontraditional executives appear to have adapted their behavior to fit current corporate cultures. However, it is unclear whether nontraditional managers in subsequent generations will be similarly willing to make these accommodations. Also, the ample career opportunities outside traditional corporate settings have opened up many more options for today's talented managers and executives than were available in prior decades, suggesting that retention of nontraditional executives may continue to pose a significant challenge unless organizations become more inclusive and responsive to these executives' needs.

Despite the considerable barriers that they face, women and people of color appear to be making slow but steady progress in climbing the corporate hierarchy to attain executive-level positions. For example, the annual Catalyst surveys revealed that women have progressed from holding less than 9 percent of the corporate officer positions in Fortune 500 companies in 1995 to holding almost 12 percent of these positions in 1999 (Catalyst, 1999a). Another cause for optimism is the increasing numbers of ambitious, career-oriented women and people of color who are obtaining the necessary college degrees to prepare themselves for business careers. As companies struggle to fill key positions in today's tight labor market, hopefully more organizations will do a better job of providing appropriate opportunities for talented women and people of color. Finally, as women and people of color move into the executive ranks, it will be interesting to observe their influence on their organizations as well as the opportunities of those who follow.

References

Acker, J. (1990). Hierarchies, jobs, bodies: A theory of gendered organizations. *Gender and Society, 4,* 139–158.

Adler, N. J. (1984). Expecting international success: Female managers overseas. *Columbia Journal of World Business, 19*(3), 79–85.

American Psychological Association. (1991). In the Supreme Court of the United States *Price Waterhouse* v. *Ann B. Hopkins* Amicus Curiae Brief for the American Psychological Association. *American Psychologist, 46,* 1061–1070.

Bell, E.L.J.E., & Nkomo, S. M. (1994). *Barriers to work place advancement experienced by African-Americans. A monograph prepared for Glass Ceiling Commission.* Washington, DC: U.S. Department of Labor.

Bierema, L. L. (1996). How executive women learn corporate culture. *Human Resource Development Quarterly, 7,* 145–164.

Brett, J. M., & Stroh, L. K. (1997). Jumping ship: Who benefits from an external labor market career strategy? *Journal of Applied Psychology, 82,* 331–341.

Brooks, N. R. (1997, February 24). Careers/Management: Managers often at odds with family-friendly perks. *Los Angeles Times,* pp. D2–13.

Burt, R. S. (1992). *Structural holes: The social structure of competition.* Cambridge, MA: Harvard University Press.

Buttner, E. H., & Moore, D. P. (1997). Women's organizational exodus to entrepreneurship: Self-reported motivations and correlates with success. *Journal of Small Business Management, 35,* 34–46.

Cannings, K., & Montmarquette, C. (1991). Managerial momentum: A simultaneous model of the career progress of male and female managers. *Industrial and Labor Relations Review, 44,* 212–228.

Carli, L. L., & Eagly, A. H. (1999). Gender effects on social influence and emergent leadership. In G. N. Powell (Ed.), *Handbook of gender and work* (pp. 203–222). Thousand Oaks, CA: Sage.

Catalyst. (1996). *Women in corporate leadership: Progress and prospects.* New York: Catalyst.

Catalyst. (1998). *Advancing women in business—The Catalyst guide: Best practices from corporate leaders.* San Francisco: Jossey-Bass.

Catalyst. (1999a). *1999 Catalyst census of women corporate officers and top earners.* New York: Catalyst.

Catalyst. (1999b). *Women of color in corporate management: Opportunities and barriers.* New York: Catalyst.

Cianni, M., & Romberger, B. (1995). Perceived racial, ethnic, and gender differences in access to developmental experiences. *Group and Organization Management, 20,* 440–459.

Cole, J. (1999). E&Y creates office of retention and turnover rates drop. *HR Focus, 76*(4), 7.

Collins, S. M. (1997). Black mobility in white corporations: Up the corporate ladder but out on a limb. *Social Problems, 44,* 55–67.

Cox, T., Jr. (1994). *Cultural diversity in organizations: Theory, research and practice.* San Francisco: Berrett-Koehler.

Cox, T. H., & Harquail, C. V. (1991). Career paths and career success in the early career stages of male and female MBAs. *Journal of Vocational Behavior, 39,* 54–75.

Cox, T. H., & Nkomo, S. M. (1991). A race and gender-group analysis of the early career experience of MBAs. *Work and Occupations, 18,* 431–446.

Daley, D. M. (1996). Paths of glory and the glass ceiling: Differing patterns of career advancement among women and minority federal employees. *Public Administration Quarterly, 20,* 143–162.

Davidson, M. J., & Cooper, C. L. (1986). Executive women under pressure. *International Review of Applied Psychology, 35,* 301–326.

Davies-Netzley, S. A. (1998). Women above the glass ceiling: Perceptions on corporate mobility and strategies for success. *Gender and Society, 12,* 339–355.

Deutsch, C. H. (1996, December 1). Diversity training: Just shut up and hire. *New York Times,* Sec. 4, p. 4.

Douglas, C. A., Ruderman, M. N., & Davidson, M. N. (1999, August). *A comparison of developmental job experiences in the lives of African-American and white managers.* Paper presented at the Academy of Management Meeting, Chicago.

Dreher, G. F., & Cox, T. H., Jr. (1996). Race, gender, and opportunity: A study of compensation attainment and the establishment of mentoring relationships. *Journal of Applied Psychology, 81,* 297–308.

Dreher, G. F., & Cox, T. H., Jr. (2000). Labor market mobility and cash compensation: The moderating effects of race and gender. *Academy of Management Journal, 43,* 890–900.

Dreher, G. F., & Dougherty, T. W. (1997). Substitutes for career mentoring: Promoting equal opportunity through career management and assessment systems. *Journal of Vocational Behavior, 51,* 110–124.

Eagly, A. H., Makhijani, M. G., & Klonsky, B. G. (1992). Gender and the evaluation of leaders: A meta-analysis. *Psychological Bulletin, 111*(1), 2–33.

Friedman, R., Kane, M., & Cornfield, D. B. (1998). Social support and career optimism: Examining the effectiveness of network groups among black managers. *Human Relations, 51,* 1155–1177.

Gallagher, C. (2000). *Going to the top: A road map for success from America's leading women executives.* New York: Viking.

Gerhart, B. A., & Milkovich, G. T. (1989). Salaries, salary growth, and promotions of men and women in a large, private firm. In R. T. Michael, H. I. Hartmann, & B. O'Farrell (Eds.), *Pay equity: Empirical inquiries* (pp. 23–43). Washington, DC: National Academy Press.

Glass Ceiling Commission. (1995). *Good for business: Making full use of the nation's human capital.* Washington, DC: Glass Ceiling Commission.

Glick, P., & Fiske, S. T. (1999). Sexism and other "isms": Interdependence, status, and the ambivalent content of stereotypes. In W. B. Swann, J. Langlois, & L. A. Gilbert (Eds.), *Sexism and stereotypes in modern so-*

ciety: The gender science of Janet Taylor Spence (pp. 193–221). Washington, DC: American Psychological Association.

Greenhaus, J. H., & Parasuraman, S. (1993). Job performance attributions and career advancement prospects: An examination of gender and race effects. *Organizational Behavior and Human Decision Processes, 55,* 273–297.

Grover, S. L., & Crooker, K. J. (1995). Who appreciates family-responsive human resource policies: The impact of family-friendly policies on the organizational attachment of parents and non-parents. *Personnel Psychology, 48,* 271–288.

Gutek, B. A. (1993). Changing the status of women in management. *Applied Psychology: An International Review, 42*(4), 301–311.

Hartmann, H. I. (1987). Internal labor markets and gender: A case study of promotion. In C. Brown & J. Peckman (Eds.), *Gender in the workplace* (pp. 59–92). Washington, DC: Brookings Institution.

Heilman, M. E. (1983). Sex bias in work settings: The lack of fit model. In B. M. Staw & L. L. Cummings (Eds.), *Research in organizational behavior* (Vol. 5, pp. 269–298). Greenwich, CT: JAI Press.

Heilman, M. E. (1995). Sex stereotypes and their effects in the workplace: What we know and what we don't know. *Journal of Social Behavior and Personality, 10*(2), 3–26.

Heilman, M. E., Battle, W. S., & Barocas-Alcott, V. (1998, April). *Penalties for sex-role violation in job choice and work effectiveness.* Paper presented at the Society for Industrial and Organizational Psychology conference, Dallas, Texas.

Heilman, M. E., Block, C. J., Martell, R. F., & Simon, M. C. (1989). Has anything changed? Current characterizations of men, women, and managers. *Journal of Applied Psychology, 74,* 935–942.

Heilman, M. E., Block, C. J., & Stathatos, P. (1997). The affirmative action stigma of incompetence: Effects of performance information ambiguity. *Academy of Management Journal, 40,* 603–625.

Heilman, M. E., Martell, R. F., & Simon, M. C. (1988). The vagaries of sex bias: Conditions regulating the undervaluation, equivaluation, and overvaluation of female job applicants. *Organizational Behavior and Human Decision Processes, 41,* 98–110.

Howard, A., & Bray, D. (1988). *Managerial lives in transition: Advancing age and changing times.* New York: Guilford Press.

Hurley, A. E., & Sonnenfeld, J. A. (1998). The effect of organizational experience on managerial career attainment in an internal labor market. *Journal of Vocational Behavior, 52,* 172–190.

Ibarra, H. (1997). Paving an alternative route: Gender differences in managerial networks. *Social Psychology Quarterly, 60,* 91–102.

Jackson, P. B., Thoits, P. A., & Taylor, H. F. (1995). Composition of the workplace and psychological well-being: The effects of tokenism on America's Black elite. *Social Forces, 74,* 543–557.

Jamieson, K. H. (1995). *Beyond the double bind: Women and leadership.* New York: Oxford University Press.

Judiesch, M. K., & Lyness, K. S. (1999). Left behind? The impact of leaves of absence on managers' career success. *Academy of Management Journal, 42,* 641–651.

Kanter, R. M. (1977a). *Men and women of the corporation.* New York: Basic Books.

Kanter, R. M. (1977b). Some effects of proportions on group life: Skewed sex ratios and responses to token women. *American Journal of Sociology, 82,* 965–990.

Korn/Ferry International & Columbia Business School. (1998). *Diversity in the executive suite: Creating successful career paths and strategies.* New York: Korn/Ferry International.

Krefting, L. A., Berger, P. K., & Wallace, M. J., Jr. (1978). The contribution of sex distribution, job content, and occupational classification to job sex typing: Two studies. *Journal of Vocational Behavior, 13,* 181–191.

Landau, J. (1995). The relationship of race and gender to managers' ratings of promotion potential. *Journal of Organizational Behavior, 16,* 391–400.

Levey, L., Johnson, A. A., & Civian, J. (1999). *Moving women through the pipeline to senior leadership.* Boston: Work/Family Directions.

Lyness, K. S., & Judiesch, M. K. (1999). Are women more likely to be hired or promoted into management positions? *Journal of Vocational Behavior, 54,* 158–173.

Lyness, K. S., & Judiesch, M. K. (forthcoming). Are female managers quitters? The relationships of gender, promotions, and family leaves of absence to voluntary turnover. *Journal of Applied Psychology.*

Lyness, K. S., & Thompson, D. E. (1997). Above the glass ceiling? A comparison of matched samples of female and male executives. *Journal of Applied Psychology, 82,* 359–375.

Lyness, K. S., & Thompson, D. E. (2000). Climbing the corporate ladder: Do female and male executives follow the same route? *Journal of Applied Psychology, 85,* 86–101.

Mainiero, L. A. (1994). Getting anointed for advancement: The case of executive women. *Academy of Management Executive, 8*(2), 53–67.

Martin, P. Y., & Collinson, D. L. (1999). Gender and sexuality in organizations. In M. M. Ferree, J. Lorber, & B. B. Hess (Eds.), *Revisioning gender* (pp. 285–310). Thousand Oaks, CA: Sage.

McCall, M. W., Jr., Lombardo, M. M., & Morrison, A. M. (1988). *The lessons of experience: How successful executives develop on the job.* Lexington, MA: Heath.

McCauley, C. D., Ruderman, M. N., Ohlott, P. J., & Morrow, J. E. (1994). Assessing the developmental components of managerial jobs. *Journal of Applied Psychology, 79,* 544–560.

Meyerson, D. E., & Fletcher, J. K. (2000). A modest manifesto for shattering the glass ceiling. *Harvard Business Review, 78*(1), 126–136.

Moore, G. (1988). Women in elite positions: Insiders or outsiders? *Sociological Forum, 3,* 566–585.

Morrison, A. M. (1992). *The new leaders: Guidelines on leadership diversity.* San Francisco: Jossey-Bass.

Morrison, A. M., & von Glinow, M. A. (1990). Women and minorities in management. *American Psychologist, 45*(2), 200–208.

Morrison, A. M., White, R. P., & Van Velsor, E. (1987). *Breaking the glass ceiling: Can women reach the top of America's largest corporations?* Reading, MA: Addison-Wesley.

Nieva, V. F., & Gutek, B. A. (1981). *Women and work: A psychological perspective.* New York: Praeger.

Olson, J. E., Frieze, I. H., & Good, D. C. (1987). The effects of job type and industry on the income of male and female MBAs. *Journal of Human Resources, 22,* 532–541.

Powell, G. N. (1999). Reflections on the glass ceiling: Recent trends and future prospects. In G. N. Powell (Ed.), *Handbook of gender and work* (pp. 325–345). Thousand Oaks, CA: Sage.

Powell, G. N., & Butterfield, D. A. (1994). Investigating the "glass ceiling" phenomenon: An empirical study of actual promotions to top management. *Academy of Management Journal, 37,* 68–86.

Powell, G. N., & Butterfield, D. A. (1997). Effect of race on promotions to top management in a federal department. *Academy of Management Journal, 40,* 112–128.

Ragins, B. R. (1997). Diversified mentoring relationships in organizations: A power perspective. *Academy of Management Review, 22,* 482–521.

Ragins, B. R. (1999). Gender and mentoring relationships: A review and research agenda for the next decade. In G. N. Powell (Ed.), *Handbook of gender and work* (pp. 347–370). Thousand Oaks, CA: Sage.

Ragins, B. R., & Cotton, J. L. (1991). Easier said than done: Gender differences in perceived barriers to gaining a mentor. *Academy of Management Journal, 34,* 939–951.

Ragins, B. R., & Sundstrom, E. (1989). Gender and power in organizations. *Psychological Bulletin, 105,* 51–88.

Ragins, B. R., Townsend, B., & Mattis, M. (1998). Gender gap in the executive suite: CEOs and female executives report on breaking the glass ceiling. *Academy of Management Executive, 12*(1), 28–42.

Richie, B. S., Fassinger, R. E., Linn, S. G., Johnson, J., Robinson, S., & Prosser, J. (1997). Persistence, connection, and passion: A qualitative study of the career development of highly achieving African American black and white women. *Journal of Counseling Psychology, 44,* 133–148.

Robinson, G., & Dechant, K. (1997). Building a business case for diversity. *Academy of Management Executive, 11,* 21–31.

Ruble, T. L., Cohen, R., & Ruble, D. M. (1984). Sex stereotypes: Occupational barriers for women. *American Behavioral Scientist, 27,* 339–356.

Ruderman, M. N., & Hughes-James, M. W. (1998). Leadership development across race and gender. In C. D. McCauley, R. S. Moxley, & E. Van Velsor (Eds.), *The Center for Creative Leadership handbook of leadership development* (pp. 291–335). San Francisco: Jossey-Bass.

Ruderman, M. N., Ohlott, P. J., & Kram, K. E. (1996). *Managerial promotion: The dynamics for men and women* (Technical report 170). Greensboro, NC: Center for Creative Leadership.

Ruderman, M. N., Ohlott, P. J., & McCauley, C. D. (1990). Assessing opportunities for leadership development. In K. E. Clark & M. B. Clark (Eds.), *Measures of leadership* (pp. 547–562). West Orange, NJ: Leadership Library of America.

Sackett, P. R., DuBois, C.L.Z., & Noe, A. W. (1991). Tokenism in performance evaluation: The effects of work group representation on male-female and white-black differences in performance ratings. *Journal of Applied Psychology, 76,* 263–267.

Schein, V. E. (1973). The relationship between sex role stereotypes and requisite management characteristics. *Journal of Applied Psychology, 57,* 95–100.

Schein, V. E. (1975). Relations between sex role stereotypes and requisite management characteristics among female managers. *Journal of Applied Psychology, 60,* 340–344.

Schneer, J. A., & Reitman, F. (1994). The importance of gender in mid-career: A longitudinal study of MBAs. *Journal of Organizational Behavior, 15,* 199–207.

Schwartz, F. N. (1989). Management women and the new facts of life. *Harvard Business Review, 67*(1), 65–76.

Shelton, B. A., & John, D. (1996). The division of household labor. *Annual Review of Sociology, 22,* 299–322.

Silverman, R. E. (2000, September 5). Career journal—Focus on women: The jungle. *Wall Street Journal,* p. B14.

Society for Human Resource Management. (1999). 1999 barriers to advancement survey. Available online: http://www.shrm.org/diversity/fortune.pdf.

Stroh, L. K., Brett, J. M., & Reilly, A. H. (1992). All the right stuff: A comparison of female and male managers' career progression. *Journal of Applied Psychology, 77,* 251–260.

Stroh, L. K., Brett, J. M., & Reilly, A. H. (1996). Family structure, glass ceiling, and traditional explanations for the differential rate of turnover of female and male managers. *Journal of Vocational Behavior, 49,* 99–118.

Thomas, D. A. (1990). The impact of race on managers' experiences of developmental relationships. *Journal of Organizational Behavior, 2,* 479–492.

Thomas, D. A., & Ely, R. J. (1996). Making differences matter: A new paradigm for managing diversity. *Harvard Business Review, 74*(5), 79–90.

Thomas, D. A., & Gabarro, J. J. (1999). *Breaking through: The making of minority executives in corporate America.* Boston: Harvard Business School Press.

Thompson, C. A., Beauvais, L. L., & Lyness, K. S. (1999). When work-family benefits are not enough: The influence of work-family culture on benefit utilization, organizational attachment, and work-family conflict. *Journal of Vocational Behavior, 54,* 392–415.

Tosi, H. L., & Einbender, S. W. (1985). The effects of the type and amount of information in sex discrimination research: A meta-analysis. *Academy of Management Journal, 32,* 662–669.

U.S. Department of Labor, Bureau of Labor Statistics. (2000). Table 11: Employed persons by detailed occupation, sex, race, and Hispanic origin. *Employment and Earnings, 47*(1), 178–183.

U.S. Equal Employment Opportunity Commission. (1998). Table 1. Occupational employment in private industry by race/ethnic group/sex and by industry, United States, 1998. Available online: http://www.eeoc.gov/stats/jobpat/tables-1.html.

Van Velsor, E., & Hughes, M. W. (1990). *Gender differences in the development of managers: How women managers learn from experience* (Technical report 145). Greensboro, NC: Center for Creative Leadership.

Walsh, M. W. (2000, September 3). Where G.E. falls short: Diversity at the top. *New York Times,* Sec. 3, pp. 1, 13.

Ward, P. A., Orazem, P. F., & Schmidt, S. W. (1992). Women in elite pools and elite positions. *Social Science Quarterly, 73,* 31–45.

White, M. B. (1999). Women of the world: Diversity goes global at IBM. *Diversity Factor, 7*(4), 13–16.

CHAPTER 10

E-Executives
Leadership Priorities for the New Economy
D. Douglas McKenna,
Robert B. McKenna

Business as usual is a formula for disaster in the world of e-commerce. Andrew Grove, chairman of Intel Corporation, has challenged the relevance of even fundamental concepts like ROI in the new world: "What's my return on investment in e-Commerce? Are you crazy? This is Columbus in the New World. What was his ROI?"

Analogies like this are often helpful in making sense of radically new situations. So let's try another. Imagine the Starship *Enterprise* without Captain Kirk or Captain Picard. To blast into space seeking new worlds and civilizations would clearly be foolish without ambitious, adventure-driven leaders well-prepared to boldly go where no one has gone before! Who would set the course, tap individual genius to solve novel problems, pull the crew together when needed, exploit the ship's technology to learn and survive, and make life-and-death decisions—all while traveling at warp speed? Only a captain of mythological proportions, of course.

Before you dismiss us for using a simple-minded pop culture analogy to begin what should be a serious analysis of executive leadership in the New Economy, consider the following:

- If you spend a morning with almost any executive in a company with an Internet-driven strategy, you will hear the word *space* at least nine times (as in, "our goal is to pre-empt this or that player in the small to medium business space").

- If you listen carefully, it will also be clear that while your executive has a strong sense of general direction (as in "we're going to play in the B2B, but in not the B2C or P2P space"), she is really making it up as she goes along. She is creating strategy, making decisions, taking action, seeing what works and what doesn't in real time—exploring uncharted, unpredictable territory where you live on your wits and grit.
- If your executive is universe-class, she will have conversations on technology with marketers (remember Bones) and on marketing with technologists (remember Spock) that will leave you muttering and wondering about your own bandwidth limitations. How did she ever learn all these acronyms, let alone understand how to use them to execute a new business model?
- If your executive's company has a bright future, you'll be staggered by the brilliance, expertise, and missionary zeal of its staff (remember Data and Troy). You don't want to go flying off into space without an incredibly talented, diverse, and dedicated crew.
- If your executive has been playing in the New Economy for at least a year, she'll be able to tell you about the competitors who became partners (remember the Klingons) and the new competitors who refused to stay on their own side of established business boundaries (remember the Romulans).
- And finally, if your executive truly has the New Economy in her blood, you'll hear constant echoes of Andy Grove–like paranoia—stories of the 200 dot-coms across the United States that disintegrated in Internet recently. Someone has always got to be on the bridge, 24x7.

So we hope you'll agree that the *Star Trek*–New Economy analogy is at least interesting if not profound. Either way, we believe it illuminates a leadership problem in the making. Many of our current executives grew up and learned to be effective in a pre-Internet world very different from what they face today. The Internet explosion and digital technology revolution are creating a new business space in which executives and their organizations must be more adventurous, dedicated, risk taking, intelligent, creative, collaborative, independent, decisive, resilient, and above all, faster than ever before.

Some executives, particularly those who've led the PC revolution of the past 25 years, are better prepared than others to deal with this new space. However, even executives in IT companies like Microsoft, Intel, Hewlett-Packard, Sun Microsystems, and Oracle are finding that the pace has quickened, business rules are being rewritten, and old ways of leading and doing business are rapidly becoming obsolete. As Bill Gates has said, a "fundamental new rule of business is that the Internet changes everything" (Gates & Hemingway, 1999, p. 72).

Though new patterns of effective executive leadership in the e-world are emerging in a Darwinian fashion, we see an opportunity to intervene and speed the adaptation process along. As this book demonstrates, there is a wealth of theory, research, and practice standing ready for application to the challenge of electronic executive—*e-executive*—effectiveness. For this to happen, however, we will need to get focused—quickly—on the fact that within the next five years, almost all executives will need to become e-executives. Indeed, we anticipate that there will be no need for a special chapter on e-executives in the second edition of this book. By that time, we expect that the impact of information technology on executive work will be so profound that every chapter will be about e-executives! In the meantime, however, the purpose of this chapter is to identify the priorities and attributes that we believe will characterize the effective e-executive for the next . . . dare we say . . . five years.

To date, the topic of e-executives has received more popular than scholarly attention and the business landscape is changing very quickly. So most of what we say will be based on others' observations and our own personal experience in the software industry. But in many ways, this is the nature of e-business—if you wait until you really know what's going on, you'll never get in the game.

We will begin by proposing that organizations are taking different strategic postures vis-à-vis the Internet and digital technology. We will use these postures to differentiate e-executives from traditional, pre-Internet-economy executives. Next we will identify five technology-enabled changes occurring in the world of e-business:

connectivity, collaboration, navigation, personalization, and *speed.* These are the gravitational forces that are creating the new business space that executives and organizations are challenged to navigate and explore. As we discuss each of these forces, we will speculate on their implications for the priorities of e-executives. We will conclude the chapter by identifying five key implications of these priorities for e-executives and those of us interested in helping them become more effective.

E-Organizations and E-Executives

As the new e-business space has opened up, organizations and their leaders have taken different strategic postures. Some have bet their futures on the new space, others have sent out probes, and still others have stayed home. Those who have launched into the new space are finding that different forms of organizing are more effective than others. They are at the forefront of figuring out the anatomy and physiology of an effective e-organization. The executives in this group are also adapting their priorities and learning new skills to suit the new e-business space.

Strategic Postures in E-Business Space

A continuum of strategic postures has begun to emerge. It is based on the degree to which a company's business model or functioning depends on the Internet and digital technology. A simple question differentiates organizations along this continuum: What percentage of this company's business model is dependent on the Internet?

At this point in time, we see four postures along this continuum: explorers, hybrids, migrators, and laggards. Each strategic posture places different demands on organizations and executives.

Explorers. Explorers are pure Internet players. Without the Internet, they wouldn't be in business. Dot-coms like Priceline.com, AOL, Yahoo, Homegrocer.com, and Expedia are all clearly explorers with 100 percent of their business dependent on the Internet. Internet infrastructure providers like Cisco Systems are also explorers. Clearly, executives in explorer companies are e-executives. But it's equally clear that there is great variance in effectiveness among executives at these companies, with many failing badly just within the past six months. In fact, by the time this chapter is published we may very well see some of these explorer organizations disappear or become something else while still others will appear on the horizon. Regardless, the e-executive has a tough job that requires a different mind-set, different priorities, and different attributes from those of the near past.

Hybrids. Hybrids are in the process of changing key company systems and strategies to exploit the potential of the Internet. Barnes and Noble, Circuit City, IBM, and Bank of America are examples of hybrids, selling to customers and working with partners in traditional as well as Internet-enabled ways. Hybrids in retail businesses have been dubbed "bricks and clicks." With its pure Internet plays (MSN) and its traditional franchise businesses (Windows, Office), Microsoft stretches across the strategic posture continuum from explorer to hybrid. But the company's Net strategy reveals its intention to bet its future success on its ability to be an explorer in Internet space.

We typically see a mix of traditional and e-executives in hybrid companies. And it is common to see these two groups in conflict over strategy and resource allocation in a hybrid organization. The successful e-executive in such a company must function as a change agent, dealing constantly with resistance from those who have a vested interest in maintaining legacy business assumptions, metrics, systems, and practices that were effective in the old economy. Resilience, political savvy, and a fair amount of evangelical zeal are required of e-execs in hybrid companies.

Migrators. Migrators continue to work with customers and partners in traditional ways, but have transformed and streamlined their internal operations through the use of information technology and digital tools (such as e-mail, finance, human resources, manufacturing systems). Heavy manufacturing companies (such as Boeing), pharmaceuticals (such as Merck), and professional service firms (such as McKinsey and KPMG) typically are positioned in this part of the e-organization continuum, although they may have some functions and business units that are more like hybrids.

While migrators value technically savvy executives, they typically place them in staff roles such as chief information officer rather than in operational roles. To our way of thinking, an e-exec runs a line business unit with a fundamental dependency on the Internet for its success. So we see technology executives at migrator companies as just outside the boundary of our definition of e-executive.

Laggards. Finally, there are the laggards. These are organizations that have chosen to ignore, avoid, or minimize the impact of the Internet and digital technology in their business. Many of these organizations will die protecting franchises and business models that worked in a pre-Internet business environment. Some executives in laggard organizations may justify their lack of interest and investment by explaining that their value proposition is based on personal, proximal contact and interactions with customers (as with restaurants, psychotherapists, home cleaning services, universities). While it may never be possible or desirable to totally replace human interaction with virtual interaction in many of these businesses, it is hard to imagine a business in which the Internet could not be exploited in some way to enhance customer interactions and streamline operations. Indeed, there seem to be explorers, hybrids, and migrators in almost every business category, thus putting the ultimate survival of laggards in question. We would not expect to find e-executives in a company with a laggard strategic posture. And placing a genuine e-executive in such an organization is a formula for frustration if not disaster.

Having described those we regard as e-executives, we will turn to a discussion of the technology trends that are driving e-business and the priorities we think are critical for e-executives in explorer and migrator organizations. Table 10.1 summaries these trends and their associated priorities for e-executives.

Connectivity

Connectivity and E-Business

The Internet and the wide, converging array of digital devices connected to it are making it possible for almost anyone to communicate instantly and inexpensively with anyone else (individuals, organizations, and communities) anywhere in the world. It's easy to imagine a time very soon when one could send copies to the world on an e-mail message. With an e-mail account, anyone has the potential to contact almost anyone else—potential buyers, sellers,

Table 10.1. Technology Trends and Priorities.

Technology Trends	Priorities
Connectivity	• Embracing and evangelizing the web lifestyle • Searching relentlessly for a "sweet spot" in the value chain • Building infrastructure ahead of demand
Collaboration	• Recognizing that the network *is* the business • Testing the limits of technology for collaboration—with customers, partners, employees • Balancing initiative and collaboration
Navigation	• Orienting everything to the customer • Knowing how you show up on the Net • Making navigation as simple and easy as possible for customers, partners, and employees
Personalization	• Stimulating perpetual fascination with the customer • Maintaining a rich, robust view of the customer • Staying in love with solving customer problems
Speed	• Pacing the business just ahead of the network's comfort zone • Attracting, inspiring, and keeping extraordinary talent • Reducing cycle times for organizing

partners—and prompt a business transaction at very low cost to both parties. Moreover, as digital devices become more sophisticated and the bandwidth of the Internet itself expands, the ability to reach anyone anywhere is enhanced with "richness" (Evans & Wurster, 2000). Voice, pictures, real-time collaboration and interaction, and other information-rich exchanges between parties can take place across the Internet; exchanges that previously required expensive travel or a global workforce.

From a business strategy perspective, the combination of reach and richness enabled by the Internet and digital devices has cut loose two forces that are shaking the world of business to its core: deconstruction and disintermediation. *Deconstruction* occurs when a competitor launches an Internet-enabled attack on a segment of the value chain established over time by a successful business or industry. Amazon.com, for example, deconstructed the value chain of established book retailers by allowing customers to buy books directly from its web site, eliminating the cost of physical bookstores from its business model. By tapping directly into the databases of book distributors and transforming those into a virtual catalog with millions of books on its web site, Amazon.com was able to move into direct and successful competition with well-established non-Internet (at that time) companies like Barnes and Noble. It used the Internet to change the rules of competition in the book business, thus deconstructing its established value chain. Of course, Amazon.com has yet to make a profit, but that goal now appears to be in sight.

Disintermediation is the second force loosed on the business world by the combination of richness and reach enabled by the Internet. When buyers and sellers can find each other directly, middleman businesses become unnecessary—disintermediated—and their business models quickly erode. As Gates (Gates & Hemingway, 1999, p. 78) describes it: "If you're a middleman, the Internet's promise of cheaper prices and faster service can 'disintermediate' you, eliminate your role in assisting the transaction between the producer and the consumer." For those aspiring to attack the territory of powerful incumbents with an installed base of customer relationships, the ability to go straight to customers via the Internet is an unprecedented opportunity to get in the game.

Connectivity and E-Executives

How is this new level of connectivity enabled by the Internet affecting the priorities of e-executives? Our observations suggest that successful e-execs hold tight to three specific connectivity-driven priorities:

- Embracing and evangelizing the web lifestyle
- Searching relentlessly for a "sweet spot" in the value chain
- Building infrastructure ahead of demand

Embracing and evangelizing the web lifestyle. In contrast to executives who are still living in the pre-Internet economy, successful e-execs have crossed or actually grew up on the e- side of the chasm. They assume, rather than question, that a great business will be digitally connected and global. They live and breathe in a networked world. This difference shows up not only in their business assumptions and strategies but in the way they work every day. Technology-based communication—enabled by devices such as the Blackberry Wireless Handheld, Internet Phone, Palm Pilot, or Pocket PC—is a way of life for e-execs. Equally important, they expect everyone in their organizations—and even external partners and customers—to communicate and work this way. Receiving and responding to several hundred e-mail messages a day is not at all uncommon for e-execs. They are true believers in the web lifestyle—at work and at home.

Nevertheless, e-execs understand that not everyone is as immersed in the web lifestyle as they are. And they understand that the size of their business opportunity depends heavily upon the rate of Internet technology adoption in the world at large. So they invest significant amounts of time and energy in evangelizing the possibilities of the New Economy in general and their business model in particular. They not only have to run a business, they have to evangelize the new perspective to employees, customers, partners, and investors on how business can be profitably conducted in a connected world. Like all pioneers before them, they must have an unwavering commitment to their vision—in this case, a web-based business and world. And they must be resilient and relentless in the face of skepticism, criticism, and sabotage from those who have good reasons to hold on to the assumptions that made them successful in an analog, low-connectivity business environment.

Searching relentlessly for a "sweet spot" in the value chain. For some time now, we have known that the sweet spot in the value chain, the factor that causes customer dependency, is developed and maintained through products and services that are valuable to the customer, that are rare in the marketplace, and that are difficult for competitors to imitate. We believe this principle is still true in e-business.

But in a superconnected world, that sweet spot is subject to constant change as customers' interests shift, competitors change their offerings, new partnerships are formed, or new employee talent is discovered, recruited, or developed. So when it comes to strategy and focus, there is no rest for the e-executive. Whether out of fear or aspiration, e-executives are perpetually forward-looking, knowing that if they stop moving forward, their survival is at risk. Change is regarded as an opportunity to level or tip the playing field in a new way to create competitive advantage—for a time. But there is a relentlessness in e-executives that keeps driving toward the next challenge, the next opportunity created by a competitor's mistake, a new way of using technology to change the rules of the game. There's a willingness to challenge long-successful business models through web, IT, and sheer business creativity.

Examples abound. Amazon.com, Microsoft, and AOL use their web presence and capabilities to leap across boundaries into new business categories like auctions, banking, and travel. Charles Schwab aggressively changes the rules of the game in its industry by providing customers with low-cost web-based transactions and rich, online market research. Priceline.com turns airline pricing on its head by auctioning customers to airlines with open seats. At their most aggressive, e-executives are so forward-looking they are even willing to cannibalize their own business models and recent successes with new approaches and offerings to stay close to the current sweet spot for their business.

Building infrastructure ahead of demand. Increasing connectivity means that the world of Internet users can access your organization as soon as they are aware of your web presence. It can happen anytime, day or night, by plan or accident. This ability to be linked with so many customers is an incredible marketing advantage for the e-organization. But it can also be deadly. Launch a web site and you may have a million visitors within a very short time. It's hard to predict the scope and scale of customer response to your offering. Max DePree's dictum—"Before you pull the trigger, know where you're going to put the body"—applies in spades in an e-business (personal communication, 1997). A high priority must be placed on building an infrastructure that is able to handle the sheer volume of interested customers who can now come through the door. E-execs must have enough technical savvy to understand the basic specifications of a web-based infrastructure and a nose for the technical talent needed to create and maintain potentially huge volumes of traffic and transactions. If the infrastructure is not ready when a customer clicks on your site, that customer is unlikely to come back. So the e-executive must place high priority on making investments in infrastructure that look risky given the current level of the business. Failure to do so will severely limit growth or even kill the company.

Collaboration

Collaboration and E-Business

The change in connectivity has stimulated another major change in the world of e-business. Using their intranets and the Internet, organizations are learning how to achieve new levels of collaboration internally and externally. These technologies are enabling rich communication and knowledge sharing and are ultimately changing the way work is done and managed within organizations. Although early results have been less than stellar, business-to-business (or B2B) collaboration and partnering is increasingly viewed as an important strategic investment as companies learn how to connect, communicate, and share data in interactive, inexpensive ways over the Internet.

Collaboration at this level obscures traditional boundaries between countries, organizations, communities, and individuals—boundaries that otherwise freeze pre-Internet business models in place and stand in the way of innovation and market evolution. When such boundaries disappear or shift, a window of opportunity for deep structural change in business and society opens wide.

Collaboration and E-Executives

The opportunity for Internet-enabled collaboration puts pressure on e-execs to keep their eyes clearly on three priorities:

- Recognizing that the network *is* the business
- Testing the limits of technology for collaboration—with customers, partners, employees
- Balancing initiative and collaboration

Recognizing that the network is the business. For over 50 years, Peter Drucker has been preaching "defining the business" as an executive's first priority. So what's new? What's new is that e-executives find themselves in a business environment where the Internet has made it possible to run and grow businesses in fundamentally different ways than in the past. Deconstruction and disintermediation put virtually every traditional business model at risk. Increased competitiveness drives e-organizations to focus on those segments of the value chain where they have unique capabilities and competencies. Trying to be all things to all customers has never worked well, but it's even more disastrous in the current environment.

Consequently, e-executives are constantly looking to partner with other e-organizations in delivering complete solutions to their customers. In theory, the Internet provides the connectivity and tools needed for partners to share critical business information in real time and work as a single virtual organization whose internal boundaries are transparent to the customer. In practice, working seamlessly with partners across company boundaries continues to be hard work. Nevertheless, the necessity of maintaining a clear competitive focus based on unique strengths will continue to prompt e-executives to form intensive partnerships, alliances, and joint ventures.

Testing the limits of technology for collaboration—with customers, partners, and employees. While much publicized, B2B efforts based on Internet-enabled technologies have been disappointing to date. Business exchanges between partners and companies are often complex, and our technologies either do not provide the richness necessary for effective real-time collaboration or companies don't really know how to take advantage of the technological capabilities available to them. Even in the face of these partnering challenges, the e-executive keeps pushing the collaboration envelope, knowing that companies that figure out how to collaborate most effectively online will gain a foothold with customers and partners that may be difficult for others to overcome.

To get others to test the limits of the technology for collaboration, e-executives understand that they walk a fine line between successful and unsuccessful collaborative efforts. Pushing the limits of what can be done puts everyone in the path of potential failure as well as great success, and sometimes allows collaborative efforts to break down as quickly as they are built. But collaboration enabled by technology with allies and even rivals is a business necessity.

Balancing initiative and collaboration. This challenge haunts every e-executive we know. Just as the Internet and digital tools make external partnerships feasible in ways not previously possible, intranets and e-mail can enhance internal collaboration and coordination across groups within a company. For example, connectivity through e-mail enhances "mutual adjustment" (individuals actually having direct, two-way conversations) which is the most flexible but least scaleable mechanism for coordinating work across organizational structures and units (Mintzberg, 1978). But where e-mail use becomes the default way to communicate in an organization, mutual adjustment can scale far beyond what could be achieved in its absence. Intensive e-mail use increases the number of people with whom one can have rich coordinating communications in a given period of time, potentially knitting together cross-organizational processes and interdependencies that inevitably remain after reporting structures are put in place. In theory, even matrix organizations might actually be made to work.

But it's never that simple. E-executives know they need initiative and action as much as they need collaboration. And many have designed selection processes to identify people who are ready to spot problems, take quick action, and learn from what happens. Because e-business moves so fast, there is also the constant risk of failing to act and losing or disappointing customers or partners. While e-organizations require highly individualistic and super-motivated people, it can be difficult to get these highly charged individuals to work together. Overcollaboration can be seen by many as a barrier to getting the job done. So although there are tremendous opportunities and need for collaboration in e-organizations, *over*collaboration can drain initiative desperately needed to respond quickly to the marketplace. Just because technology enables collaboration doesn't mean we should get overly excited about designing more interdependence into our organizations than is absolutely necessary.

Navigation

Navigation and E-Business
Finding and connecting with the people, organizations, communities, or information you need to execute a business strategy or

transaction is a fundamental challenge for any business or organization. Without the benefit of the Internet, we do this through a limited and often inefficient search process.

The Internet changes this process in a dramatic way. It shifts the balance of power between buyer and seller by enabling the buyer to engage in broad, nonhierarchical searches for products or services. Using an Internet navigator (such as Yahoo or MSN Shopping)—an online incarnation of a service like *Consumer Reports*—buyers can quickly identify virtually all vendors of a particular product or service worldwide and access objective evaluations of those vendors by the navigator.

Since the navigator's primary affiliation is with the buyer and not the seller, it has an interest in ensuring that evaluations are accurate and objective. This sets up a dynamic in which companies must focus primarily on doing a great job of solving customer problems versus selling and negotiating with an information-poor customer. With Internet-powered navigation services available, buyers and sellers can find each other quickly and efficiently, disintermediating middlemen who no longer add value and starving businesses that aren't responsive to customers.

Navigation and E-Executives

Navigation drives three key priorities for e-execs:

- Orienting everything to the customer
- Knowing how you show up on the net
- Making navigation as simple and easy as possible for customers, partners, and employees

Orienting everything to the customer. When customers have broad access to information about the full range of vendors, they become far more demanding. Effective e-executives understand this pressure and know that their organization is constantly subject to evaluation by both customers and navigators. The only way to be successful in such an environment is to ensure that all aspects of the organization—strategy, structure, systems, people, culture—are clearly focused on the interests of customers. There is no such thing as a successful e-organization without an intense focus on customers. E-executives take the lead in keeping this priority in front of employees, partners, and customers.

Knowing how you show up on the net. Navigators provide e-executives with incredibly leveraged marketing exposure to a global audience. But having someone else control your company's image in this way is dangerous unless it is attended to and managed. Consequently, e-execs watch very closely how they are being represented by navigators.

To influence how they appear through the market window of the navigator, e-executives invest in building proactive and positive relationships with navigators. And they respond quickly to correct problems that lead to negative exposure on the net, knowing that they may only have one chance with a customer who has exposure to a world of suppliers.

Making navigation as simple and easy as possible for customers and partners. Navigation is not just a service provided by outsiders. E-executives are passionate about making it as easy as possible for customers and partners to get to know and work with their company online. Few things are more frustrating to e-executives than the customer or partner who gives up on their company because of an inability to maneuver efficiently through the organization's online or technologically enabled interfaces. Once again, you can't assume you'll get more than one chance at a customer or partner in an e-business environment.

Personalization

Personalization and E-Business
The fourth major change in the world of e-business is in the degree to which information on the behavior or preferences of large numbers of individuals can be gathered and mined for information that can be used to craft and deliver personalized messages or advertising to that individual. Evans and Wurster (2000) call this the "Segment of One."

As individuals move through a company's web site choosing to investigate certain products or pages more closely, their movements are easily tracked and their interests inferred. When a product is purchased from an e-tailer, that information is captured and stored at almost zero cost to the company. Purchase patterns can then be mined from these databases, enabling the company to personalize information on the interface each customer pulls up when signing onto the company's web site (offering music recommendations, auctions of interest, chat rooms likely to appeal to that customer).

Although there are issues of personal privacy that must be addressed as these methods become more and more sophisticated, the potential benefit of personalization to users is immense. The low cost and efficiency of data gathering and data mining enabled by the Internet and digital technology makes the prospect of mass market reach combined with the power of segment-of-one marketing a near-term reality.

Increases in personalization go beyond marketing in companies like Dell Computer, where the customer is able to go online to configure and order a PC or server to meet his personal requirements. When followed with fast delivery and responsive customer technical support, this kind of personalized interaction raises the bar on customer expectations. As we become accustomed to being treated in a personal way, our tolerance for generic product and service offerings falls rapidly. Companies that fail to exploit the advantages of technology to understand and be more responsive to their customers' specific interests and needs are likely to fall quickly behind those who can exploit this capability.

Personalization and E-Executives

As if she didn't have enough to worry about with the previous nine priorities, the trend toward increasing personalization of business offerings surfaces three more urgent priorities for the e-executive:

- Stimulating perpetual fascination with the customer
- Maintaining a rich, robust view of the customer
- Staying in love with solving customer problems

Stimulating perpetual fascination with the customer. This fascination must be developed from the inside out as it challenges the way we think about those we serve and for whom we provide products. In the New Economy, e-executives aren't alone in their search for new ways to connect, collaborate, and navigate. Many customers are aware that their market power has drastically increased and that they may be able to command much more personal attention from would-be suppliers than ever before.

For the e-executive, such high expectations from customers must be viewed as an opportunity rather than a problem. He must be genuinely and perpetually fascinated with customers and potential customers. The e-executive must have and model a contagious passion and curiosity for understanding, interpreting, and empathizing with individual customers: how do they live, what do they want and need to do with their time and resources, how do they want to be treated, how are these things changing? The e-executive is once again relentless in keeping this fascination and commitment to the customer vital among everyone in the company.

Maintaining a rich, robust view of the customer. Though the data mining technologies hold incredible possibilities for getting to know individual customers and defining market segment trends, e-executives are a forcing function in their organizations for maintaining a richer, deeper view of customers than just what quantitative data will allow. Overreliance on quantitative data can introduce a view of the essentially mythical *average customer.* This can lead to decisions that fail to unveil critical variance in customer needs, interests, and behaviors. Organizations with chronic oversimplification have a way of pouring resources into campaigns and strategies that will miss the customer's interest like an arrow sailing by the straw target it was intended to hit. E-executives look to a variety of resources—dialogue, data, intuition—to understand how the customers are reacting, what they think about what the organization is doing, and how all these reactions and perceptions are changing.

Staying in love with solving customer problems. Literally hundreds of e-executives have failed in the past year. One virtually certain path to failure in an e-business is to fall in love with the market opportunity, the technical challenges, or with the chance to become rich overnight.

E-executives with staying power are crystal-clear that a successful business—whether e-business or traditional business—must create value or solve problems for customers. A successful e-business is certainly not about a web site or having a web presence, it is about delivering customer value. Like their successful predecessors in the pre-Internet economy, e-executives never let their people or their partners forget this fact in the midst of all the marketing hype that has accompanied the rise of the Internet.

With the increase in customer power afforded by the capabilities of the Internet—connectivity, collaboration, navigation, and personalization—keeping a top priority on delivering customer value is simply more important than ever before. So it's a critical priority for e-executives.

Speed

Speed and E-Business

We've seen steep increases in the speed of business due to technology innovation and adoption before; for example, with the printing press, the railroad, the telegraph, the automobile, the airplane, the telephone, the television. But with its capacity to connect buyers, sellers, and suppliers instantly, inexpensively, and interactively anywhere in the world at any time, the Internet has increased the pulse of business to an unprecedented level. As Richard McGinn, chairman and chief executive officer of Lucent Technologies, says, "You either move with speed or die. It's the converse of 'speed kills.'"

Even companies in the software industry that are accustomed to fast product development cycles have had to speed up to keep pace. Before the Internet, development cycles for major software products like operating systems or productivity applications were 24 to 36 months. This cycle time was already twice as fast as IBM development cycles for mainframe operating systems. Not only did it take 24 to 36 months to build the major products, but deployment costs for upgrades or new systems made customers reluctant to move more quickly than that. But the implementation of "software as a service" across the Internet will change this scenario dramatically. When deployment and system administration is done by the software vendor across the Internet, it becomes possible to control and deliver almost continuous upgrades of major products. This will drive software service vendors like Microsoft, Sun, and Oracle to development cycles in their core software businesses that approximate those of Internet portals like AOL, MSN, and Yahoo, where changes in service occur in a matter of weeks rather than months.

Bill Gates describes the increase in the velocity of business this way:

> If the 1980s were about quality and the 1990s were about reengineering, then the 2000s will be about velocity. About how quickly

the nature of the business will change. About how quickly business itself will be transacted. About how information access will alter the lifestyle of consumers and their expectations of business. Quality improvements and business process improvements will occur far faster. *When the increase in velocity of business is great enough, the very nature of business changes.* A manufacturer or retailer that responds to changes in sales in hours instead of weeks is no longer at heart a product company, but a service company that has a product offering [Gates & Hemingway, 1999, p. xiii, italics added].

Speed and E-Executives

The pulse of e-business may be the single most important difference between the world of the traditional executive and that of the e-exec. E-executives think, decide, and act more quickly. They develop and adapt products and services faster. They respond to customer needs more quickly. They communicate in higher volumes at higher speeds both internally and externally. They change strategies, policies, and organization structure and processes constantly and quickly to keep people and groups aligned with and focused on what's happening now in the network of the business. Speed is necessary for survival in e-business and e-executives set their priorities accordingly:

- Pacing the business just ahead of the network's comfort zone
- Attracting, inspiring, and keeping extraordinary talent
- Reducing cycle times for organizing

Pacing the business just ahead of the network's comfort zone. Going too slow is deadly for an e-business, but so is going too fast. There are inherent risks in going too fast and changing too often. As Microsoft CEO Steve Ballmer has said: "The fact of the matter is that customers can't take cataclysmic change every three months. The organization also can't. You can ship products quickly. But you can't say, 'Oh, we have a radically new strategy' every three months" (quoted in Cusumano & Yoffie, 1998, p. 306).

The two areas where going too fast is a particular risk for e-executives both involve interactions with people. Going too fast for customers can lead to the permanent loss of not only that customer but thousands of others who hear about it through the wonder of the Internet. Once a navigator starts evaluating potential vendors, then everybody else gets those evaluations. At that point you become exposed to an evaluation that can be immediately distributed all over the world. Going too fast with employees can also be deadly for the e-executive. In an environment where success will be determined by the ingenuity of your employees in dealing with unpredictable business challenges, failing to take the time necessary to recruit and select the best people available will have dire consequences for the organization. And failure to notice and respond to signs of employee overwork and stress leads to retention problems that will inevitably slow down even the most strategically savvy and financially successful company.

Hiring extraordinary people with extraordinary quickness. There is no substitute for extraordinary talent when you are inventing your business every day. E-executives who hope to create a great e-organization understand that their single most important priority is to create an environment in which extraordinary people believe they have the opportunity to do the best work of their career.

Extraordinary employees for e-organizations are driven by a variety of values, but a sense of purpose, making a contribution, growing their competence, and getting immediate rewards for great work are at the top of the list. To assume that the promise of great wealth will be enough to attract extraordinary talent is naive and dangerous for the e-executive. People with extraordinary talent want to grow and use their talent. Just like e-customers, extraordinary employees will click quickly to the next employer if their needs for competence, contribution, and fun are not being met—today.

E-executives ensure that the hiring profile includes the ability to think fast under pressure and act decisively without being sure of the outcome. They also make sure that the hiring process of their organization values keeping the bar high versus filling the immediate need.

Reducing cycle times for organizing. It's not uncommon at Microsoft to hear people tell newcomers: "If you don't like your manager, just wait three months for the next reorganization."

E-organizations function best when the overall direction or vision for the company is clear and compelling. But within the bounds of that direction, there is a common understanding that there is no clear road map to that destination. Individuals and groups are expected to pay close attention to what's happening now and create solutions to problems as they arise. It is understood that periodic reorganizing is necessary as strategy and tactics must adapt in response to current challenges and feedback from customers, partners, employees, and others.

While high-technology organizations have a reputation for maintaining flat structures, we would argue that flat is less important than flexible. E-organizations can neutralize the more negative effects of hierarchy by using the connectivity, collaboration, and navigation capabilities of information technology (such as e-mail and intranet knowledge management).

E-executives understand that dynamic markets and strategies will require constant adaptations in the way work is organized and managed. So they preach the same sermon clearly and consistently: Reorganization is not bad; it's essential to our survival; it's a way of life. Of course, their goal is not to reorganize and disrupt execution just for the sake of variety. This happens far too often in e-organizations. Their goal is organizing in a way that delivers maximum customer value, at an acceptable cost, while providing motivating work for employees.

When reorganizing, the e-executive's priority is to make the necessary organizational adjustment while minimizing downtime, that is, the amount of time during which goals and roles are unclear and execution is disrupted. This is critical to minimize disruption of service to customers and partners, and also to ensure that employees have a strong sense of progress, momentum, and contribution. Extraordinary employees will not suffer inept leadership and reorganization more than a couple of times before they move to greener pastures.

Implications for Enhancing E-Executive Effectiveness

This chapter was written with three audiences in mind: e-executives, those who want to be e-executives, and those who are in the business of helping e-executives be more effective. We think our discussion of trends and priorities has implications for each of these audiences. We've framed these implications for each audience in terms of several key questions that can help clarify thinking and action in real situations that these audiences are dealing with today.

Implications for E-Executives

No executive can function successfully with 15 top priorities, so in a sense we've already done a disservice to e-executives by not compressing our discussion down to a more manageable list. We won't do this for you, but the following questions should help you gain a deeper understanding of your leadership challenges and what actions will be most helpful to your effectiveness:

Why do you personally care about building this business? An evangelist is either a true believer or a charlatan. Eventually, customers, employees, partners, and investors will figure out which you are. To be effective in evangelizing a radically new perspective and vision for an e-business, you must be crystal-clear about your own motivations and be willing and able to share them with others. There is no substitute for conviction, courage, and clarity for the e-executive.

Where is the sweet spot in the network that is your business today? After the recent carnage, most e-executives are clear that eventually their company needs a business model that will make money— probably sooner rather than later. Given the customer opportunity you've chosen to pursue, your organization's unique strengths and weaknesses, and the relative positions of your partners and competitors in the business today, you need to be able to articulate what your sweet spot currently is and how it should be measured. As Peter Drucker states so clearly: a leader must able to identify what constitutes meaningful performance for the organization (Hesselbein, Goldsmith, & Beckhard, 1996). In the case of e-business, this definition must be revisited on a regular basis to hit the current sweet spot.

Have you hired people with extraordinary talent—or have you hired people with extraordinary talent for the e-business environment? The old saying that the "best predictor of performance is past performance under similar circumstances" has never been more true. Particularly the part about under similar circumstances. The strategic and technical demands, the intellectual and emotional flexibility, and the speed required in the world of e-business are all at least a step above what most companies—even high-tech—companies have experienced in the last decade. Challenging the circumstances under which a candidate built a great track record may be the wisest investment of time you make in the selection process.

Are your accelerator and your brakes working effectively? Too many executives get caught up in the need for speed without taking a moment to weigh the risks of moving too fast. Confusing customers and partners, undermining operational execution, and burning out employees with too much speed and change can be disastrous. Simple awareness of how fast you're going in different parts of your business is the first step to managing your speed. And since most e-execs have a bias for too much speed, it is important to check in with others—employees, customers, partners—to get their views of your current and optimal speed in each of these areas.

Implications for Potential E-Executives

It's obvious that the demand for e-executives will grow as the e-business expands. So the opportunity is there for those who would like to prepare to be an e-executive or those who are currently in traditional executive roles and would like to make the transition. If you fall in this category, here are key questions for you to ask as you explore this possibility:

Are you living the web lifestyle or are you willing to make the leap? Unless you are willing to incorporate the web and emerging digital devices into your life and work, it will be difficult to be a credible e-executive who can attract and inspire others in an e-business. Only by getting fully engaged in the web lifestyle will you be able to think and feel like a customer or partner. Only by investing yourself in understanding and using the technology will you be able to imagine new ways of delivering value to customers in a distinctive, web-enabled fashion. Are you sufficiently enthusiastic about technology to make it at least a hobby, if not a personal passion?

Are you ready to invest the time and energy necessary to build a business that must constantly reinvent itself? A start-up mentality and commitment level is essential for success as an e-executive. Given the stage of development of e-business, you have to be ready to work very long hours and tolerate a high level of personal risk. Many executives from traditional businesses who have made the crossover have found the price just too high. In addition, you'll need a much higher level of tolerance for uncertainty, change, and speed in e-business than in traditional business. Talking with e-executives—successful and unsuccessful—about the realities of their work and non-work lives is essential to discovering whether you should make the leap.

Are you willing to make partnership a way of life? As the priorities clearly show, successful e-executives must operate in a complex network of collaborative relationships—internal and external. Before launching your career in e-business, it's important to assess your interest and ability in building and maintaining effective working relationships with others. An e-business opportunity may look like taking a break from the dependencies that often feel like gridlock in a traditional large organization, but as an e-executive you are likely to find yourself engaged in an even larger and more complex network of relationships. Taking initiative will still be critical to success, but doing it at the expense of your business partners, customers, and employees will be disastrous in e-business.

Are you willing to do all it takes—or are you just testing an e-business strategy? We are fairly certain that most organizations will be encouraged, if not forced, to embrace technologies that allow them to connect, collaborate, navigate, personalize, and speed up. Therefore, to some extent, your transformation is inevitable. However, we also see significant problems for those who attempt to take on some of the characteristics of an e-business while ignoring others. To draw extraordinary talent and fail to provide them with the resources and support they need to keep pace with customers, competitors, and partners could be fatal. To put your organization out there on web, inviting your world of stakeholders to see you without the infrastructure to respond to their needs, would be equally dangerous. The difference will be in the extent to which you understand the implications of a dabbling sort of approach to an Internet-based strategy versus a full on commitment to e-business.

Implications for E-Executive Helpers

For those involved in the business of helping e-executives be more effective—either directly through coaching and development or indirectly through selection and placement—there are fascinating questions that flow from the priorities we've identified in this chapter.

What are the differences between highly effective and less effective e-executives? This chapter is at best speculative. There is a tremendous opportunity for research on the individual, organizational, and contextual factors that affect e-executive effectiveness. Such research might focus on differentiating e-executives from traditional executives, but we think the biggest opportunity is to study variance among e-executives. Now is the time because there have been so many noteworthy failures among e-executives recently. Such research will have to deal squarely with the criterion problem in defining e-executive effectiveness. One thing is certain. The criteria are evolving right along with e-business and the technologies that are making it possible.

How can we help traditional executives evaluate themselves as potential e-executives and then prepare for the transition? Past success can be one of the greatest barriers to future success. Traditional executives have built their careers on assumptions, knowledge, and skills that apply in large, relatively autonomous organizations operating in an analog world. We can do a real service for such executives by gathering the data necessary to provide a valid, substantive picture of what successful e-executives do, how successful e-strategies are formed, and how successful e-organizations are run—particularly in comparison with traditional, Old Economy organizations. A valid, realistic, and data-based job preview for the potential e-executive is badly needed.

How effective are our traditional tools for selecting, developing, and rewarding executives when applied to e-executives? Just like the executives we serve, those of us dedicated to supporting e-executive effectiveness must reevaluate all our tools and methodologies in the context of e-business, e-organizations, and e-executives. The incredible increase in speed alone may be enough to make many of our most powerful selection and development methodologies obsolete. As a profession, we risk extinction unless we move aggressively into research and practice that is focused on the emerging, evolving e-world.

Conclusion

Our highest hopes for this chapter are that it will stimulate discussion and research on e-executives. We will be delighted if everything we've written proves to be wrong when subjected to the crucible of empirical research. But there is no time to wait years for the research results to pour in before we get on with the business of selecting, coaching, developing, rewarding, and even terminating e-executives. Just as in e-business, learning through action, feedback, and reflection is needed to move forward as quickly and efficiently as possible to enhance e-executive effectiveness. Let's get on with it.

References

Cusumano, M. A., & Yoffie, D. B. (1998). *Competing on Internet time: Lessons from Netscape and its battle with Microsoft.* Carmichael, CA: Touchstone Books.

Evans, P., & Wurster, T. S. (2000). *Blown to bits: How the new economics of information transforms strategy.* Boston: Harvard Business School Press.

Gates, B., & Hemingway, C. (1999). *Business @ the speed of thought: Using a digital nervous system.* New York: Warner Books.

Hesselbein, F., Goldsmith, M., & Beckhard, R. (1996). *The leader of the future: New visions, strategies, and practices for the next era.* San Francisco: Jossey-Bass.

Mintzberg, H. (1978). *Structuring of organizations.* Upper Saddle River, NJ: Prentice Hall.

CHAPTER 11

Growing Global Executives

John R. Fulkerson

Imagine for a moment that you are the chief executive officer of a global business with offices in 120 countries. Further imagine that your company has a proprietary technology that will allow practically unlimited growth and provide a service that can improve the lives of a great many people. Now imagine that the only thing holding your company back is the lack of experienced, wise, and savvy senior global executives who can execute your company's business plan. The problem, in shorthand, is simply an inadequate supply of executive talent. This is a problem experienced by almost every global business organization. Solving it demands nothing less than disciplined attention to the development of a process pipeline that will deliver a sustainable stream of executive talent prepared to do battle in today's global business environment.

The overall objective of this chapter is to provide both the individual executive and the executive development professional or expert with guidance on how to help grow the executive talent demanded by a business world that now regards international borders as less and less of a barrier to the movement of ideas, goods, and services. The principles discussed in this chapter are intended for three audiences: the executive development professional charged with the design and implementation of an executive talent development pipeline, the individual executive looking for some ideas that can be used to improve personal performance, and the individual executive who is called upon to mentor or coach others and who can use a conceptual framework to help structure development actions.

There are five key conceptual frameworks that can provide the executive development professional or the individual executive with a road map for growing the personal competencies, knowledge, and wisdom to be more effective managing in today's complex global business environment (see Figure 11.1.) A discussion of these five conceptual frameworks serves as the outline for this chapter.

First, a working definition of a global environment is needed to provide a clear target for the required development outcomes. What does it mean for an executive or organization to be global? What are the characteristics that define the global environment? Answering these questions is an essential start for deciding what needs to be developed to impact a global business.

Second, competencies associated with successful international or global executives need to be identified. These global competencies provide grounding in the behaviors and actions required of global executives. If the right competencies are defined, even more specific targeted actions can be taken to develop the global executive and ensure that the developmental outcomes are linked to business and personal success.

Figure 11.1. Five Frameworks for Growing Global Executives.

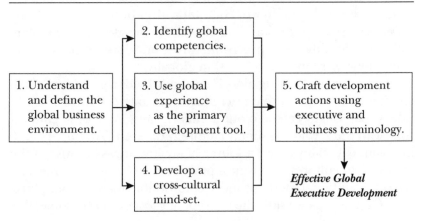

Third, certain key experiences are required to grow the skill sets needed by global executives. Much of what a global executive does requires a mind-set that thrives on complexity when confronted with situations that are emerging either for the first time or in combinations that have not appeared before. It is this experience that provides the foundation for functioning in this emerging, ever-more-complex world of global business.

Fourth, cross-cultural understanding must be seen as a foundation knowledge skill set. No global executive will succeed without a full grounding in, and understanding of, how different cultures have different business practices. Being cross-culturally effective is a fundamental prerequisite for better global business results. Without that understanding, the motivation and alignment of a global workforce is not possible.

Fifth, it is essential to understand personal growth and development from the executive's viewpoint. All too often, the executive development professional looks at development from a social science perspective rather than from the perspective of the executive. Understanding how chief executive officers and presidents think and actually learn provides key insights on how to structure the learning and growth experiences that will maximize executive development.

Understand and Define the Global Business Environment

Before discussing how to grow global executives, it may be helpful to start by developing a working definition of what is meant by *global*. A working understanding of what "being global" means can, with considerably more precision, direct our development of the competencies required to function globally.

The concept of "being global" currently holds a great deal of fascination, and some of that fascination is negative. On the positive side, *global* usually refers to our familiarity and increasing connectivity with those who are simply culturally different. An understanding of global reality is also a source of creative ideas because of the exposure to cultures or business practices that cause us to reexamine our traditional, perhaps more comfortable ways of doing business. On the negative side, the concept of *global* means, to some, that organizations and businesses that are better equipped to compete across international borders are also better equipped to mount competitive challenges within one country. This raises the question of whether globalization means that more economically powerful cultures eventually supplant weaker ones. This negative side of business globalization has been derogatorily referred to as corporate imperialism.

These perspectives raise a host of issues related to the understanding of how laws and trade practices govern the practice of international business. Any executive working across international borders today is likely to be confronted by issues like those just mentioned, which are well beyond the heavy demands of normal business operation and competition. Though this discussion may seem an odd way to begin a discussion of how to develop global executives, the point must be made that fundamental changes are under way in how business is conducted across international borders. To the international executive, clashes of culture and changing trade rules are a daily occurrence. Because these issues impact the competitive effectiveness of a business, executives must develop new and different skills to deal with social and political issues with the same intensity they develop skills in business practices. Global competition is happening, not just in terms of goods and services but also in terms of ideas and the intellectual and human capital needed to run a competitive global enterprise. Because of the increasing demand for human capital (a talented workforce), executives must spend a much larger proportion of their time on people and organization issues. Senior executives of global corporations spend as much as half of their time on such issues. This means an entirely different approach may be needed to develop the executives who are in the midst of living the complexity that comes with increased global competition.

Most social science discussions about the concept of global are couched in terms of management practices and the impact that cultural differences or similarities have on those practices. On the other hand, writings from the business community generally assume that the meaning of global is clear and then move forward with the thesis that all businesses must be more global if they want to survive in an increasingly competitive and connected world. These two perspectives on the meaning of global have different implications for developing executives and suggest that two tracks may be needed to produce a truly effective global executive. The social science perspective has more of a focus on process and organization effectiveness while the business track focuses more on the product or service delivery. The social science perspective is primarily competency driven while the business perspective is based on what and how things get done to provide a competitive advantage.

The primary developmental challenge coming from the social science perspective is that global executives must be cross-culturally effective. Rhinesmith (1993, p. x) defines a global executive as "the facilitator of personal and organizational development on a global scale." This social science definition sheds a little light on what a global executive does, but still does not tell us how to recognize one if we see one.

Back to the business perspective, Aaker and Joachimsthaler (1999, p. 137) state that "as more companies come to view the entire world as their market, brand builders look with envy upon those that appear to have created global brands whose positioning, advertising strategy, personality, look, and feel are in most respects the same from one country to another." The primary developmental implication from the business perspective is that executives must seek business and economic synergies while minimizing differences that add expense to a company's bottom line. Both of these views suggest, however, that if something (a practice, a process, a product, an individual executive) is global, it or they are everywhere in the world.

For the purposes of this chapter, a working definition of a global executive is a business leader who is effective regardless of where in the world the executive may focus attention or energy. In our working definition, geography and physical location are not sufficient to define global. The working definition suggests global can mean, for example, just thinking about an issue in another country from a home office located in a different country. As we use the term *global,* we are also referring to the mind-set that drives the actions that in turn help businesses and organizations succeed regardless of where the person or the issue is located. In this sense, *global* refers to a mind-set that takes into account the complexities of doing business anywhere in the world. Defining global in this manner takes us down a complex developmental path that suggests that a global executive must be simultaneously as facile as a diplomat and as rigorous as a systems engineer—and also able to juggle cultural differences to get people and far-flung organizations to work together for a common purpose. Our working definition of global forces a much more rigorous acceptance of the complexity that global executives must deal with and a more rigorous focus on learning about how to cope with that complexity than has been covered by traditional development methodologies.

More than a decade ago, Ohmae (1990, p. 18) wrote that "however managers do it, however they get there, building a value system that emphasizes seeing and thinking globally is the bottom line price of admission to today's borderless economy." Ohmae's comment would suggest that development must be focused on developing ways to see and think more broadly if one is to be an effective global leader. His description demands that an effective global executive understand how events in one part of the world affect those in another. If a factory in Thailand goes on strike, there well may be repercussions in Europe or the United States because delivery schedules are not met. Ohmae's comment also suggests that global executives must have a set of generalizable principles or values from which to make decisions or they will be forced into a dead end of tactical, knee-jerk decisions regarding every specific problem that arises. In the author's experience, effective global executives must have a mind-set that embraces and understands complexity from a broad frame of reference and experience.

A relatively new element added to this complexity mix is described by Tapscott, Ticoll, and Lowy (2000), who describes how the revolution in digital technology is further transforming business practices and impacting global executives. For effective global executives, the digital revolution means the potential for instantaneous connectivity with every market or office individual in their charge. It means global executives do not need to be physically "in country" to know all of the relevant metrics that measure how a given business or team or individual is performing. A global executive only needs to be connected to a company intranet or the web to know exactly what is happening to their businesses at any defined moment. The working definition of global must now be mixed with a sea of information inside a sea of global complexity.

The dust jacket on Thomas L. Friedman's (1999) book, *The Lexus and the Olive Tree,* describes globalization as "the integration of capital, technology, and information across national borders, in a way that is creating a single global market and, to some degree, a global village" Friedman (1999, p. 20) notes that the relevant market today is the planet earth, and further points out that Yale historians Paul Kennedy and John Lewis Gaddis are exploring how to broaden their curriculum offerings in order to develop a new generation of strategists who can think more as globalists than as particularists.

The developmental challenge that is emerging, driven by technology and its concurrent connectivity, is to decide how to help executives grow in the midst of enormous complexity while they are simultaneously running an enterprise. The challenge to a growing global executive is a little like building an airplane while flying it. Development is no longer a set curriculum bounded by a schedule or a well-defined career ladder tied to specific competencies. Global development is more likely to be defined in terms of just-in-time lessons, leading to actions needed in the moment, against situations that have not happened before. Events and circumstances are changing so rapidly that the business practice that was true yesterday may not be true tomorrow. This means that executive growth and development must take place in a literal sea of change and complexity encompassing geopolitical, environmental, cultural, governmental, organizational, and technological components in addition to traditional business requirements. Covering all the subsets of potential circumstances makes growing global executives an exciting challenge.

Davis and Meyer (2000, p. 6) make a case for why the complexities found in our new digital global economy also require new ways of thinking. They identify three current and future business principles that can be extended to help us to begin reframing how global executive development might be accomplished. First, the speed of change and the constant requirement for businesses to reinvent themselves will be much more likely to lead to healthy enterprises than will attempts at building business stability. As new ways of competing and new technologies emerge almost daily, the global executive must embrace rapid personal as well as business change. Constant learning and change must then become as natural as breathing for the effective global executive. Without embracing change, neither a business nor an individual executive will be likely to survive competitively.

Second, connectivity and information sharing are now part of the fabric of how all successful businesses operate. Ideas can now flow, because of digital technology, at a rate and speed unimaginable only a few years ago. This connectivity means improved alignment and contact between global decision-making groups. Schlender (2000) cites examples of how GE's Jack Welch and Sun Microsystems' Scott McNealy, both chief executive officers, communicate daily with their respective staffs with global e-mail. What follows, according to Davis and Meyer, is that open dialogue systems and executives will thrive while closed ones will wither. Ideas are everywhere and only open, continuous dialogue will deliver the rate of innovation required to drive businesses forward. Our successful global executives must be idea factories, using the weight of their office to find and spread new ideas and practices around the globe.

Third, Davis and Meyer state that the virtual will trump the physical in the emerging digital business world. This means that ideas and intellectual capital are fast becoming a primary source of competitive advantage, and global executives must grow constantly by gathering ideas from every country, culture, and individual employee. To do this well, global executives may not need to be webheads, but they will need to be increasingly technologically savvy. Putting Davis and Meyer's principles in developmental terms means that those charged with growing global executives will need to appreciate the need for global executives to have instant responsiveness to competitive challenges, to sort through vast quantities of relevant and irrelevant information, and to develop a conscious, passionate objectivity about finding better ways of doing things. It may well be that the nurturing and leveraging of human and intellectual capital will become more important, as a business practice, than the physical plant that produces a product. This suggests that growing global executives will require even more attention to the competencies needed to align and motivate global organizations. In shorthand, any global executive development system we construct must be fully in tune with a 24-hour, 7-days-a-week, 365-days-a-year, global, connected, and increasingly digital business world. Global executives will be required to think and act differently in this emerging competitive and complex business landscape. They will need to constantly learn new technology and ways of leading organizations whose employees have access to the same information as the executive and are, because of that access, increasingly suspicious of authority.

Identifying the Right Stuff: Global Competencies

Armed with an understanding of what it means to be global, specific competencies associated with being an effective global executive in that environment need to be identified. Clearly the ability to handle complexity is a primary competency that should receive a significant majority of developmental attention. Handling complexity means a global executive must have the ability to deal with issues ranging from normal business actions to trade policy, political actions, cross-cultural issues, and international law, as well as the more traditional personal effectiveness and organization leadership skills. And if our working definition of global is correct, then our superhero global executive must also be able to handle any of these issues anywhere and everywhere in the world. Fortunately, there has been a great deal of work done in the past decade to identify competencies that appear to be common to global executives. These competencies provide an excellent starting point for identifying what needs to be developed to produce a truly global executive.

Fulkerson and Schuler (1992) provided a list of empirically derived global success factors that helped distinguish between average and very strong international executives at Pepsi-Cola International (see Exhibit 11.1).

An examination of these success factors after the benefit of time suggests that they still reflect the realities of global business. The factors are rank ordered with the most important listed first. Importance was defined as having the largest differentiating power between average and very strong international executives. The executives who were studied to produce the factors were from a broad, multicultural sample. It is interesting to note that technical knowledge was eighth on the list and that handling business complexity was first. This rank order reinforces the notion, found in

Exhibit 11.1. Global Success Factors.

Factor	Actions
• Handling business complexity:	Figuring out what needs to be done and charting a course of action
• Drive and results orientation:	Focusing on an outcome and driving for completion
• Leads and manages people:	Directing the work of and motivating others
• Executional excellence:	Putting ideas into action
• Organization savvy:	Knowing how the organization works and how to maximize it
• Composure under pressure:	Staying focused in the internal pressure cooker and still getting things done
• Executive maturity:	Always acting with maturity and good judgment
• Technical knowledge:	Understanding and applying technical knowledge
• Recruits and develops good people:	Making the organization and individuals better
• Positive people skills:	Knowing how to get along with people from all cultures
• Effective communication:	Knowing how to communicate cross-culturally
• Impact and influence:	Being able to get things done when faced with obstacles

other studies of successful executives, that technical knowledge is rarely seen as the most important factor in determining success (McCall, 1998). All of the success factors in Exhibit 11.1 were defined in simple business outcomes or action language. This definitional simplicity made the factors understandable across cultures and allowed a common language to be developed that could potentially be discussed anywhere in the world. Even though the original language was primarily Western in form, a little work made the factors translate readily into other cultures. Because the competencies were essentially Western in origin, people from cultures with a strong Eastern flavor (such as China and Japan) had to work a littler harder to shift the definitions to their semantic space. In one focus group with a number of Indian executives in New Delhi, it took very little time for those executives to slightly modify the language to make the concepts applicable in their culture. It should be noted that most global business in India is conducted in English. Drive and results orientation, for example, quickly became simply making the business successful by working hard and not giving up. Once culturalized, the factors were then used to guide selection, development, and promotion actions. Most important, the factors provided a common language that worked across borders.

Using the twelve success factors, it is possible to paint a broad picture of the things a global executive must do. Subsequently, it also helps to guide the identification of an executive's deficiencies and the developmental actions that should be directed against those deficiencies. In summary, a truly distinguished global exec-utive should be able to accomplish the following:

- Decide on a course of action when confronted with a host of complicated business issues.
- Work hard and relentlessly to overcome obstacles to business actions.
- Lead and manage people from many different cultures.
- Take complex or difficult ideas and find ways to successfully execute them in the marketplace.
- Know how to get things done in a complex global organization.
- Remain composed, and still get things done, when under pressure.
- Be as mature and rational as possible in the face of uncertainty and ambiguity.
- Possess the technical and business information needed to reach optimal solutions for the business.
- Find and recruit the best people regardless of their nationality or culture.
- Maintain positive relations with a wide spectrum of people at all levels of the organization and the international geopolitical environment.
- Communicate effectively with and in multiple cultures.

- Make a difference or influence a course of action when faced with obstacles or problems.

This list of success factors, of course, represents an idealized executive—only a very select few are strong across the majority of the factors. What is important, for our purposes, is that the factors provide a language for drafting a developmental strategy around any or all of these success factors. What is most important for the executive development professional is that some competency system is needed to drive the development of a shared understanding of what developmental success might look like.

An example of a slightly different and less detailed competency model may be found in Black, Morrison, and Gregersen (1999). This model has four key components and starts first with the notion that curiosity or inquisitiveness is the core element for successful global leadership. The other three components of the model specify how executives look at the world (perspective), their emotional connection and integrity (character), and their clear sense of what needs to be done (savvy). The authors believe these four competencies are quite sufficient to describe a successful global executive. Black et al. also propose a simple four-by-three matrix that links four methods of development with the three career stages: early, midcareer, and late. For these researchers, there are only four developmental activities: traveling and working with global issues, working on global teams, action learning and networking, and transferring or physically moving from assignment to assignment and geography to geography. The author of this chapter believes the exact dimensions of a model are less important than the consistency with which a competency model is applied. The important action for the executive development professional is to apply and modify the same competencies over time. This will help build commonly understood measures of the competencies as well as commonly applied methodologies for developing them.

As a practical matter, if an attempt is made to build a development strategy for all competencies and their individual components simultaneously, that effort may be simply too complex to execute for any given executive. A more practical approach is to select a limited number of factors to work on at a time until some developmental objective is met and then move on to the next developmental priority. It is recommended that priorities for development be assigned based on what can provide the greatest and most immediate business or personal impact. This not only provides a greater likelihood of immediate positive feedback but links the development to meeting real-world, competitive business needs.

For maximizing the utilization of often scarce developmental resources, it must be pointed out that development is not the only method for delivering competencies to an organization. Some competencies are best "developed" through selection decisions—while some are best developed by supplying explicit, factual knowledge and others are best grown over longer periods of time through cumulative experience. For a better understanding of this three-part development scheme, see Exhibit 11.2.

Such a classification scheme can lead to a more intelligent allocation of resources and thereby increase the likelihood of developmental success. The first group of factors is representative of the core personality of a given executive. This core is somewhat resistant to change without the enormous application of resources and energy. With these core personality success factors, selection may be the most efficient way to get the skills into an organization. The second or explicit knowledge group is more specific to the business, industry, or profession and may be best learned from an understanding of the facts required, for example, to produce a product or complete a financial transaction. The third or tacit knowledge group of factors requires an understanding that comes from the ability to create higher orders of meaning from many discrete piles of situational information and data. This third group represents the art rather than the science of business, and is developed or grown primarily from an accumulation of wisdom based on having seen, learned from others, or experienced many similar situations.

For each group of success factors there are interventions that have a greater likelihood of success. Just as the core personality group is best developed by the selection of individuals who already have those qualifications, the business- or industry-specific competencies are best learned from explicit exposure to the hard facts of how things get done. The last grouping, tacit knowledge, represents the success factors that are best learned through experience-based exposure and require the teaching of skilled mentors or managers.

**Exhibit 11.2. Strategies for Developing
Global Success Factors.**

Factors	Group Definition	Primary Development Strategy
Core Personality Factors		
• Drive and results orientation • Composure under pressure • Executive maturity • Positive people skills • Effective communication	• Factors are learned during formative years from life experiences, considered part of core personality and operating style, and represent a core value system.	• Select rather than attempt to grow.
Explicit Knowledge		
• Executional excellence • Technical knowledge	• Factors are highly explicit and related to factual knowledge of the business, and the science of the business.	• Teach facts and processes with traditional, data-based delivery mechanisms.
Tacit Knowledge		
• Handling business complexity • Lead and manage people • Organization savvy • Recruit and develop good people • Impact and influence	• Factors are tacit and combine with other factors to lead to actions that move organizations, individuals, or business process forward. These reflect the art of business.	• Provide opportunity to learn over time—primarily through experience, practice, and diligent coaching and mentoring.

While it is true that none of these developmental approaches stands alone; the executive development professional or executive is simply advised to consider developing different competencies with distinctly different and appropriate methodologies.

The Role of Experience

Kets de Vries (1999) has spent the majority of his career teaching senior executives how to be and become more effective. In *The New Global Leaders,* he takes a close look at three highly successful global executives of significant stature to see what makes them more effective than others. He provides an in-depth look at how chief executives Richard Branson (Virgin Group), Percy Barnevik (ASEA Brown Boveri), and David Simon (British Petroleum) function in their respective global business environments. Combining these three cases with his extensive experience, Kets de Vries paints a picture of success factors much broader than the competencies outlined earlier. He suggests that when raw intuitive ability is combined with a series of ongoing business experiences, an effective global executive may be the result. It is experience that is the teacher rather than a set of codified facts. McCall, Lombardo, and Morrison (1988) provided a seminal work on how experience is often the best teacher. Their work provides a detailed look at how practitioners and individual executives can identify and structure experience to deliver powerful developmental lessons.

Kets de Vries (1999) says that at the highest conceptual level, "CEOs currently face two critical issues: going global and fostering employee loyalty at a time when organizations can no longer make meaningful long-term promises to their people" (p. xix). These issues are so broad and require such a range of skill that it is unlikely any curriculum can provide all of the knowledge and wisdom required to address them. It is through cumulative experience that a global executive develops a skill set adequately to address the issues faced in global business. Based on his research and experience, Kets de Vries outlines the many characteristics he sees as defining the global executive. The author of this chapter has taken the liberty of listing and reorganizing the points that Kets de Vries uses to define what an idealized global executive must be, have, or do (see Exhibit 11.3). The points are from Kets de Vries while the structure is from the chapter author.

The characteristics mentioned by Kets de Vries that may apply to any executive regardless of work setting are shown on the left-hand side of Exhibit 11.3. On the right-hand side of the exhibit, the author has again taken the liberty of specifying actions or abilities believed to be more specific to the global environment. In addition, asterisks on the generic side of the matrix mark several characteristics that, in the author's experience, are actually foundation requirements for a global environment, but certainly apply to both global and nonglobal environments.

Organization alignment, as defined by Kets de Vries, is necessary for any executive, and is certainly not limited to a requirement

Exhibit 11.3. Global Executive Characteristics.

Characteristics with Generic Executive Implications	Characteristics with Specific Global Implications
Organization Alignment	*Business Strategy*
• Mobilize people • Sustain change and innovation • Act as change agent • Team player • Collegial leadership style • Cultivate an authoritative not an authoritarian manner • Build organization structures aligned with the business • Motivate people to actualize their specific vision of the future	• Design a multicultural strategy • Tackle intensifying worldwide competition • Strategic awareness of socioeconomic and political scenes in other countries • Build a multi-country, multi-environment, multi-functional, globally connected strategy • Build a global mentality in the ranks
Personal	*Experience*
• Strong relational skills • Talented verbal and nonverbal communicator • Can step out of comfort zone • Sense of adventure • Take risks • Unwilling to give up	• Have humanities or engineering degree and an MBA • Work in foreign subsidiaries • Work with people with diverse cultural backgrounds • Speak more than one language • Acquire rich knowledge of a culture other than their own
Mind-set	*Mind-set*
• Not judgmental; acknowledging and valuing people's differences* • Willing to learn and acquire new attitudes and patterns of behavior* • High tolerance for frustration • Live comfortably with ambiguity* • Foster corporate values that answer basic human needs	• Proven competence in dealing with a world of rapid continuous change • Possess cross-cultural empathy • Strong sense of self and own cultural bias • Recognize diversity is the name of the game • Open to thinking across borders as much as national ones • Curious about foreign environment

Note: * indicates characteristics more highly valued in global environments than in single-country environments.

only for the global executive. The generic organization alignment characteristics, however, do have a flavor that reflects the New Economy and the attitudes most often associated with executives who are sensitive to the retention of a workforce that has more choices than they have ever had in the past. In particular, the ideas of sustaining change, collegial leadership, and working with and respecting others have assumed a level of importance not seen in historic competency lists.

Turning to the more specifically global characteristics described by Kets de Vries, being able to design a multicultural strategy (handling complexity), again emerges as a core overall characteristic. Our global business executive must be able to think across borders and get the organization to do the same. In the author's opinion, the characteristics listed by Kets de Vries are seen as a developmental end product best developed through cumulative experience. Most of the global characteristics are unlikely to be either wholly innate or learned in a classroom. While some of the characteristics may certainly be more natural to a given executive, to be fully developed, they require a lifetime accumulation of experience.

On the globally specific side of the ledger, the experiences of a global executive are also seen as heavily slanted toward working with or in different cultures and countries. Successful global executives will readily admit that having a sufficient number of life experiences outside their home country produces a much greater acceptance of differences and tolerance for ambiguity. Some of the most successful global executives see events or circumstances they have never seen before as simply different and are unlikely to put a "bad" or "good" label on them. This mind-set allows the executive to remain more dispassionate and objective about finding the right solution to a problem rather than operating from a position of personal bias. The generic characteristics suggest all executives should be able to take risks and seek new experiences, but—contrasted with the successful global executive—some executives are short of a visceral and personally experienced understanding of cultural differences.

In the last grouping, labeled mind-set, are found the characteristics that may be the most important in differentiating between a good and a great global executive. The generic executive has an open mind and is willing to learn and acquire new ways of doing things, but the global executive seems to possess a deep-seated and fundamentally different mind-set about the world and its cross-cultural similarities and differences. Being open, curious, and accepting of different cultures and customs allows the global executive to more readily adopt new ideas. This openness also allows a global executive to see possibilities where others are trapped in a narrower understanding or perspective of the world. In the author's opinion, the single most important developmental challenge to growing a global executive is to foster the ability to be initially nonjudgmental about how things are accomplished. This does not mean to be nonjudgmental about values or integrity but rather to suspend judgment until a situation and its circumstances are fully understood. The successful global executive recognizes there are many paths to accomplish the same end. As a practical example, consider the delivery of a consumer product—which can be carried on foot, on a bicycle, on a truck, or on an airplane; it doesn't matter as long as the product gets delivered. The global executive must develop a mind-set that is very objective and flexible but lacking in an excessive preconceived operational bias about how things work. A development of these mind-set characteristics demands a great deal of experience before the learning can be consistently and efficiently translated into action.

Rosen, Digh, Singer, and Phillips (2000) have a more simplified version of the things global executives must learn from experience than the one Kets de Vries proposes. Rosen et al. choose four global literacies to frame where experience-based learning should lead: personal, social, business, and cultural literacy. Personal literacy is about understanding and valuing yourself. Social literacy is about engaging and challenging others. Business literacy is about focusing and mobilizing an organization, and cultural literacy is about valuing and leveraging cultural differences. As in the matter of competencies, the exact system is less important than the consistent application of a shared understanding about what constitutes a successful global executive. Simply put, experience may truly be the best teacher.

The lesson that should be drawn from a comparison of what was said about competencies and broader, experience-driven characteristics is that a global executive must be constantly exposed to cross-border business and leadership issues. True global awareness takes place only when an intellectual awareness is coupled with the visceral and emotional feel of personal experience. This means developmental events like living in-culture and hopefully having a series of mentors—both home-country and in-country—who are available to guide the consolidation of learning.

Cross-Cultural Understanding

Behind any list of the specific characteristics of successful global executives, there is clearly a recurring theme of the importance of cross-cultural understanding. This basic understanding of cross-cultural differences is one of the most critical pieces of the mind-set puzzle that makes a global executive effective. For a more complete treatment of the importance of cross-cultural differences and how they may be managed, see Trompenaars (1994) and Fulkerson (1998). For our purposes here, it is clear that a mind-set that is thoroughly entrenched in multicultural issues is a basic foundation for any global executive. For anyone to claim to be global, a heavy immersion in cultures and cultural practices that are very different from the one in which they were born is required. This immersion is not simply a matter of an intellectual awareness of how things are different. There must be, in any global executive, a visceral understanding of how problems can be creatively solved if approached with a global, cross-cultural mind-set. It is this awareness that leads to an openness to new ideas and concepts and realization that ideas may come from any source, anytime, anywhere on the planet.

Trompenaars (1994) specifies seven powerful, essentially bipolar comparisons on the key dimensions of culture that represent how different cultures and countries differentially view the world. These dimensions are shown and briefly defined in Exhibit 11.4. Examples of cultures that predominantly hold to one side of the dimension are also represented. It is unlikely that any executive will be able to articulate the Trompenaars dimensions in an academic sense, but he must be able to articulate country-specific behaviors such as the sequential nature of the Germans, the synchronic tendencies of the Arab, and the indirect nature of the Japanese.

The key point is that, developmentally, a global executive has a mind-set that is grounded in the acceptance of differences and

Exhibit 11.4. Seven Dimensions of Culture: Representative Cultures.

Dimension 1

Universalism	versus	Particularism
(Rules apply to everyone)		*(Rules are bent depending on the particular individual or situation)*
(Canada, United States, Switzerland)		(South Korea, Venezuela, Russia)

Dimension 2

Individualism	versus	Collectivism
(Individuals are always accountable)		*(The group or organization is more accountable than the individual)*
(Canada, United States, Norway)		(Nepal, Kuwait, Egypt)

Dimension 3

Neutral	versus	Affective
(Emotions and feelings should be excluded from actions and decisions)		*(Emotions and feelings are integrated into all decisions)*
(Japan, Indonesia, United Kingdom)		(Italy, France, United States)

Dimension 4

Specific	versus	Diffuse
(Actions are taken in the light of the specifics of a situation or a relationship—for example, share information only about a specific topic)		*(Actions are not specific, but rather done based on the value of the action with limited regard for the specifics—for example, share information about everything)*
(Sweden, United States, Denmark)		(Yugoslavia, Hungary, China)

Dimension 5

Ascription	versus	Achievement
(Personal status is driven by descent, sex, age, wealth, and so on)		*(Personal status is based solely on personal achievements)*
(Egypt, Turkey, Argentina)		(Norway, United States, Canada)

Dimension 6

Internal	versus	External
(Actions are taken on the basis of what the individual thinks is important)		*(Actions are taken on the basis of what the market demands or others want)*
(United States, Switzerland, Pakistan)		(East Germany, China, Egypt)

Dimension 7

Sequential	versus	Synchronic
(Order, logic, and time are paramount)		*(Order, logic, and time all flow, if not randomly, certainly not sequentially)*
(United States, West Germany)		(Indonesia, Russia, Venezuela, Saudi Arabia)

Source: Adapted from Trompenaars, 1994.

sees those differences as sources of information and inspiration that help solve problems. Growing a global executive requires an identification of experiential ways to make the internal maps and mind-sets of that executive broader and more flexible. The reason for doing this goes well beyond the simplistic notion of cultural awareness. Knowing that Americans and Germans are different, for example, is useful—but it is more important to be able to translate that knowledge into the steps that permit collective business-building actions.

Essentially, cross-cultural effectiveness is learned by exposure to and practice with different cultures. This is an example of where a combination of exposure to material explaining how cultures differ and living in a culture will build effectiveness. Developmentally, the practitioner as well as the executive must make a conscious effort to determine how cultural practices are different and what the implications of those differences are for business actions. There are very effective cultural immersion programs as well as a significant body of literature explaining how different cultures operate and perceive the world. An effective global executive must have— and make the effort to build—a skill set that allows an effective understanding of many different cultures.

Development from the Executive's Perspective

Interestingly enough, global executives do not generally think about their personal development in the same terms used by the executive development professional. Fulkerson (1999) offers what is termed an "operating system" that specifies how global leaders organize the complex world in which they live. In this model, global executives add value by bringing cohesive meaning or a highly personalized operating system to the complexity they confront. The value added by a given executive comes from the organization of four major ways of viewing the world: a vision or a plan for the future of an enterprise, cross-cultural awareness, a set of personal values that, in turn, provide a foundation for sustainable principled action, and finally an inherent preferred decision or thinking style. Growing an effective global executive means adjusting the way all four components are organized and focused on a problem. These four components make up an executive's operating system or preferred way of dealing with the world. An operating system is somewhat predictable and allows the identification of developmental steps that can make an executive more effective. Development actions should focus on understanding how the individual executive organizes personal experience and using that understanding to design targeted developmental actions.

After working with a global organization composed entirely of chief executive officers and presidents from almost every country in the world, joined together for the sole purpose of educating themselves, a very different perspective emerged for the author about how executives conceptualize their personal development. The author's representation of a global executive's perspective on development is shown in Figure 11.2. In summary, the figure illustrates a thinking- and experience-driven form of development that is intensely personal and unique for each individual executive and his respective business.

First and foremost, these practicing executives do not generally think in terms of competencies the way an executive development professional does. They start from the position that they need to do something better or to make their respective businesses more profitable. Their development agenda is simply a product of their personal life and business proposition at any given moment. In this sense, the development agenda may literally change from moment to moment depending on what is happening to their business and their personal experience of that moment. After observing this elite group of young chief executive officers and presidents, it is apparent their development starts when something in their external or internal environment changes. Development takes place in the day-to-day business world rather than in any structured, contrived way. Development for senior executives is usually not a well-thought-out or carefully considered path but rather a complicated mix of intentions, ideas, information, and connectivity all viewed through the lens of personal experience and needs. Development for these executives is driven by the need to "be better"—which is, in turn, determined by their unique needs, their business issues, and their current life stage. Development for these individuals often can be nothing more than a simple fact that turns out to be useful. Development can also be a conscious, longer-term effort to understand something like a complicated business process or rollout of

Figure 11.2. Development from the Global Executive's Perspective.

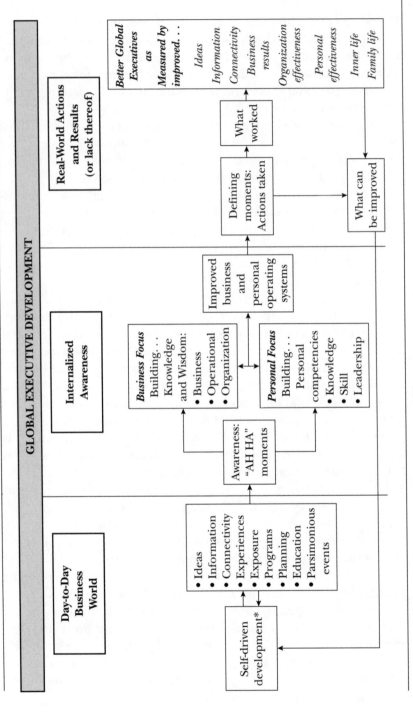

Note: * Factor determined by needs, business issues, and life stages.

a new product. It is, however, almost always done in the context of running a business.

For the executive, *development* and *learning* are essentially synonymous. Both terms refer to the total of all the actions required to do things differently or better. Executives do not start with a specific thought about how to develop or learn something, but rather about how to get a particular outcome or result. In this sense, development or learning are the by-products of getting results. These executives have experiences or thoughts or feelings that produce an awareness that suggests that what was valid is now altered. The altered awareness is the "AH HA" moment that drives a focus on how to understand what is happening or has happened, but more important, what "TO DO" about that altered awareness. The "TO DO" is usually to take some action or do something different and see if things get better. It should be noted that quite often doing nothing and waiting for more data can also be a very sound strategy.

If senior executives are driven to achieve, and they are, then motivation is not a developmental problem. The developmental challenge is where to focus their attention at a given moment. The driven need to achieve leads these executives to be constantly exposed, by choice, to a wide range of topics related to their current business or personal demands. This exposure may be referred to as an ongoing series of mini-learning events that occur in the course of running a business. The vast majority of development takes place on the run and is internalized as attention to a simple fact or an "AH HA" moment. Development for the senior global executive is fragmented and composed of the experience of factoids and things that simply happen. This total awareness is then coded into either a business or personal understanding bucket. There is often some internal awareness that something has changed and that awareness is either filtered or stored in their personal operating system. The learning, however, is not something that becomes permanent until some action is taken or some feedback is received. If the action leads to a positive outcome, then it is likely to be repeated when appropriate. If the action is not so successful, it will still be stored away as something to avoid in the future.

From the successful global executive's perspective, development is constant and a part of ongoing business and personal life.

Development—that is, learning—is like the air they breathe. It simply is. For the executive development professional, it is a mistake to attempt to build too much structure into executive development. When dealing with self-motivated, achievement-oriented senior executives, development is something that is best tied to the real world of global issues as opposed to something that is done with the express intent of learning something specific or academically interesting. Global executives drive their respective businesses in a process similar to the way children learn language. They do development as a daily course of action. If something works, it is repeated and if it does not work, it is not repeated—but it is filed away as something to avoid in the future.

Integrating the Concepts

The five conceptual frameworks that have been covered to this point should all be considered when attempting to grow global executives. Each of the preceding sections contains some ideas and thoughts about how to grow global talent. There are, however, some specific considerations for development that deserve mention.

Understanding Global

Understanding the breadth and scope of the global environment provides both context and content for development actions. Our working definition of global focuses us on the content that must be included in the development of a global executive. That content must deal with a wide range of knowledge and understanding. The topics included for understanding must be well beyond those associated with simple business functions or organizational effectiveness. The topics must include geopolitical understanding, economic understanding, political (country or geopolitical) understanding, along with cultural issues and differences. To build an understanding of what it means to be global, the executive should constantly be on the lookout for different ways of doing things, in constant discussion with peers from other parts of the globe, and constantly asking questions about how things are done. Even something as mundane as reading a publication like the *Economist* on a regular basis can add to global skills.

Competencies

Competencies can provide a useful look at the specific skill sets that global executives must possess. The empirically derived competencies mentioned in this chapter establish a starting point for developing a common language and actions to drive development. Some competencies should be part of the selection process while others can be taught as facts, and still others must be developed with years of experience and practice in the art of the business. One of the most effective methods of identifying and developing competencies is the use of 360-degree feedback process. In the author's experience, a sound 360-feedback process will highlight and prioritize things that can be done to be more personally effective.

Experiential Skills

Kets de Vries's (1999) discussion of talents and skill requirements for global executives suggests that the bulk of development is likely to take place in the context of daily experience rather than through formal programs. This means the development practitioner must be constantly on the lookout for events that teach. Fundamentally, these characteristics are learned by doing and through a great deal of practice, hopefully under mentoring and coaching by those with even more experience. While it may be a cliché to say that experience is the best teacher, there really is no substitute for learning by doing. Learning by doing involves an intellectual and emotional (visceral) understanding about how to approach problems. World-class athletes and world-class global executives both need to build a strong experience base.

Cross-Cultural Skills

Cross-cultural skills are certainly a requirement for the global executive, but they cannot be fully learned in an classroom. An understanding of culture must be developed with a heavy dose of seeing, touching, and experiencing different cultures. To even explain the Trompenaars dimensions verbally, in an introductory way, is not easy. To fully appreciate a culture different from one's own requires a significant immersion in and experience with that culture over time.

The time spent, in the chapter author's experience, minimally demands a year to develop fundamental cross-cultural skills. There is simply no substitute for living and working outside of one's familiar or home culture. In addition, quality time with an individual from another culture can be used to explore levels of meaning associated with business and management practices like empowerment or the limits of authority. A simple discussion of concepts that seem second nature to the developing executive explored through the eyes of a different cultural perspective is always a learning experience.

Executive Perspective

Finally, the integration of global awareness, key personal competencies, experiential learning, and cross-cultural effectiveness takes place in a framework most executives cannot articulate even though they do it. This means that the best learning will take place when there is an internal motive or drive to succeed or achieve and learning takes place in the context of servicing that need. Further, it is useful for the executive development professional to develop a real understanding of how individual executives conceptualize their unique development. This step can provide insights on how to better structure learning and development that is linked to business results.

Mini-Cases Illustrating the Concepts

Understanding Global Business for an American

Ted Johnson, an American marketing executive for a consumer products company, was given accountability for running Southeast Asia as a general manager. This was Ted's first international assignment and suddenly he was responsible for marketing in such diverse countries as Thailand, Australia, New Zealand, Philippines, Malaysia, Taiwan, and Indonesia. The regional office was in Singapore.

Ted was seen as an outstanding prospect for the future and this assignment was seen as a way to round out his skills and improve his ability to make decisions in a very complex and diverse part of the world. In mind-set, he was somewhat linear, and had been trained in typical Western marketing disciplines. In the diverse Southeast Asia assignment, he had to struggle with differences in trade practices, cultures, and language. He was fortunate enough to have a mentor who was quite familiar with that part of the world who also took the time to coach him through some very complex situations involving government approvals.

Ted developed an appreciation for how nonbusiness considerations can make it difficult to simply run a global business. At the end of a three-year assignment, he had a much broader understanding of how business fits into the much larger global picture. Specifically, he learned how to be more patient and ask questions before acting. He learned that in many Asian cultures personal familiarity must precede business action and language does not always convey a literal message. In Western terms, he developed a great deal of emotional intelligence around the tacit requirements and perceptions found in Asia.

Competencies for a Malaysian

Shafik Haddad, a Malaysian executive, was moved to the United States with his family for an 18-month assignment to learn how U.S. manufacturing was done and then to take that knowledge and return to his home country. Shafik and his family were provided cross-cultural training to help them adapt to living and working in the United States. The pace of life and the huge number of consumer choices made it difficult for the family to adjust. The list of competencies discussed earlier was used as a tool to engage him in conversations about what would be required for him to work more effectively in an American environment, as well as how to help his family adapt. The competencies and cultural differences that exist between Malaysians and Americans were also discussed at length with the American team hosting the executive. The competencies provided a starting point for a common language to develop around what was expected from both sides.

When a complex business procedure was discussed, for example, both cultural sides would refer to the procedure as learning how to handle business complexity. This had the added benefit of making the learning reside outside of the individual's ego and pride thereby making tough lessons less personally threatening.

Positive people skill competency discussions provided an opportunity for Shafik to develop an understanding of practices uncommon in Malaysia, such as having a woman in charge of a business. In a situation when he was leading and managing people who were generally more skilled than the ones he had worked with back home, a discussion of the leads-and-manages competency served as a starter to help teach him to be much more collaborative and that it was not always necessary to operate from a position of authority. The entire set of competencies were used as standard and became a tool for ongoing dialogue about what needed to be done and learned.

Experiential Learning

Alex Brandt, a Canadian who had lived his entire life in Canada, was tapped to move to Egypt to manage several difficult franchise owners. One of the franchisees was an arm of the government while the other was privately owned. Not only were there differences in culture between the Canadian and the Egyptians, but local business practices differed between the government and private sectors. There was no book on how this situation should be managed and nothing could have fully prepared any executive for dealing with it. What was required was a trial-and-error learning style based on carefully cultivating the personal relationships that managed the two franchisees. Every aspect of the business, from installing new manufacturing equipment to dealing with Customs to get equipment into the country to figuring out how to encourage the franchisees to work differently had to be learned. Alex was careful to ask many questions and cultivated a listening style that played well with both franchisees. As the months went by, he had a rapid learning curve based on his experience with the franchises and the culture of Egypt.

Experientially, Alex learned to appreciate the synchronicity of Egyptian culture. He learned he could not force a business action until the local thought process had played itself out. This is an excellent example of how no amount of classroom exposure could have prepared an executive to deal with this type of thinking. To fully understand it, he had to have full experiential, intellectual, and emotional immersion in the business process.

Cross-Cultural Wisdom

Henry Jacobson, an American general manager, was given an assignment that included China as part of his territory. He had been both a venture capitalist and a chief financial officer, but he wanted the experience of being a general manager. China was a real test. He understood what was required to make the products, to run an organization, and to deal with government red tape as well as the complexities of an economy that was not yet open in a Western sense. He also knew that it was important, as a Westerner and an American, that he work hard at building relationships with his Chinese partners and learn to look at the world through their eyes.

He did so by reading Chinese history and by finding a willing senior executive who was Chinese-American and who was willing to offer counsel. On a regular basis Henry would debrief and take time to reflect on what happened to the content of meetings and the cultural nuisances that he might have missed or overlooked. As a willing student, he became quite skilled at understanding Chinese customs and business practices and was able to put his knowledge to work building more a successful business.

Learning from the Executive's Perspective

Robert Hamilton, a retired American chief executive officer, was called upon to turn around a troubled business in the Philippines that had been rocked by poor management and the violation of local law. It took a lot of persuasion to convince him to come back from retirement to take on the assignment of fixing and turning the business around. The arrangement was that he would work only for a year and then turn the business over to a local manager, if that manager was ready, or to another American who would run the business until the local manager was ready.

Robert had as much experience as anyone, but all of that experience was in the United States. It would have been a fatal error to assume he knew exactly what to do in a tough turnaround in a country with which he was unfamiliar. The developmental challenge was to leverage all of his business experience while recognizing that he might not have all the answers. In this case, Robert used his staff to help him understand all the nuances of Philippine business and test his instincts and experiences before taking action. He learned by relying on advice from every member of his staff about what was needed. He focused on what was needed at the moment for fixing the business and that agenda drove the content of his learning.

A Summary of Lessons for Growing Global Executives

The preceding discussion suggests some generic lessons that may be drawn to help the practitioner or the executive develop into a more effective global executive. This summary is presented in the order that seems most useful, based on the author's experience.

Select Well

There is no substitute for sound selection. If the would-be global executive does not have a fair amount of the right stuff, then no amount of developmental effort is likely to fix the issues. Fundamentally, selection must start with a passion for working in a global environment coupled with an open mind that does not get locked up in a bias founded on a home-country understanding. There are many competency or selection lists, including the ones presented here, that may be useful. The important consideration is to find a set of selection criteria, apply it over time, and add modifications as wisdom increases.

Explicit Is Easy, Tacit Is Hard

Factual knowledge can be relatively easy to impart to anyone, and can be codified and presented in a manner that is easily integrated by an executive. On the other hand, there is no substitute for time and experience to develop skills in the art of business. The majority of business lessons are not going to be factual in nature. Much of business requires confronting new situations (such as the digital economy). Development should be viewed as a constant effort to expand the experience base of the executive.

Self-Interest Is the Best Motivator

Development should be wrapped in the context of an ongoing business combined with the enlightened self-interest of the individual executive. If an executive needs to learn something and that something can be immediately put to use, learning is more likely to stick. The most useful instructional approach is to focus on positive business or personal outcomes. When working with executives—who are by preselection already motivated to learn—it is the practitioner's role to simply put that learning in a context that the executive believes will be most personally useful. This means the executive should be engaged as a full partner in defining both the content and methodology for learning.

Experiences Teach Best

Adults learn by doing and executives learn best when they have the full experience of doing and learning. The practitioner will be most effective by finding and identifying those experiences that teach both the explicit and the tacit. This is actually the oldest learning technique of all: on-the-job. The modern adaptation of this technique is that competition and technology require ongoing and constant reinvention of business and individual skills. Projects—or more specifically, team-based action learning projects—provide a wealth of opportunity for individuals to learn. When these action-bearing projects take place across borders with team members from different countries, learning takes place in a much more meaningful way. If action learning is taking place in an environment where the results of the project are sure to be implemented, learning and growth are a sure bet.

Teach to Learn

Learning is most effective when the lessons must ultimately be taught to others by the learner. Tichy (1997) explains a system for making every leader a teacher and coach and integrating teaching into ongoing business activity. When an individual executive knows that there is a need to teach others, learning will be organized in a way that can be replicated. In the international or global world, there is always an opportunity to act as teacher even if it is nothing more than sharing a best practice that worked somewhere in the world and might be adapted to work in a current environment or circumstance. If *teaching* seems too pedantic as a term, think of it as feedback or coaching. At the heart of teaching to learn is the popular notion of knowledge sharing. Great global executives are pollinators who help move ideas and best practices from country to country.

Debrief and Discuss Often

Most senior executives are too busy and driven to pause and reflect on what is happening in their business or personal lives. When the opportunity to pause and reflect or debrief does occur, the result is very powerful. In the heat of the business moment, there is little opportunity to do anything more than act on a problem. After that experience, an objective discussion can help build powerful mental maps of what went right, what went wrong, and what should be done next time or in similar situations. The executive development professional is uniquely suited to act in that role.

Coach and Mentor

Real global executive development rarely takes place in the classroom. Real development is high-touch, one-to-one, personally experienced, on-the-fly development. Learning takes place when defensiveness is low and the information or knowledge is coming from a trusted source. For the senior executive, the author believes that coaching and mentoring are the best use of time and energy given the hectic pace of commerce. Ram Charan, coauthor with Noel Tichy of *Every Business Is a Growth Business* and a leading business strategy consultant, cites the example of how Jack Welch of General Electric takes the time to write a personal note to his senior managers after key business meetings that outlines what needs to be done and why. That is personalized coaching at the highest level (personal communication, 2000). Coaching and mentoring differ from debriefing in that debriefing simply allows an executive to reflect on experience. Coaching and mentoring, on the other hand, have a much more directive and explicit component. It is worth noting that coaching and mentoring are learning experiences in and of themselves. The coach or mentor often learns as much as the student.

Emphasize Change and Innovation as Key Values

And finally, the most important dimension or mind-set for the global executive must be constant change and innovation. At the start of this chapter, there was a discussion of the need for constant change. No global executive will be successful without a mind-set focused on changing business practices ahead of or in rapid response to the changing competitive environment. For both the executive development professional and the global executive, there is no single better way to grow than the constant, relentless pursuit of open-ended questions: Why did that happen? How could that be done more effectively? How can we be more competitive in the future?

Growing Global: Simplified Summary

Growing global executives at its most simple core is the thoughtful exposure of aspiring executives to as many varied experiences as practical in the context of actually growing a business. Growing globally is first and foremost exposure to all the elements defined by our working definition of global while making the growth an integral part of running a business. Successful global executives are curious, achievement driven, and incredibly open about what they know or don't know. The executive development professional and the developing executive can add the most value by identifying the right experience at the right time and helping solidify those experiences as part of the executive's operating system.

References
Aaker, D. A., & Joachimsthaler, E. (1999). The lure of global branding. *Harvard Business Review, 77*(6), 137–144.
Black, J. S., Morrison, A. J., Gregersen, H. B. (1999). *Global explorers.* New York: Routledge.

Davis, S., & Meyer, C. (2000). *Future wealth.* Boston: Harvard Business School Press.

Friedman, T. L. (1999). *The Lexus and the olive tree.* New York: Farrar, Strauss & Giroux.

Fulkerson, J. R. (1998). Assessment across cultures. In P. R. Jeanneret and R. Silzer (Eds.), *Individual psychological assessment,* pp. 330–362. San Francisco: Jossey-Bass.

Fulkerson, J. R. (1999). Global leadership competencies for the twenty-first century: More of the same or a new paradigm for what leaders really do. In W. H. Mobley (Ed.), *Advances in global leadership,* pp. 27–48. Stamford, CT: JAI Press.

Fulkerson, J. R., & Schuler, R. (1992). Managing worldwide diversity at Pepsi-Cola International. In S. E. Jackson and Associates (Eds.), *Diversity in the work-place,* pp. 248–276. New York: Guilford Press.

Kets de Vries, M.F.R. (1999). *The new global leaders.* San Francisco: Jossey-Bass.

McCall, M. W. (1998). *High flyers: Developing the next generation of leaders.* Boston: Harvard Business School Press.

McCall, M. W., Lombardo, M. M., & Morrison, A. (1988). *The lessons of experience: How successful executives develop on the job.* New York: Free Press.

Ohmae, K. (1980). *The borderless world.* New York: Harper Business.

Rhinesmith, S. H. (1993). *A manager's guide to globalization.* Burr Ridge, IL: Business One Irwin.

Rosen, R., Digh, P., Singer, M., & Phillips, C. (2000). *Global literacies.* New York: Simon & Schuster.

Schlender, B. (2000, May 1). The odd couple. *Fortune, 141*(9), 106–126.

Tapscott, D., Ticoll, D., & Lowy, A. (2000). *Digital capital.* Boston: Harvard Business School Press.

Tichy, N. M. (1997). *The leadership engine.* New York: Harper Business.

Trompenaars, F. (1994). *Riding the waves of culture.* Burr Ridge, IL: Irwin Professional.

CHAPTER 12

Getting an Executive View
An Interview with a Chief Executive Officer
Lawrence A. Bossidy, Marcia J. Avedon

This chapter is based on an interview with Lawrence A. Bossidy, chairman and CEO of Honeywell International (formerly AlliedSignal, Inc.). Larry Bossidy has been cited in many business articles for his superior financial performance and transformational leadership during his nine-year tenure as chief executive of AlliedSignal (Stewart, 1992, 1999; Franco, 1999; Maynard, 1994). In 1998 Larry Bossidy was selected among his peer CEOs as CEO of the year (Dolan, 1998). "Larry Bossidy led one of the most remarkable turnarounds in corporate history," says J. P. Donlon, editor-in-chief of *Chief Executive*.

The interviewer and author of this chapter, Marcia Avedon, has had the opportunity to work with Larry Bossidy at AlliedSignal and Honeywell on recruiting and selecting executives, determining executive compensation, and providing development opportunities and succession plans.

On the Role of Executives

What are your thoughts about the role of executives, how their role may differ from other managers in companies, and how you may have seen the role change over your career?

First, the role has to be one of leadership. I think that is much different than it was 5 years ago, let alone 15 years ago, when *manager*

335

was the operative word. I don't think management is the key any longer because the workforce is sufficiently independent and eclectic. Therefore, people want and expect leadership as opposed to being managed.

Different people have different meanings for leadership, but in my view, it is a set of characteristics that make an executive effective at influencing events and people. The first of these is energy. An executive must have personal energy and be able to energize the organization. Second, an effective executive has a vision of where the company or unit needs to be. This vision when articulated helps to explain to people why they are doing things or why their leader is asking them to do things. There must be a goal line, a point that everyone is striving for. The vision provides a way of getting people together. So creating a common purpose that everyone can strive for is a critical part of the role.

Executives need to have some big ideas that suggest to those they lead that we are doing something special, something different. Exciting new ideas propel people to a point of view that makes them want to stay and contribute more. These big ideas create an environment where people feel they can personally grow and prosper, not stagnate. For example, when I first took over AlliedSignal we introduced Total Quality. This initiative created an exciting set of changes in the company, with our customers and suppliers. Employees began to feel more empowered and part of a team, decisions became more fact-based, focus on the customer increased, and the quality of our products improved. We trained every employee in the company. This investment in training got everyone involved, told people we were serious and that this was something big. This is only one example of a big idea. Later we evolved to Six Sigma and most recently we focused on e-business. The point is that leaders must drive these big ideas to move their organizations and people in a new direction. Such initiatives also serve to unify the people in the company and make them feel connected. This does not just happen naturally in big organizations, particularly a diversified conglomerate like our company. The executive leaders need to make this type of change happen.

An executive must also have almost unparalleled determination. There are lots of things in the course of a day, week, month, or year that can sidetrack you away from the goal or purpose. So the ability to stay focused on what you set out to do is very important. I believe to some extent the role also requires being a cheerleader. You must be objective about the accomplishments against the goals, but you have to set an environment where there's celebration and people feel that their work is acknowledged. This will motivate people to do more, rather than less.

Communication skills are increasingly important for an executive. An effective executive needs to be persuasive and not dictate to people, asking others to join in rather than telling them. People in organizations want to know more about what is going on and feel that they have a right to know. Executives need the ability and willingness to deal with people on a "straight up" basis. The role requires the leader to be willing to communicate frequently. Not all executives are great at communicating, but they must be willing to do it often and in a genuine manner. Executives need to have an interest in communicating and make it a priority. People will be forgiving if their leader is less than General Patton.

The role of senior executives also requires responding to a host of constituencies. The needs of shareholders, customers, suppliers, employees, communities, and regulatory agencies must all be juggled. Executives must stay in touch with all of the constituencies on a regular basis and determine when one constituency needs greater attention. This need is even more striking than in the past. So strong communication skills are needed externally as well as internally.

In your experience, what have been the typical failure modes or common mistakes executives have demonstrated?

There are a lot of different issues with those who are not successful, but failing to deal with reality is the most significant and common problem. I mean when an executive actually knows that something has to be done, but does not do what is required. For example, not moving on ineffective performers, or not addressing issues that confront or inhibit the business. So failure to confront reality is the most prevalent derailer, to my mind.

Second, many executives get swept up by the so-called perks that come with an executive role. For example, they attend or speak at meetings or conventions that bring no value to the company. Some use these events to get away from the pressures of the job and bathe in the respect and luxury they get in these places. These invitations can be seductive and, when overdone, ultimately can get in the way of fulfilling the requirements of an executive's job. Getting too caught up in the perks not only diverts attention from business matters, it also feeds enlarged egos and detaches executives from the people in their organization. These executives become "missing in action" and are rendered ineffective.

The third failure mode I call the *bumblebee mentality*. These are the executives who don't think the same way all the time and therefore they never have a real point of view. They move from idea to idea but never really implement any in a meaningful way. The lack of execution skills and the inability to stay focused are particularly troublesome for executives. Sometimes this failure mode also involves not being decisive or having an inability to take a firm stand or position.

As CEO, how did you decide where to spend your time and what to delegate to others to handle?

It may be different in different companies, but in managing a global portfolio, I had a lot of confidence in three primary processes we used to run the company. These three core processes were to lead people, strategy, and operations. I wanted to spend my time on those three processes or on activities that were aligned to them. So every business in our portfolio participated in our people review process twice a year, our strategic planning process annually, and our annual operating planning. We also did operating reviews quarterly to assess our ongoing business performance against plans. I was personally involved in these plans in every business and with reviewing progress against plans to hold people accountable for their commitments. I also focused on spending time with customers to make sure I understood how we were perceived in the marketplace. By and large, I looked at my calendar and checked each week that my time was spent consistently with these objectives.

You are noted for being a CEO who spent more time on the people processes such as hiring and pay decisions than many of your peers and colleagues. Why did you believe this was a key priority?

After being in business for a lot of years, even though it sounds trite, I believe that people do make the difference. It is one thing to say it, but it's another to get a discipline in the company that practices it. I thought that if the people in the company who were recruiting knew that I was interested in objective assessments of people, maybe they would do a better job. If people knew that I was interested in who got promoted and who didn't, I thought they might make better choices. So anything I could do to continually reinforce the point that people are indeed the centerpiece of all we do, the better we would be as a company. There is no doubt in my mind that the people of Honeywell today or AlliedSignal of yesterday are dramatically better than the day I came into the company. The only way that happens is because leaders are dedicated to seeing that it happens. We had rigorous sessions to appraise our people and determine who should get new opportunities and who should leave. By continuing to evaluate people against high standards and continuing to upgrade, over time you make a real impact on the place you work. This may not happen overnight, but it is an important aspect of an executive's job. I thought it was the most important thing I could do to make things happen and transform the company to be premier (see Bossidy, 2001).

On Executive Development

You have seen many different types of formal executive development programs, both at General Electric and at AlliedSignal/Honeywell. What have you found to be the most effective and least effective?

Ultimately, effectiveness of these programs is based on whether they result in people really developing. Many of these programs have peer feedback and I think that is wonderful. Also, the more the participants are dealing with real-life issues and not hypothetical textbook cases, the better the learning. In some programs, we gave teams projects that were real issues or strategic questions and they had to study them and present their recommendations to senior leadership. Typically, the participants were not familiar with the particular issue. They had to assimilate a lot of information and work together and potentially make a real impact on the company. This type of learning benefits both the participants and the company.

I also think the process where an outsider comes in to assess an executive and provides feedback and coaching can be valuable. It is particularly good in those cases where we are dealing with people who are not easily assessed. I generally think I can assess people fairly quickly because I have so much experience, but some people are more difficult to figure out. Then an outside opinion and more in-depth process can be useful. I also think that some people need coaching and that the use of outside coaches is fine as long as we know who they are and their approach is appropriate. Sometimes people are in a stretch assignment or a new environment and I am supportive of helping them through coaching.

Do you believe there is a new model of developing executives in the e-business world? We see many CEOs who are in their 30s in the dot-coms. Do cycles of learning still matter or is there a different model of preparing to be an executive?

I think that it is too soon to say that there is a new model. I believe that most of these dot-coms will come apart at the seams, and that we in industry will then inherit some people with experience the likes of which we have not seen before at that age—and that is goodness. I see instances where young people who have wonderful ideas have established these dot-coms but have no idea how to run a company. So cycles of learning, whether they like it or not, are still with us. I must note that this is probably not the primary reason for dot-coms' failing; there are many other factors.

Do you think business school training is still important and relevant to becoming an executive?

Business schools basically teach what people should have known yesterday. So, to the extent that the curriculums are relevant in terms of what matters today, I think yes. Maybe the best thing about business schools is that you are in a class with a lot of smart people and you hear a lot of different viewpoints. That is always helpful. However, I don't think that business school training is absolutely essential to being an executive, either.

What advice would you give young people who aspire to be executives? What suggestions do you have to help them succeed and to influence their expectations?

First, I'd say that you still have to have ambition. As basic as it sounds, a strong work ethic and a drive to succeed endure as requirements. Also, I think you have to learn how to get along well with people, both one-on-one and in teams. You won't be successful on your own. I really believe that if you are perceived as a person who is willing to help other people, then a lot more is going to come your way than if you are someone who looks selfish. Next, willingness to take some difficult assignments I believe is important. I see too many young people who will not take an assignment because they think it will derail them from the firm plan they have laid out. Nevertheless, that assignment might give them all kinds of growth and valuable experience that will benefit them later. So I would advise aspiring executives to take on the difficult assignments, work to get along with people, and continue to develop. To develop yourself, I suggest you ask for feedback and even the negative input helps you mature and grow as a person. Then, I would say, don't stay in the same job for too long. Keep moving into different areas, functions, or lines of business. Try not to focus on going up the ladder vertically. Rather, move as much as possible horizontally to broaden and prepare yourself for different challenges down the road.

On Executive Compensation

I know you have personally been very involved in shaping the executive compensation philosophy and practice in your company. Can you articulate what you see as the guiding principles that support your philosophy?

I think that clearly executives should be given a base pay consistent with the pay for their role at companies comparable to theirs. I think they should be given annual bonuses depending on their ability to meet goals. Third, I believe that they should get long-term compensation in terms of stock options. I am convinced that long-term stock options should be the leverage point. I don't think we should necessarily overdo either the base salary or the bonus, but executives should make a lot of money because the stock goes up. I think that is fine because it makes those executives really act like owners of the company.

There is a lot of discussion going on now about how we compensate leaders if an Internet organization is formed within our company. The primary question is whether we should give them their own class of stock or even some kind of phantom stock tied to their own performance. I think that is a big mistake. I believe that you've got to keep all the people in the boat pulling the oars together. I don't mean people in the new entity should not have separate compensation programs based on the competitive market for their talent. However, the equity should be the same as the rest of the company. Otherwise, different equity vehicles promote division, unless of course you take it public as a separate company at some point.

On Succession Planning and Talent Management

Both of your companies have had great reputations in terms of executive continuity and grooming talent for the future. Why do you think that their approaches were so effective?

In our system we are constantly looking to see whether we have a bench of sufficient size to provide for turnover in the event it happens or for a planned succession. It does a couple of things for the company. First, it shows the level of preparedness we have because we look at specific names and their backgrounds and make judgments on whether they are eligible for a higher or different role or not. Succession is crucial if things are going well in a company or unit because it prevents disruption. So the system allows us to have people internally prepared to perpetuate the performance. Now if things are going badly in a company or unit, then you may decide to go out and hire somebody to bring in a new direction.

Companies where succession planning doesn't work are those where the top leaders don't spend sufficient time on it or they don't really look and see if they have their own backups. Other companies fail at succession planning because they do look and find there are not enough backups, but don't do anything about it. Again, executing on the plan is critical. So, succession planning including follow-up has a significant role to play in terms of the continuity of corporations.

Many companies do succession planning almost as an exercise in creating a book. In your company it has not been just an exercise. What do you think is different?

We document our discussions, both the appraisals of the people and the specific actions. If we agree to a specific succession or set of moves, I follow up. Six months later we review what has happened in terms of what we documented in the last meeting. I think if you keep it in front of people, and you have good people, things will happen. If you make an idle comment and never follow up on it, then in many cases things don't happen. We view our people discussions as commitments like our budget commitments or any other business plans. That's probably the fundamental factor that makes it different from some other companies.

What do you think about high-potential programs or programs to identify people early in their careers and work to accelerate their development?

I do like these programs. I know that they are controversial and there are others who don't like them. Some think that the participants become prima donnas or crown princes. I don't think you have to publicize it as much as we tend to do in companies. At the end of every review that I did we tried to identify those people we believed had the most potential. I didn't necessarily put a new circle on their back or label them. I was interested in seeing those identified as having the most potential as leaders progress faster, and in deciding how far we thought they could go. The notion of trying to develop the entire population as leaders is ineffective. I do think identification and subsequent career acceleration of the most promising talent is a good practice.

Would you suggest telling the individuals that they are high-potentials?

No, not explicitly. Certainly it is fine to tell people they are doing a good job and we think they have a lot of potential. I wouldn't tell them we think you are one of the top ten people in the business. I think that is unnecessary and perhaps ineffective.

To what extent do you believe that leaders are born versus made—and consequently, how much would you suggest investing in hiring and selection versus development of executives?

Society needs lots of leaders, so I like to think that many people can learn to lead. I believe that certain attributes are difficult to develop in adults, such as courage, self-confidence, or ambition. So companies need to have good assessment and selection processes to determine who has these basic traits. However, there are lots of different styles of leadership that are effective. Compare General Patton to President Eisenhower, for example—one being loud and the other being quieter.

I think that we ought to be spending about four or five percent of our revenues on education. Education in my mind is all-encompassing, for everyone, not just the leaders. Some of the education should be for executive development but this level of investment is needed to ensure you're going to have a real quality workforce across the board.

What do you want to have as your personal legacy from a people management perspective? What do you believe will have an enduring impact on the company for many years to come?

I want to have people think that we had high standards. I want people to believe we were fair and that we didn't have prejudice toward women or any minority group. So when you came to work here people would say, "You know, I had a fair chance to get where I wanted to go. I was assessed with rigor and I was appraised in terms of my job performance. As a consequence, I am a better person and got further in the corporation than I might have otherwise." I hope I leave behind an environment where merit wins, where there are no winks or favoritism. So having a reputation of being fair, interested in making people better, and rigorous. Those are the things I hope I can leave behind.

Last, do you have any other advice for executives or human resource professionals tasked with ensuring their organizations have great executives?

I think that in a lot of organizations there is a continual reluctance to be as direct with people as is needed. When I say direct, I don't mean insulting or offensive. But I see many situations in business where people should be called into a room by their manager and told, "you know, that wasn't good business judgment" or "that wasn't an effective behavior" or "you need to improve yourself in this way." I wish executives would be more candid with their people. They need to give this kind of feedback to help their people improve. Maybe it is not done more because of a lack of courage or fear of confrontation? Executives need to be able to address people's needs for improvement like any other business need, directly and professionally.

Overall, I just want to impress upon executives the same understanding that I have learned after all these years about the importance of people. I could make most executives better by helping them spend more time on the people and do a better job with their people. Then they would have better people—and better people win.

References

Bossidy, L. A. (2001, March). The job no CEO should delegate. *Harvard Business Review,* pp. 47–49.

Dolan, J. P. (1998, July-August). Chief executive of the year: The CEO's CEO. *Chief Executive.*

Franco, A. (1999, October 10). A leader's eye view of leadership. *New York Times,* pp. 1, 12–13.

Maynard, M. (1994, June 23). The best CEO you've never heard of— AlliedSignal's Bossidy is a wanted man. *USA Today.*

Stewart, T. A. (1999, December 6). How to leave it all behind. *Fortune,* pp. 345–348.

Stewart, T. A. (1992, November 30). Corporate turnaround performance: AlliedSignal's turnaround blitz. *Fortune.*

Name Index

Subject Index

DATE DUE